WHILE WE SLEPT

WHILE WE SLEPT

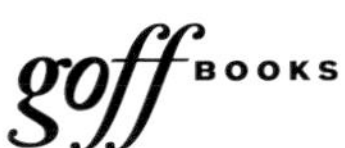

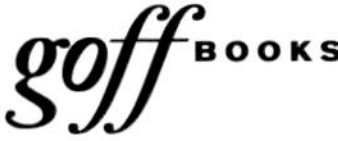

Published by Goff Books. An Imprint of ORO Editions
Gordon Goff: Publisher

www.goffbooks.com
info@goffbooks.com

Author: Pete Mauney
With Contributions from Tim Davis, Orit Peleg, David Kennerly, and Jessica Chappe
All photographs by Pete Mauney (unless otherwise noted)
Book design by Taylor Potecha
Managing Editor: Jake Anderson

10 9 8 7 6 5 4 3 2 1 First Edition

ISBN: 978-1-961856-14-1

Prepress and Print work by ORO Editions Inc.
Printed in China

Goff Books makes a continuous effort to minimize the overall carbon footprint of its publications. As part of this goal, Goff Books, in association with Global ReLeaf, arranges to plant trees to replace those used in the manufacturing of the paper produced for its books. Global ReLeaf is an international campaign run by American Forests, one of the world's oldest nonprofit conservation organizations. Global ReLeaf is American Forests' education and action program that helps individuals, organizations, agencies, and corporations improve the local and global environment by planting and caring for trees.

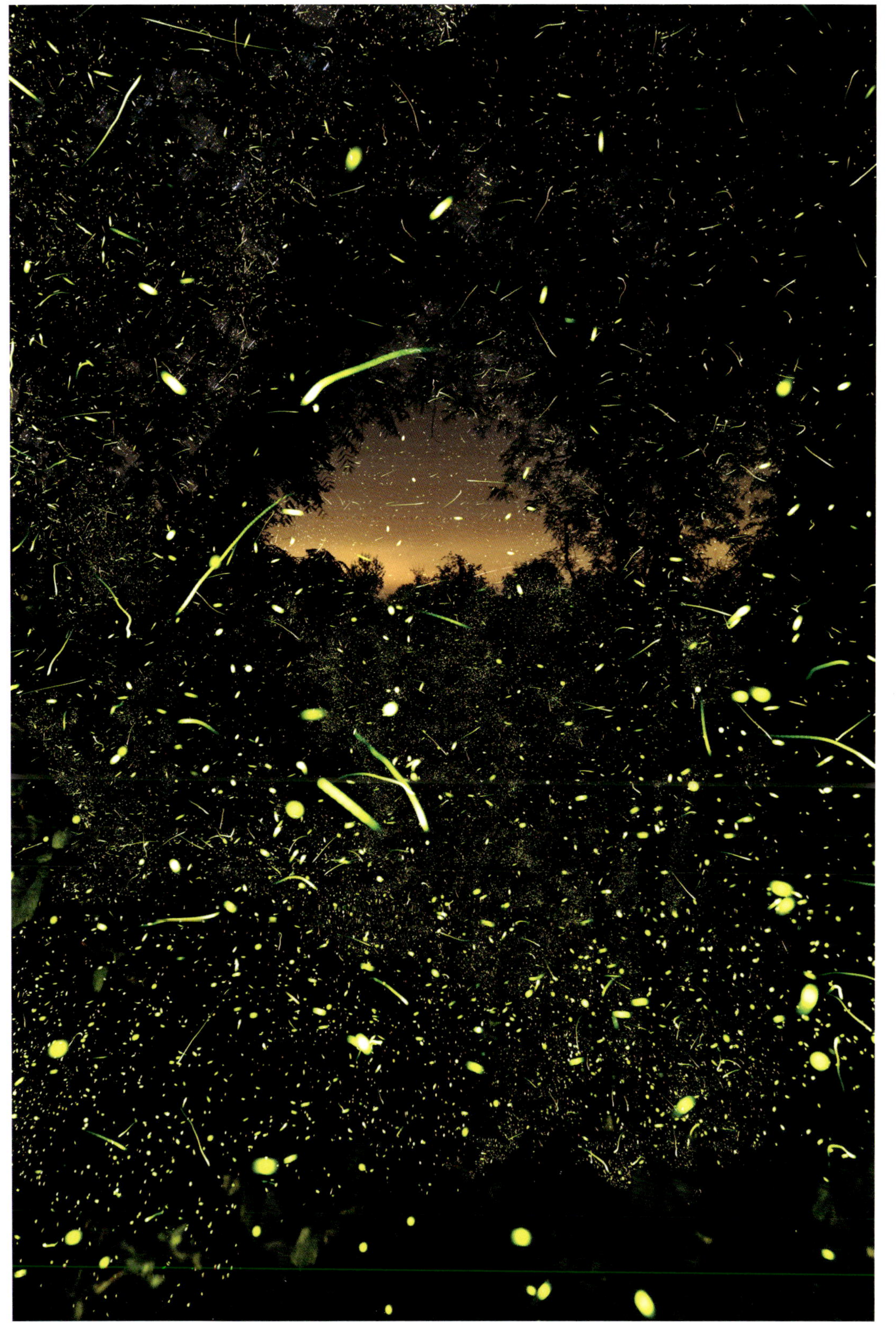

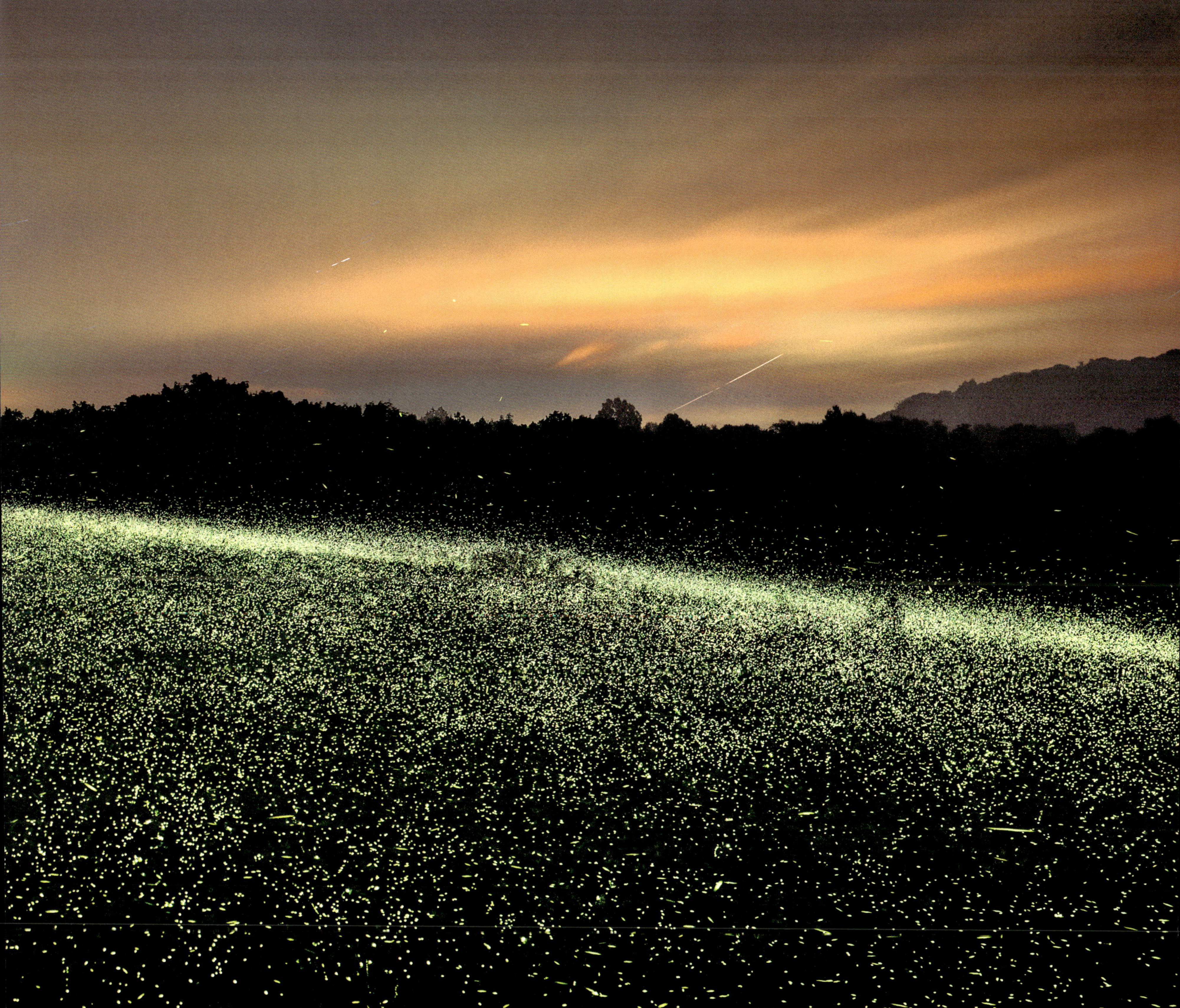

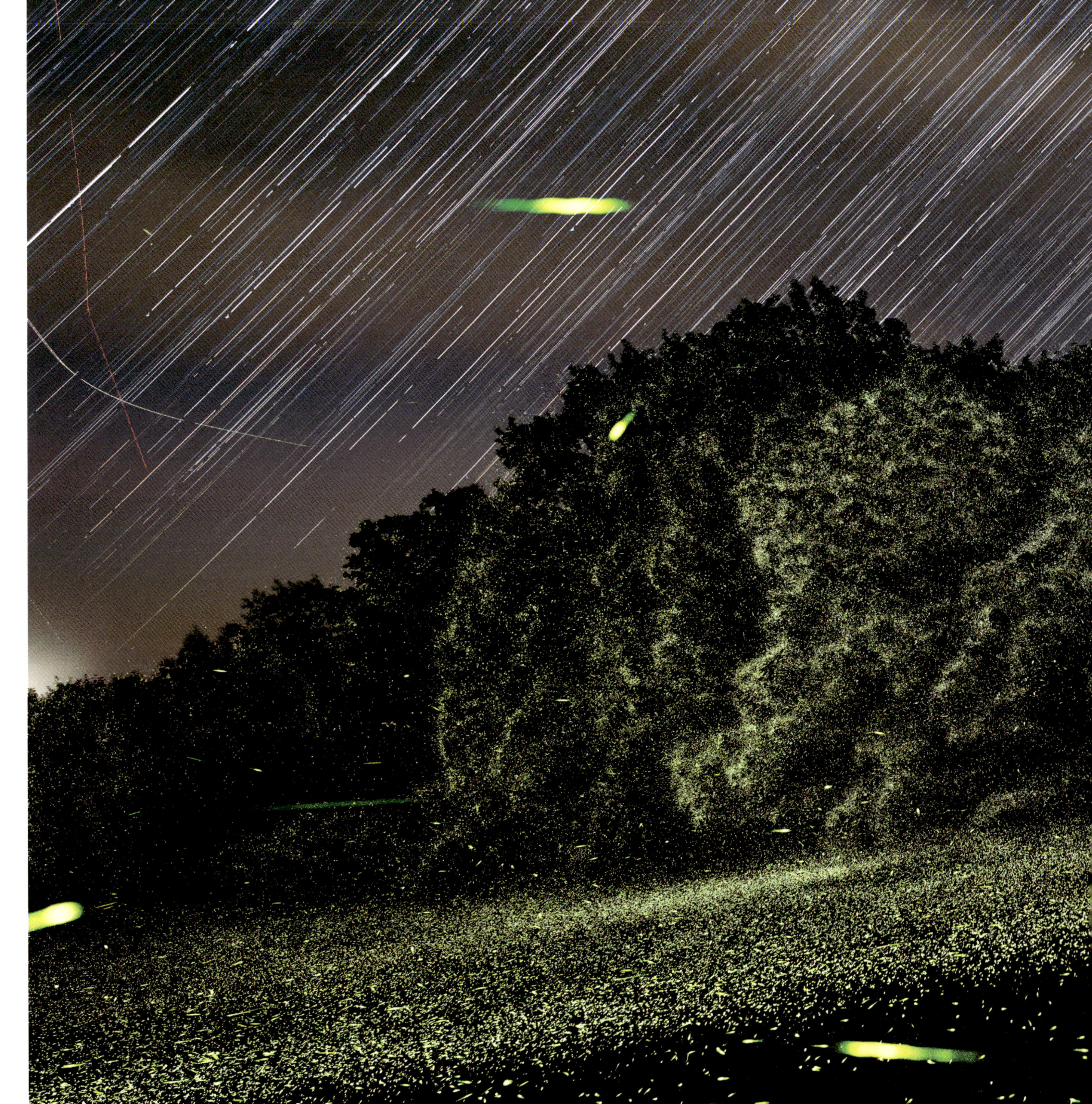

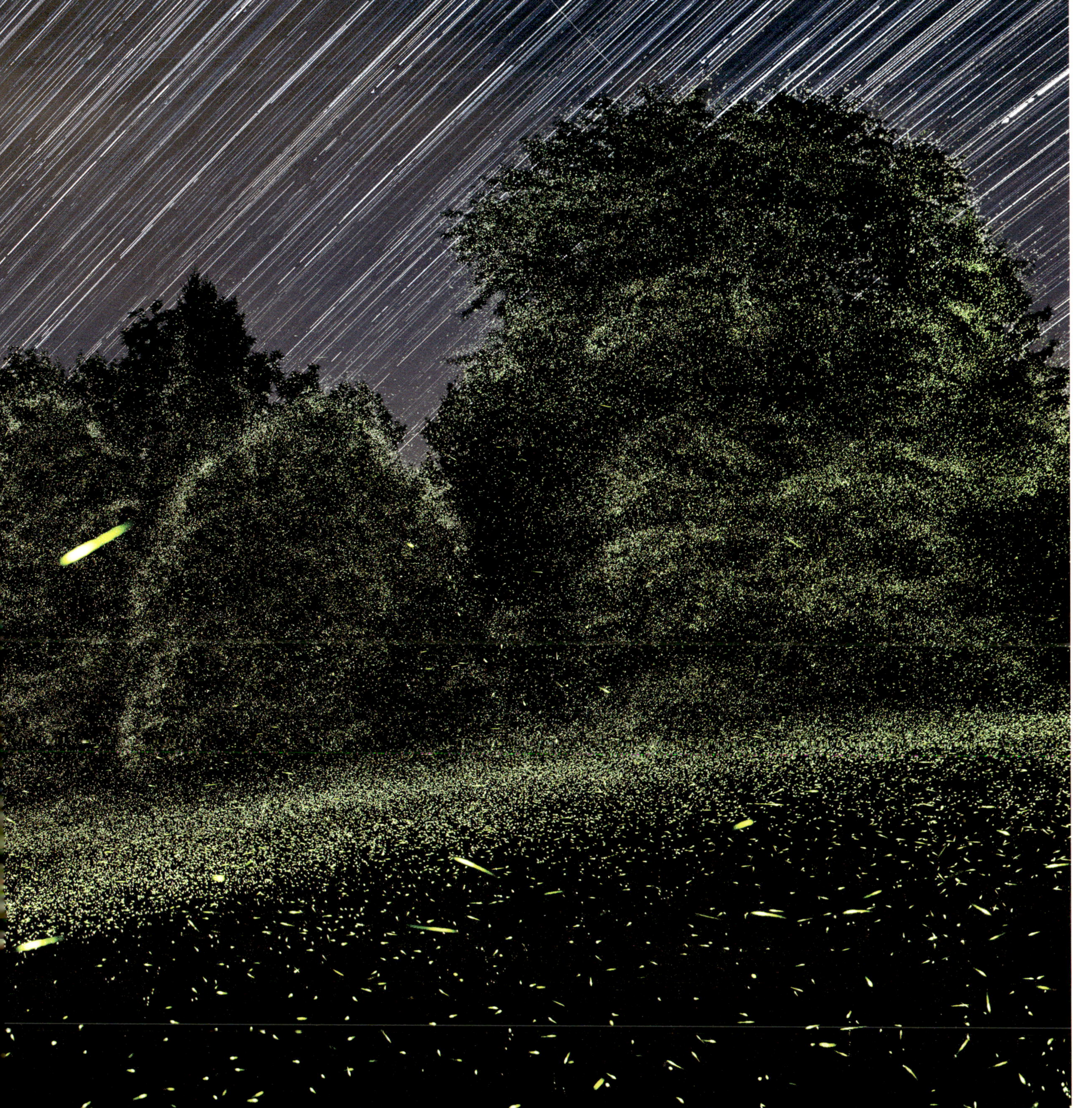

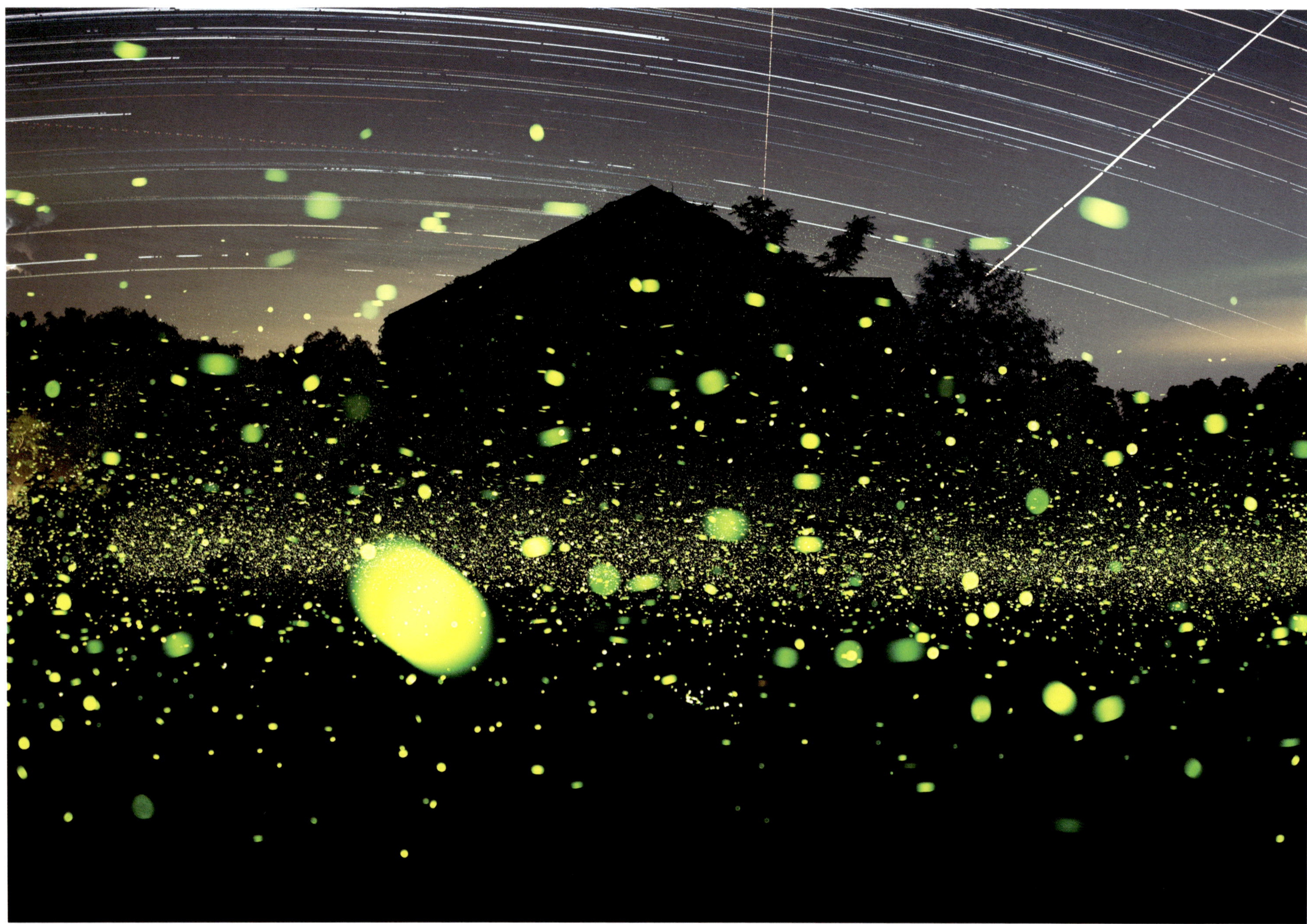

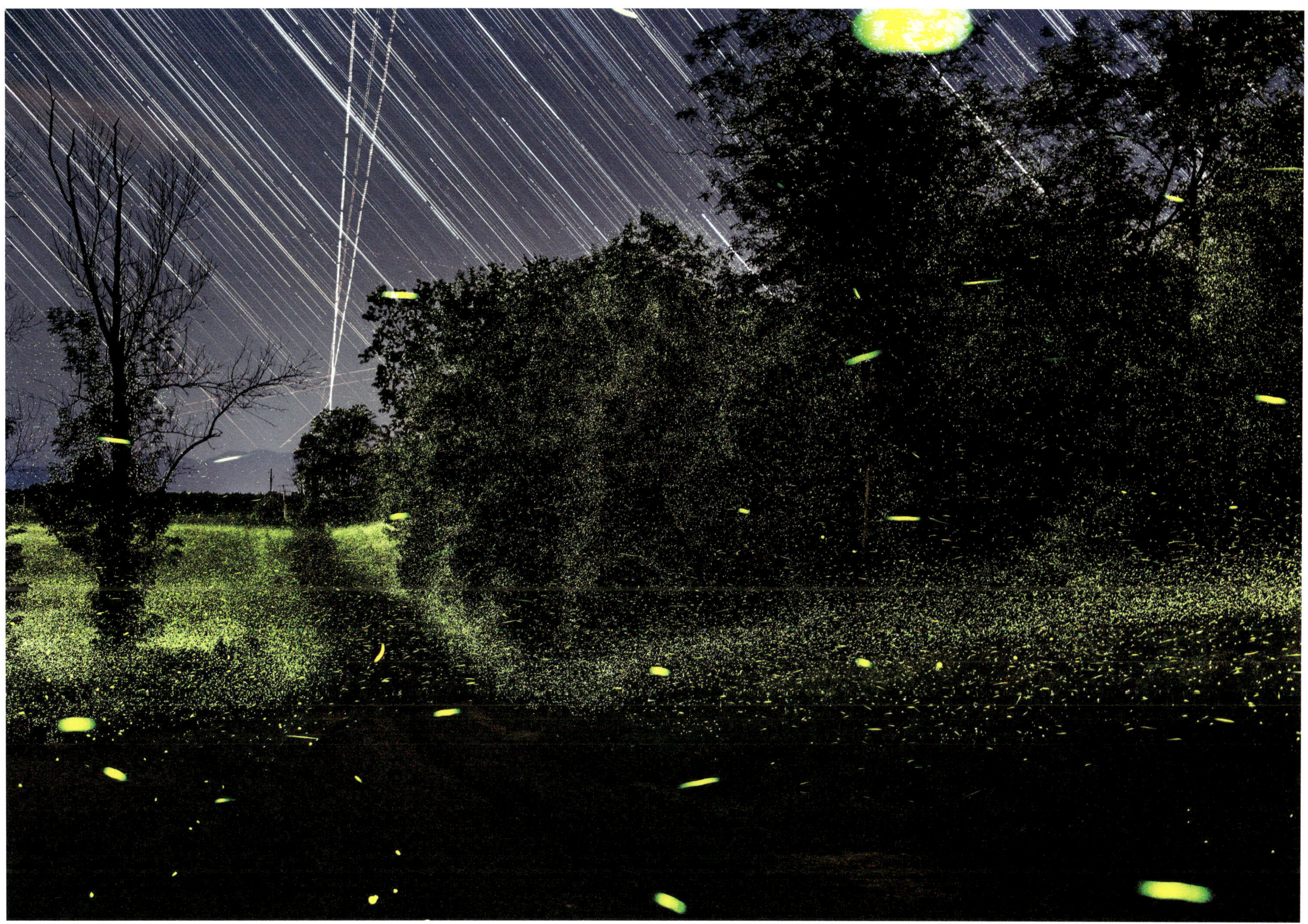

PETE MAUNEY AND THE MISSING MASS

TIM DAVIS
TIVOLI, NEW YORK 2023

The history of photography is a glass half filled with what we cannot see. However visual the medium is—and it is almost pathologically so—photographs want to talk about the invisible. Start with Daguerre's shot out the window of his studio in the Boulevard du Temple in 1838ish, the first magically clear, detailed landscape we have. The exposure probably took ten minutes, rendering the little Parisians on their busy spring morning below entirely underexposed (although a shoe shiner and his customer, stuck in one spot, manage to show up). Even the most controlled photograph in a studio is still laced through with details the photographer couldn't perceive, and the strange act of pointing the camera at the world, pressing a button, and calling it art, gets some of its juju from swallowing whole so much unknown information. Photographers are cormorants, gobbling up the writhing, formless world and digesting it later.

Pete Mauney is a photographer devoted to this missing matter, the huge percentage of the universe we can't perceive, but sense must be there. For the last ten years or more he has headed out into the dark upstate New York night to point his camera at the impossibly alive places most humans ignore, returning in the morning with evidence that galaxies of cosmic gas float in our backyards. This is a part of the world where night sends most people indoors, home, where the hearth is. There is little nightlife to speak of, a few bars and convenience stores, and most people stay home. I can't help but notice that Pete's devotion to spending his nights lassoing pinpricks of invisible firefly light coincides with the rise of social media and smartphones in the general public. Just as you started spending your nights watching your friends flash their wonderful smiles—their lives so much happier and more perfect than yours—Pete Mauney began spending his nights with fireflies. Like fireflies, photographers are aroused by light; it is the magnet in their compasses, the muezzin calling them to prayer. There are the hunter/gatherers, always turning on their diner stools to see which direction's chrome best refracts the morning sun. There are the people who stand in a parking lot for twenty minutes waiting for a cloud to pass, or (for some strange few) to arrive. Then there are the cultivators of light, who blast everything with flash in order to make the world ring with diabolical clarity. The cult of the cultivars isn't interested in how things are. They insist on an ideal world, like singers who won't work without a string section and professional horn charts.

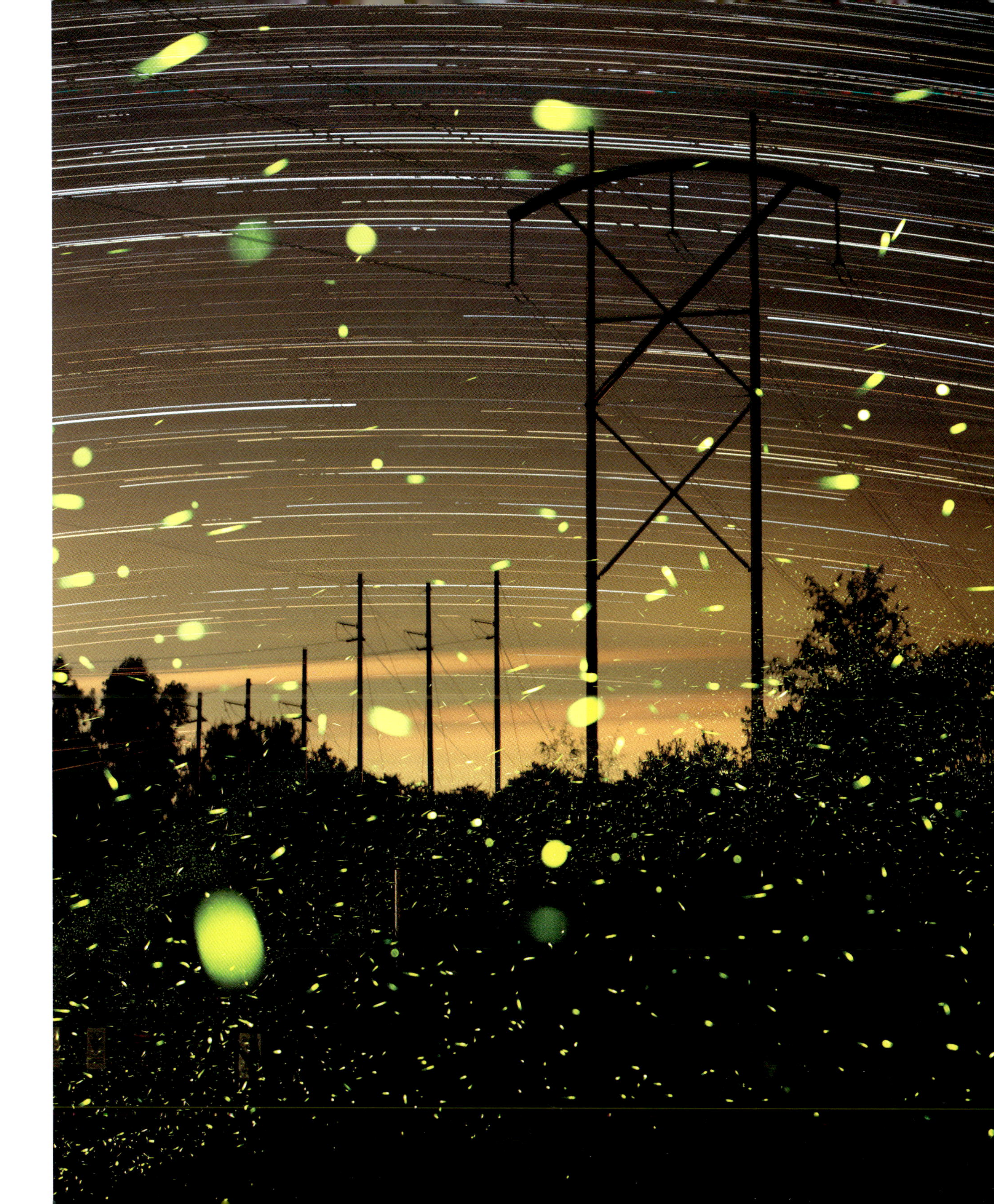

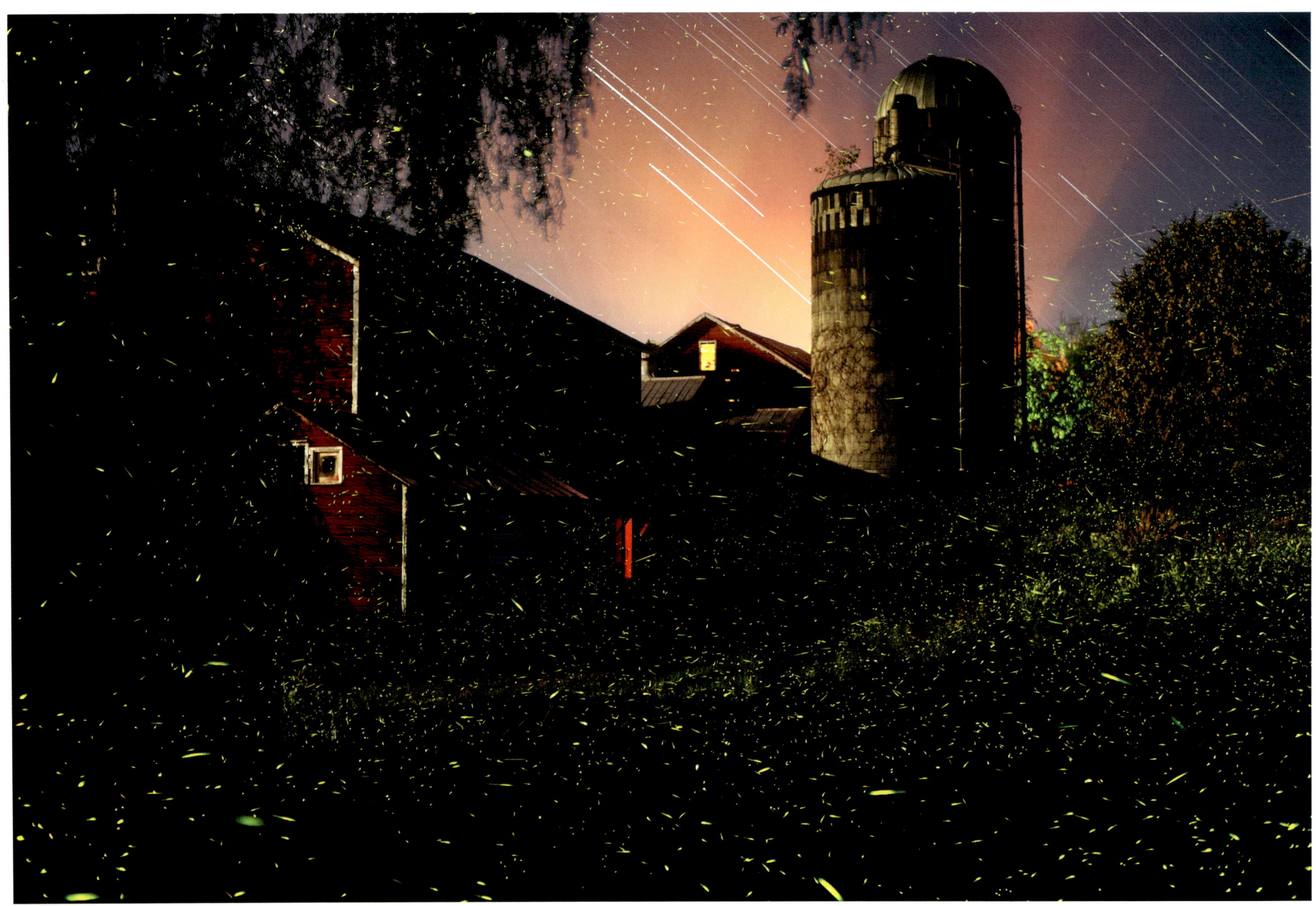

Pete Mauney's photographs don't hunt or cultivate light. They squeeze light out of an almost invisible source, trawling the deep vents at the bottom of the ocean for the purest forms of life. The photographs in this book are not images, exactly. They haven't been seen by anyone, but they are irrefutably there. Love hasn't been seen by anyone either, and certainly has never been understood, but that hasn't stopped every writer ever from shoveling novels full of it. Mauney is reminding us that there is drama in the places humans don't reckon with, as we spend our days following pheromones' trails of acquisition and aggrandizement, and our nights wiping off our mouths and recovering.

When I look at these pictures, I wonder what other light sources there may be. Could there be children developing technologies to capture static-o-graphs, rubbing their crazy unwashed hair on balloons and wrestling under blankets to produce the most wonderfully tangled tendrils any sensitized plate has ever accepted? Maybe the Vivid Bitter Oyster Mushroom will have its say, or the Hawaiian Bobtail Squid? Or perhaps there is a way to capture the light jumping between our own axons and dendrites, making pictures of the signals that tell neurons what to do. Maybe there are light sources we haven't imagined: alien fire sales or comet coma communications. But if you're the type of person who wants to lie comfortably in your chalet while guys in fluorescent vests clean the spill of Cargill Stardust™ from the jackknifed 18-wheeler out on the country road, then this book is for you. If you want to imagine what it feels like to spend the night standing in a field of smooth white beardtongue and broad-leaf sedge, of wild ginger and Virginia rose, buttonbush and bottlebush grass, with every tick in the vicinity turning toward you, the bobcats and fishers skulking away, the hellgrammites hiding under river rocks, the mute swan asleep on the duckweed pond and the red eft sifting for macroinvertebrates, the satellites passing unblinking over like unsettling dinner dates, the stars standing still as we turn under them, the owls howling your demise, then this book is for you. If you believe in both magic and sleight of hand, then this book is for you. If you believe in photography, and you do, then this book is for you.

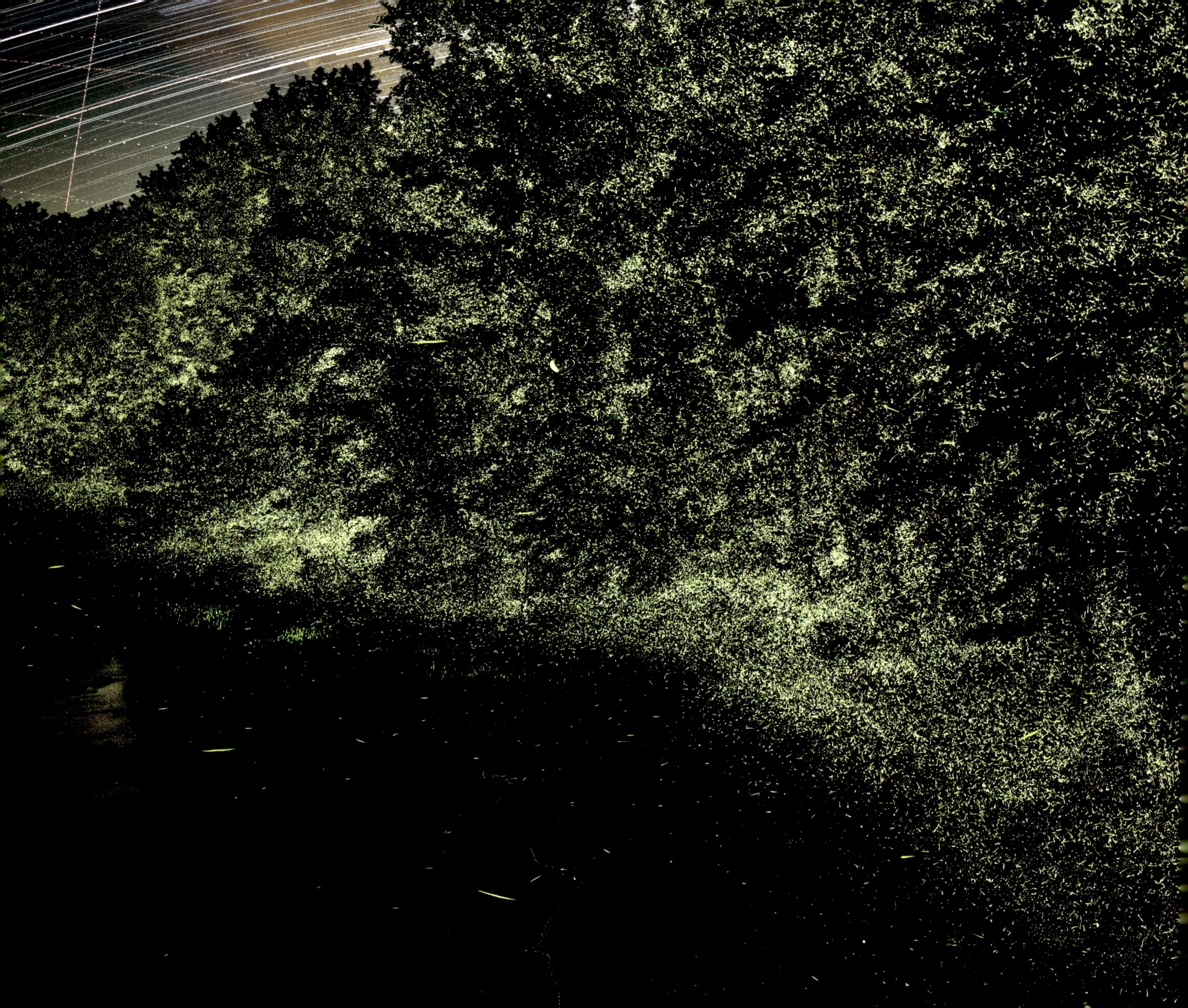

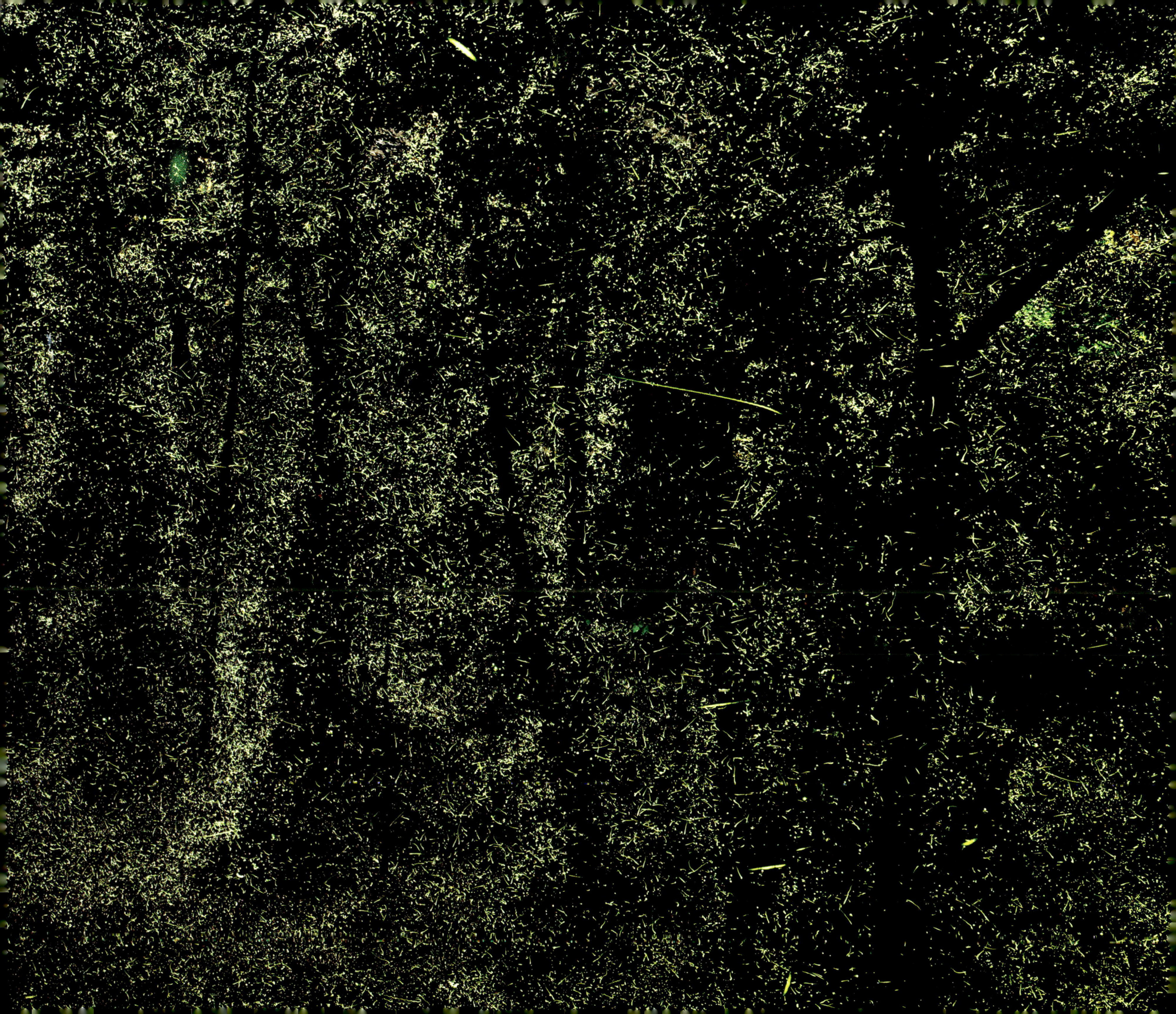

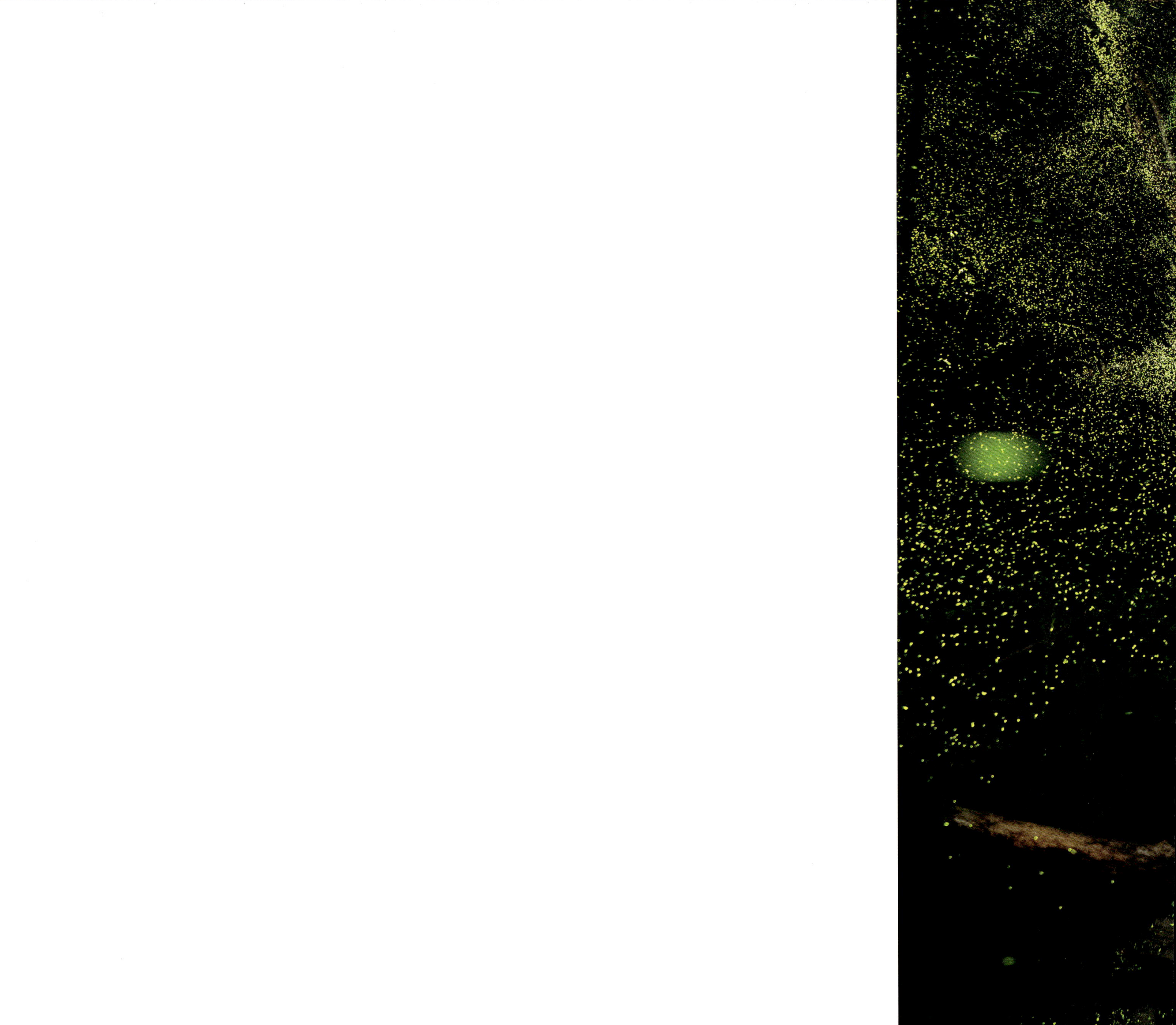

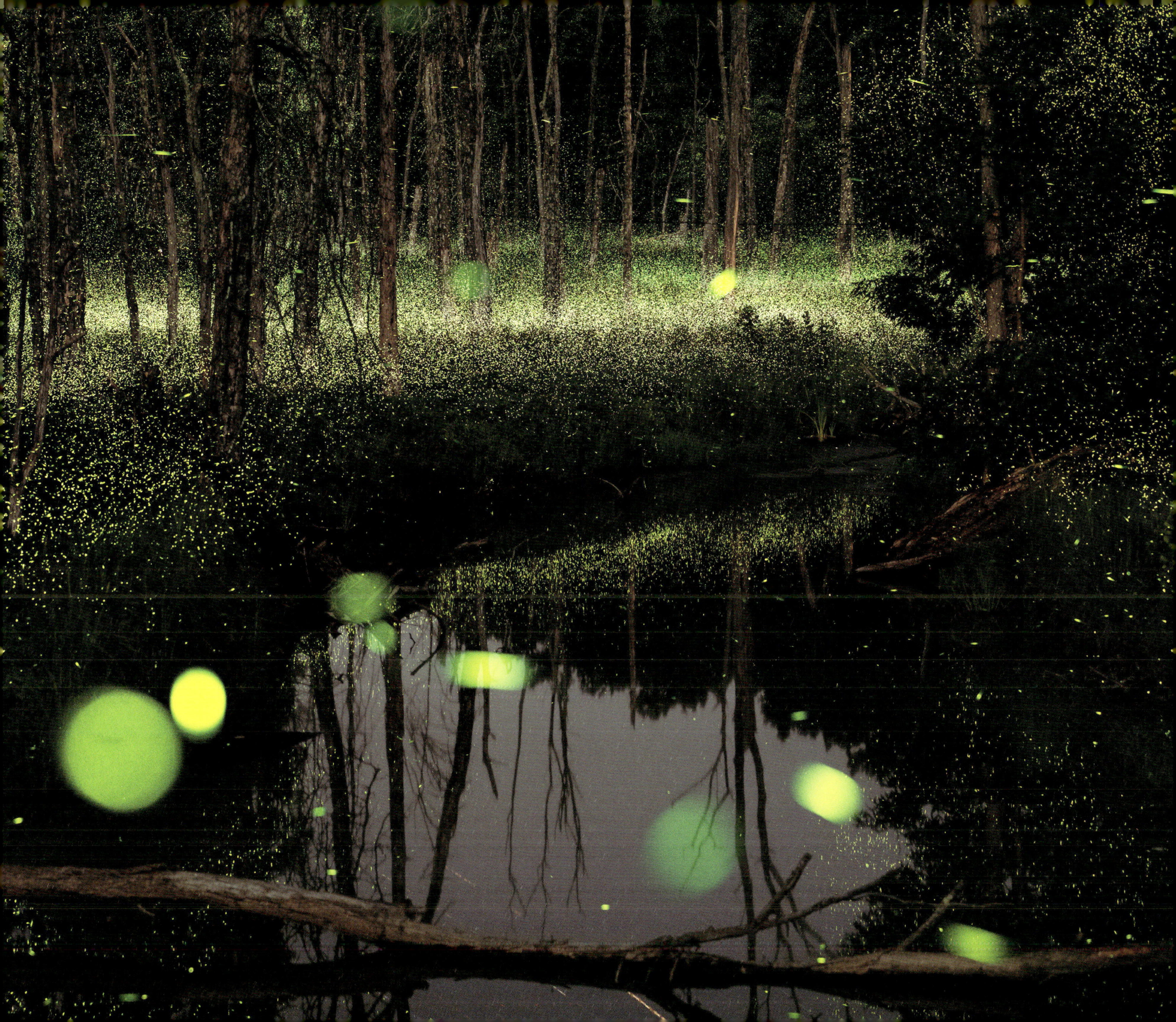

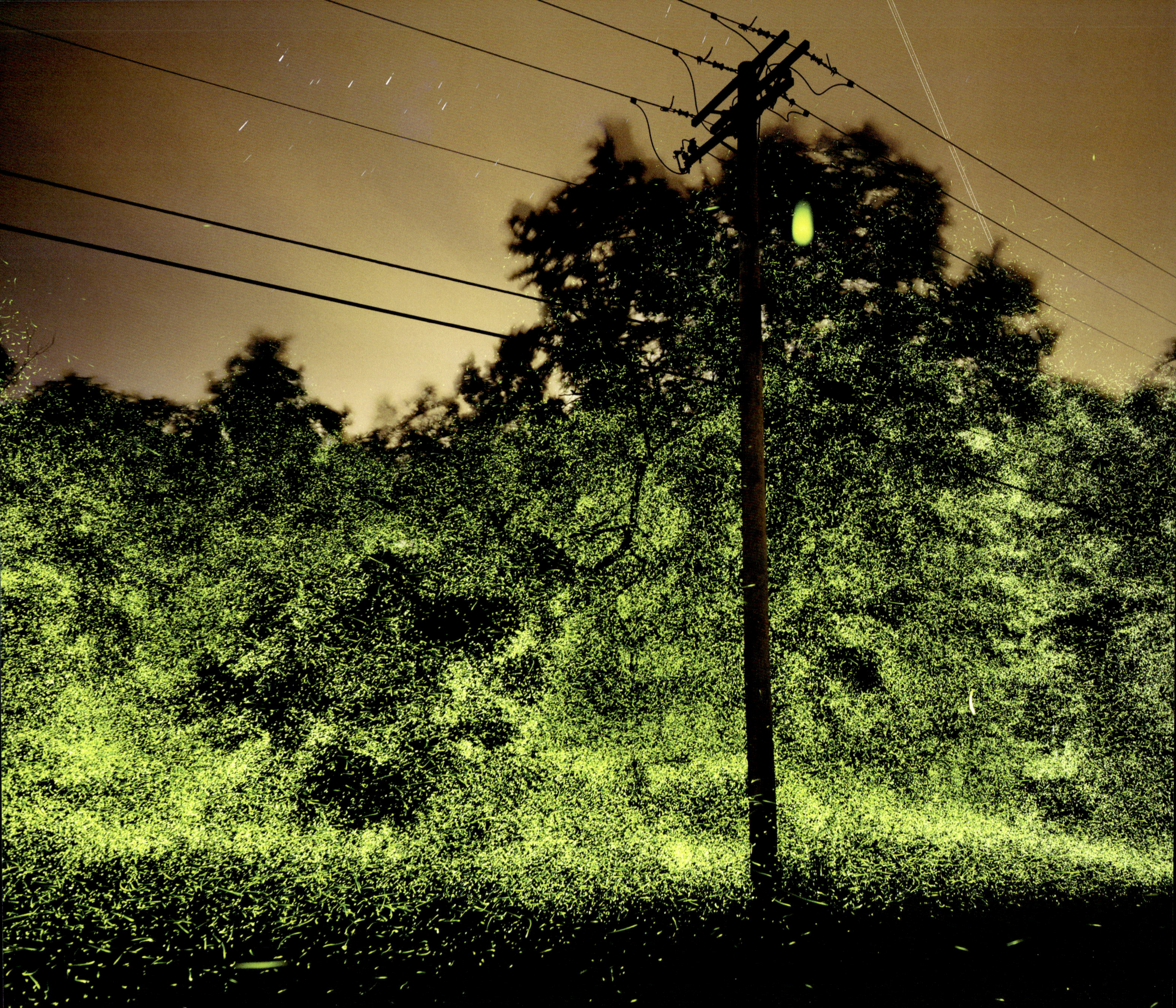

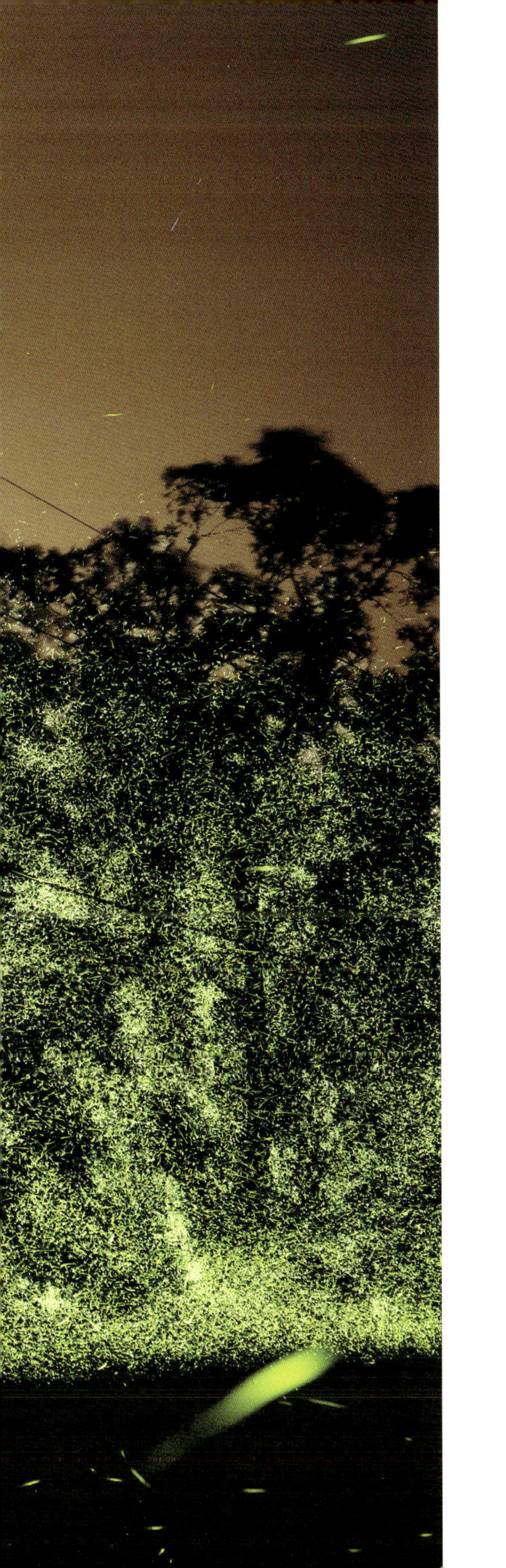

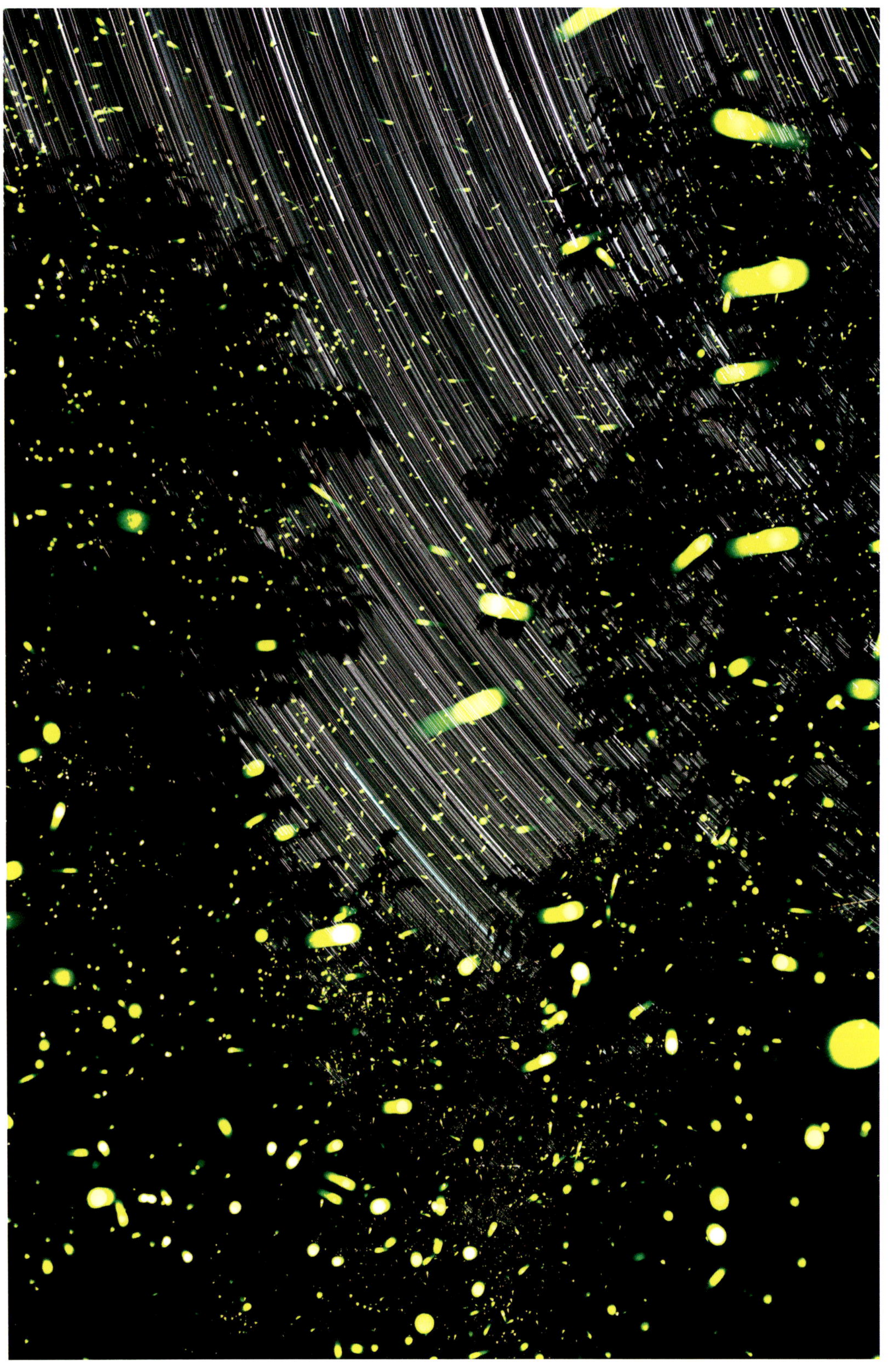

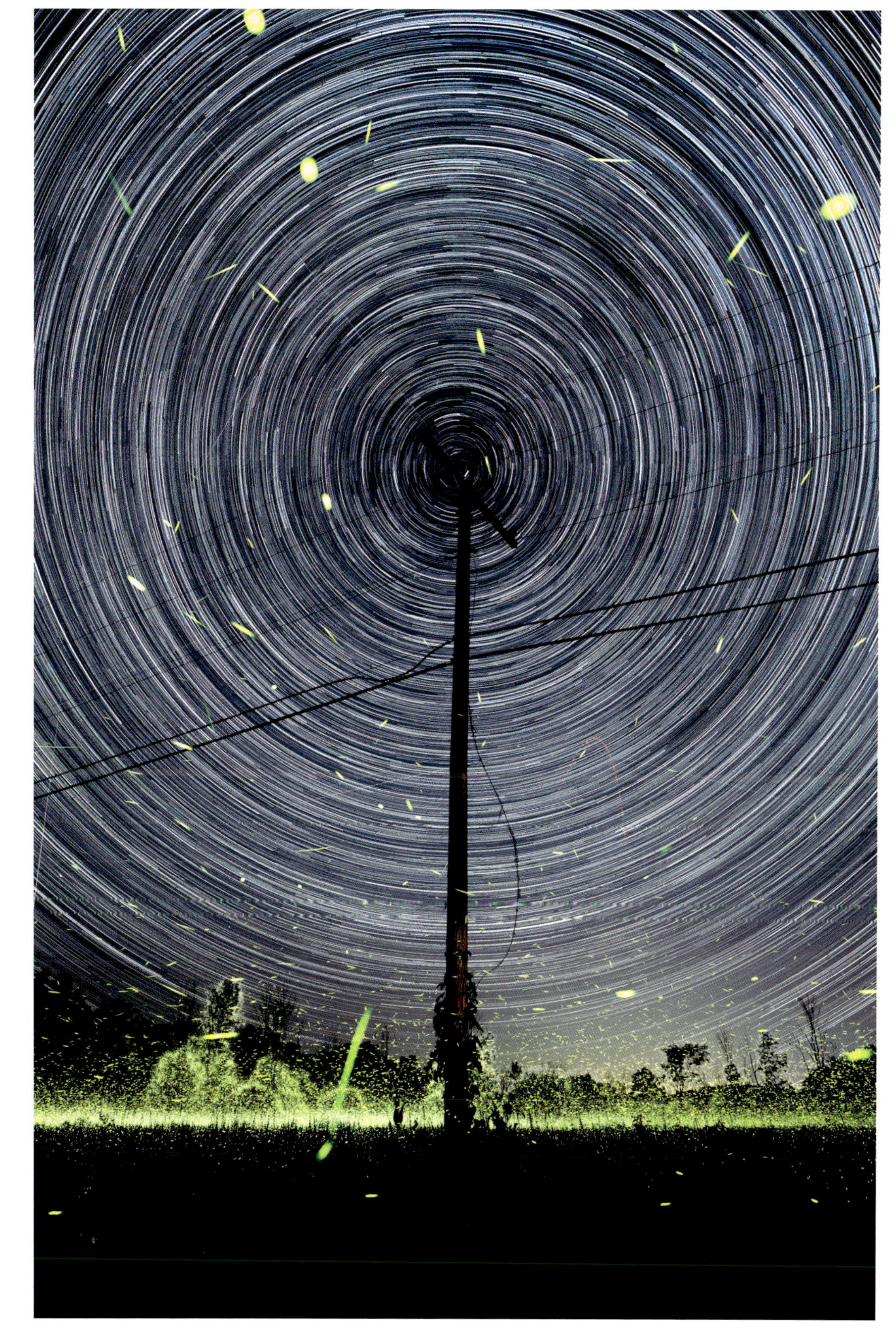

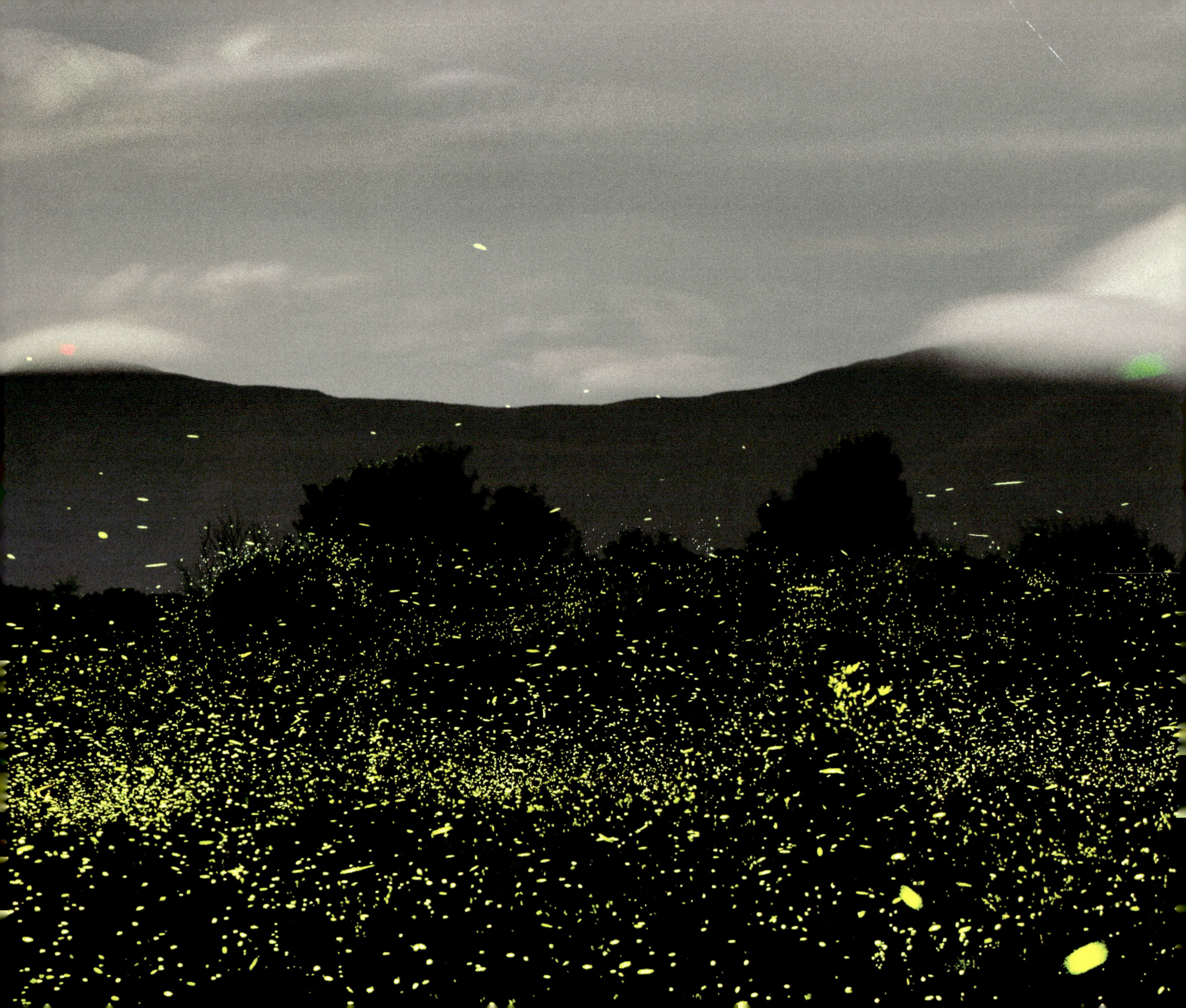

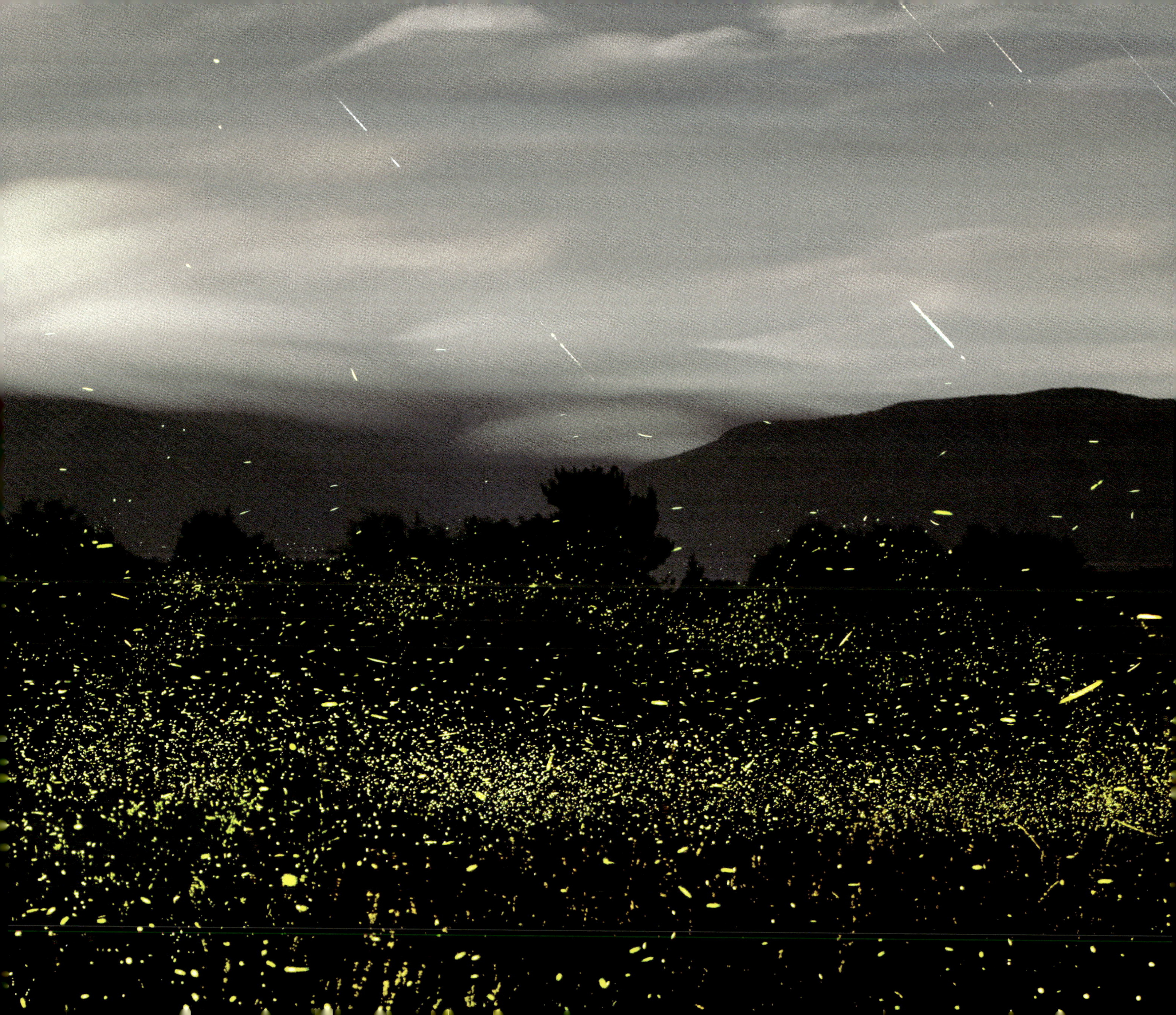

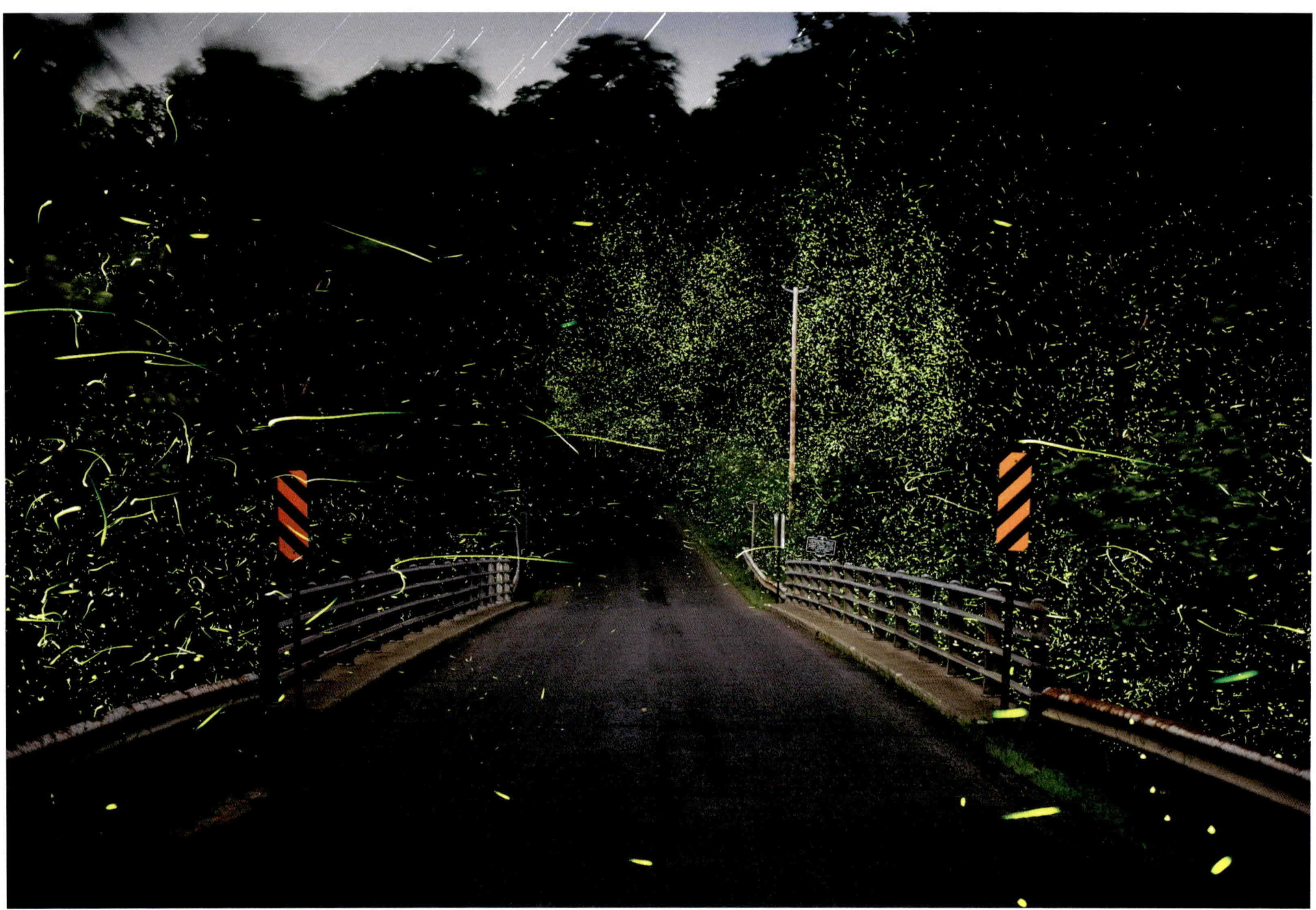

I was on a back road outside of Kinderhook one night. When I say back road, I mean there were a couple of farms in the middle and no destination of interest at either end. I had been there for about an hour and a half when the first car showed up.

It was around 1 or 2 AM, 70 degrees, and humid. They saw me, in my highway Day-Glo and reflective don't-want-to-get-hit-by-cars outfit, and came screeching to a halt. Law enforcement, county deputy, every single light on that car blazing, LED bars. The works.

"How we doing tonight?" The standard law-enforcement opening line. I pulled out my phone, The Cop Whisperer™, always pre-loaded with Instagram or my website, and launched into my well-rehearsed routine. This was not my first rodeo. I showed him some pictures, and he said, "Holy shit" and then (incredulously), "You are doing this out here? I drive this road every night, and I never see fireflies."

I said, "OK. Turn off your lights. All of them."

"Pardon me?"

"Yeah. Your lights. Turn them off and give me five minutes of your time." I wanted to say, "I am not a psycho killer, I swear," but I didn't.

To my utter and eternal disbelief, he complied with my directive, with the one exception being the dim red tactical light in the car. Acceptable. We started to talk. Kids today; that kind of stuff.

Five minutes went by, and I realized he was now looking past me into the mucky brush on the side of the road. His eyes had finally adjusted.

Slower this time (It always is), he said, "Holy shit."

My (larger) job was done. His mind was blown. I have no doubt I will find him out there again someday, this time with his lights off. Maybe with his kids. Hopefully not on their phones.

PETE MAUNEY
TIVOLI, NEW YORK 2024

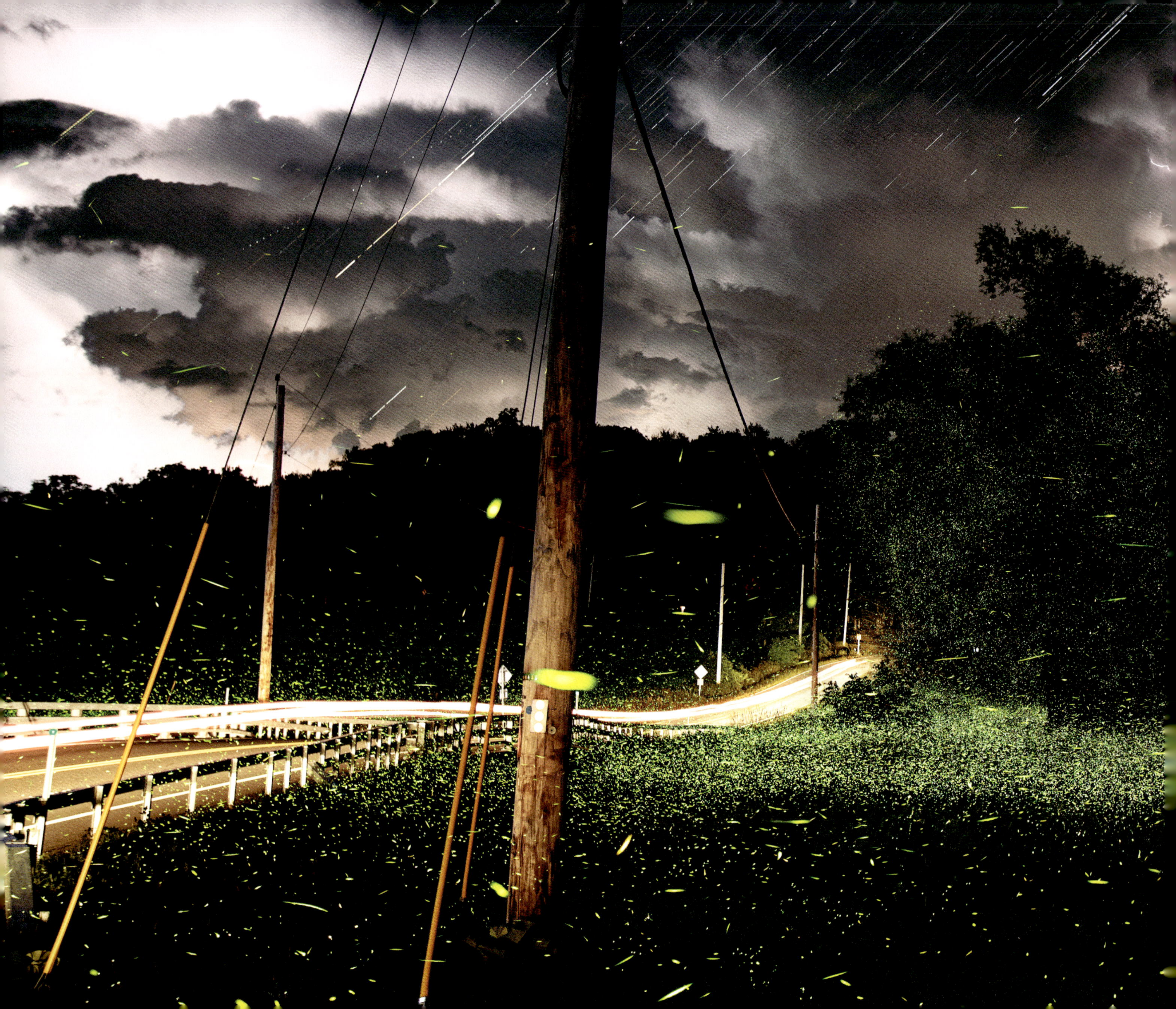

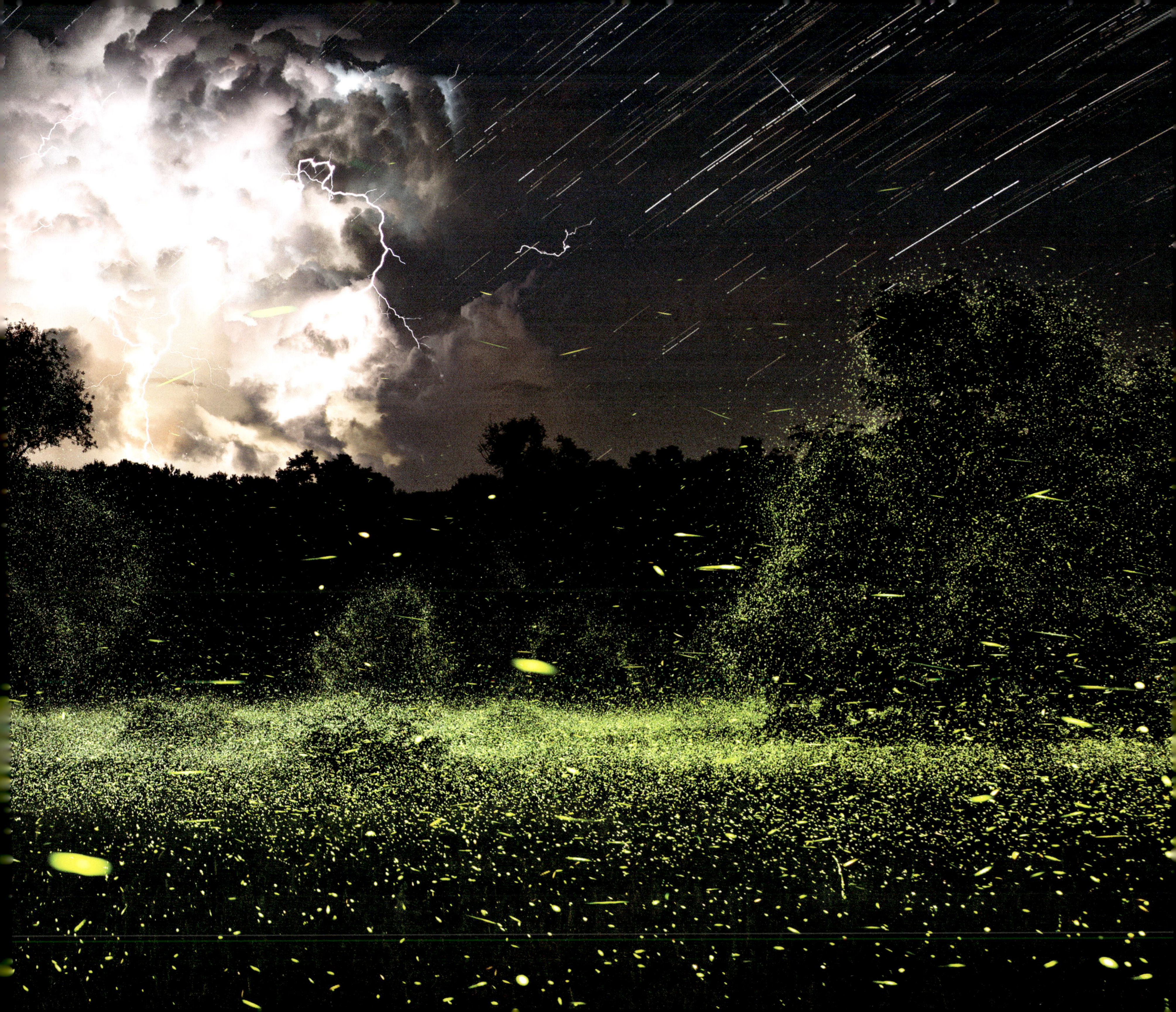

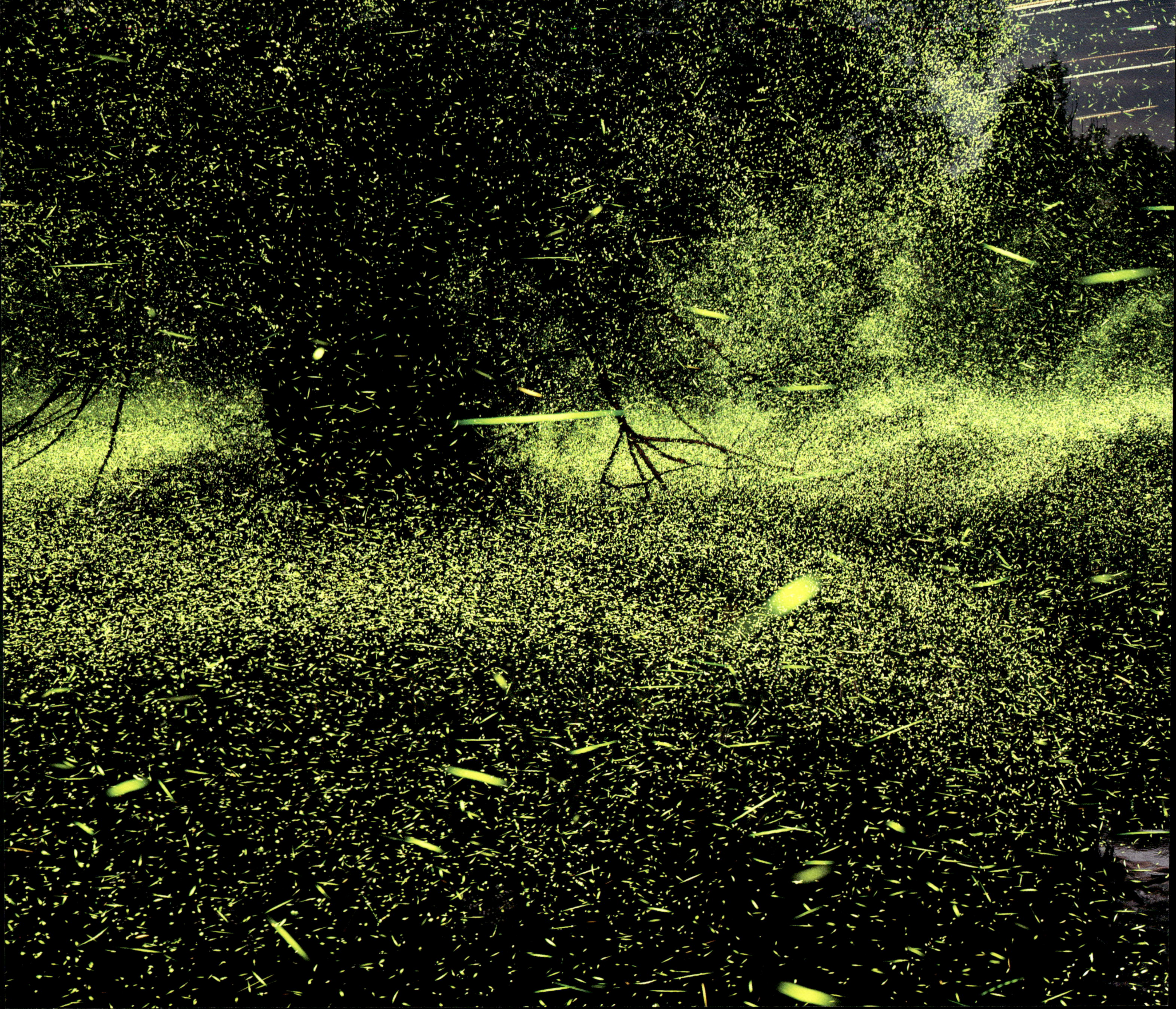

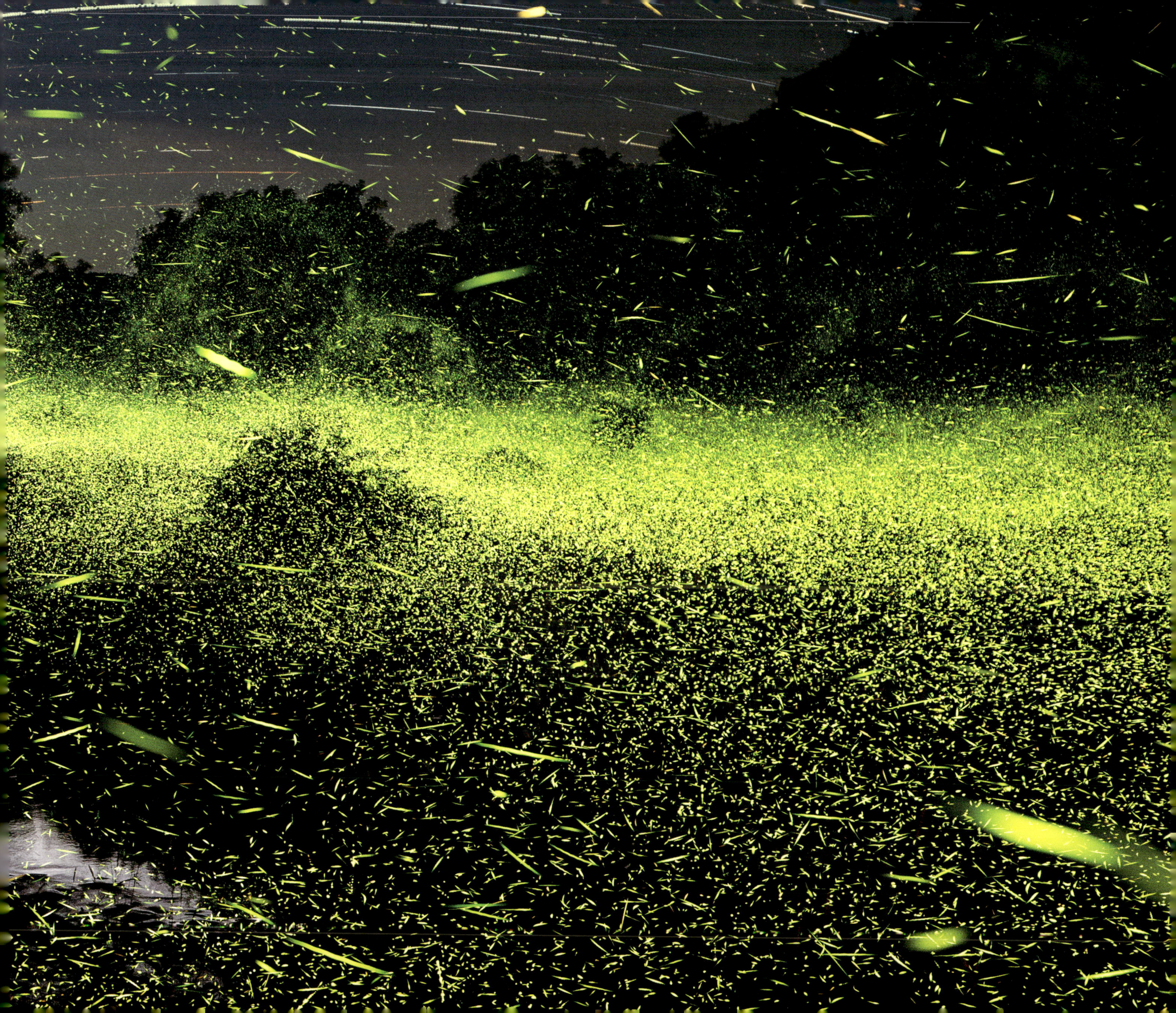

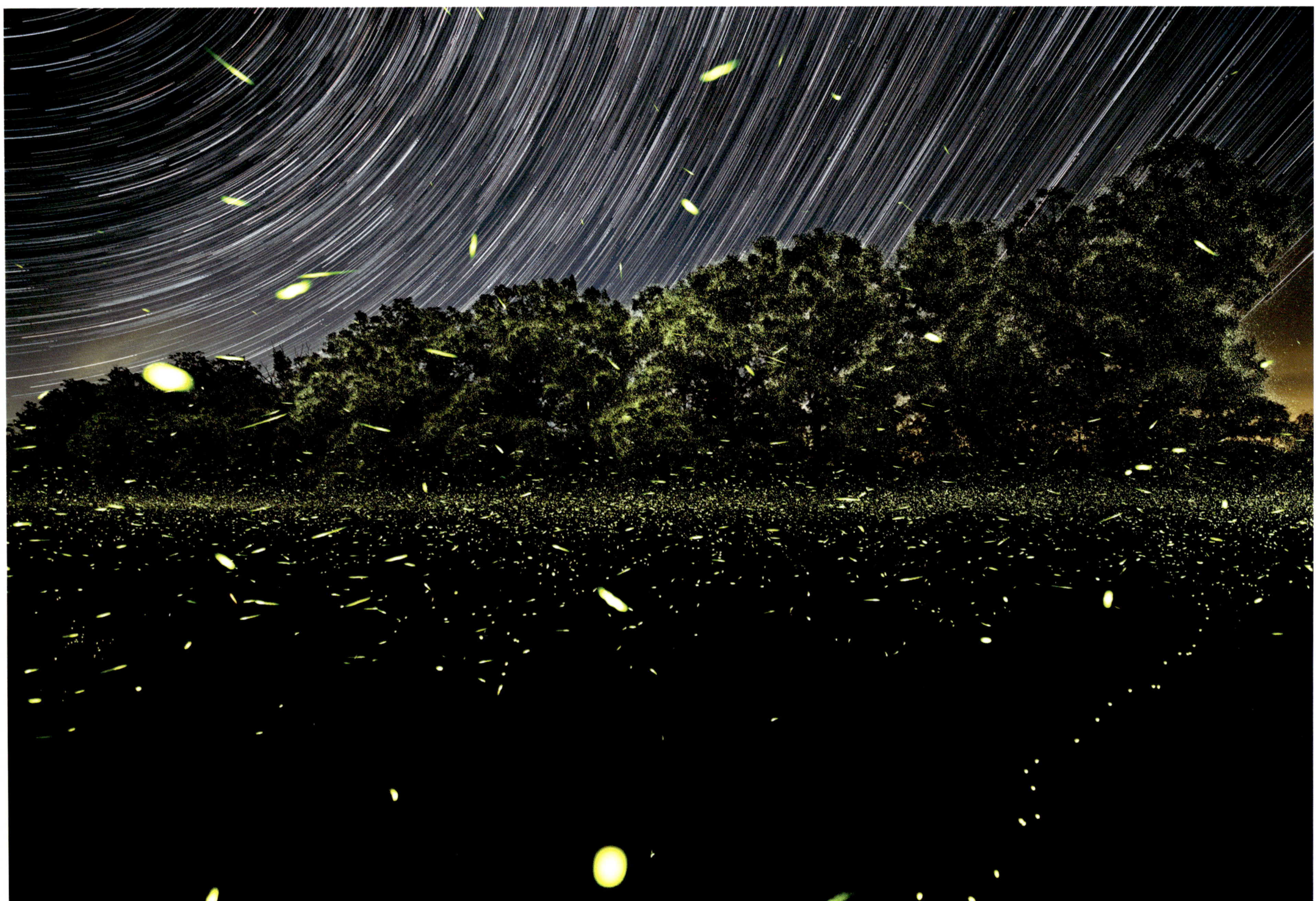

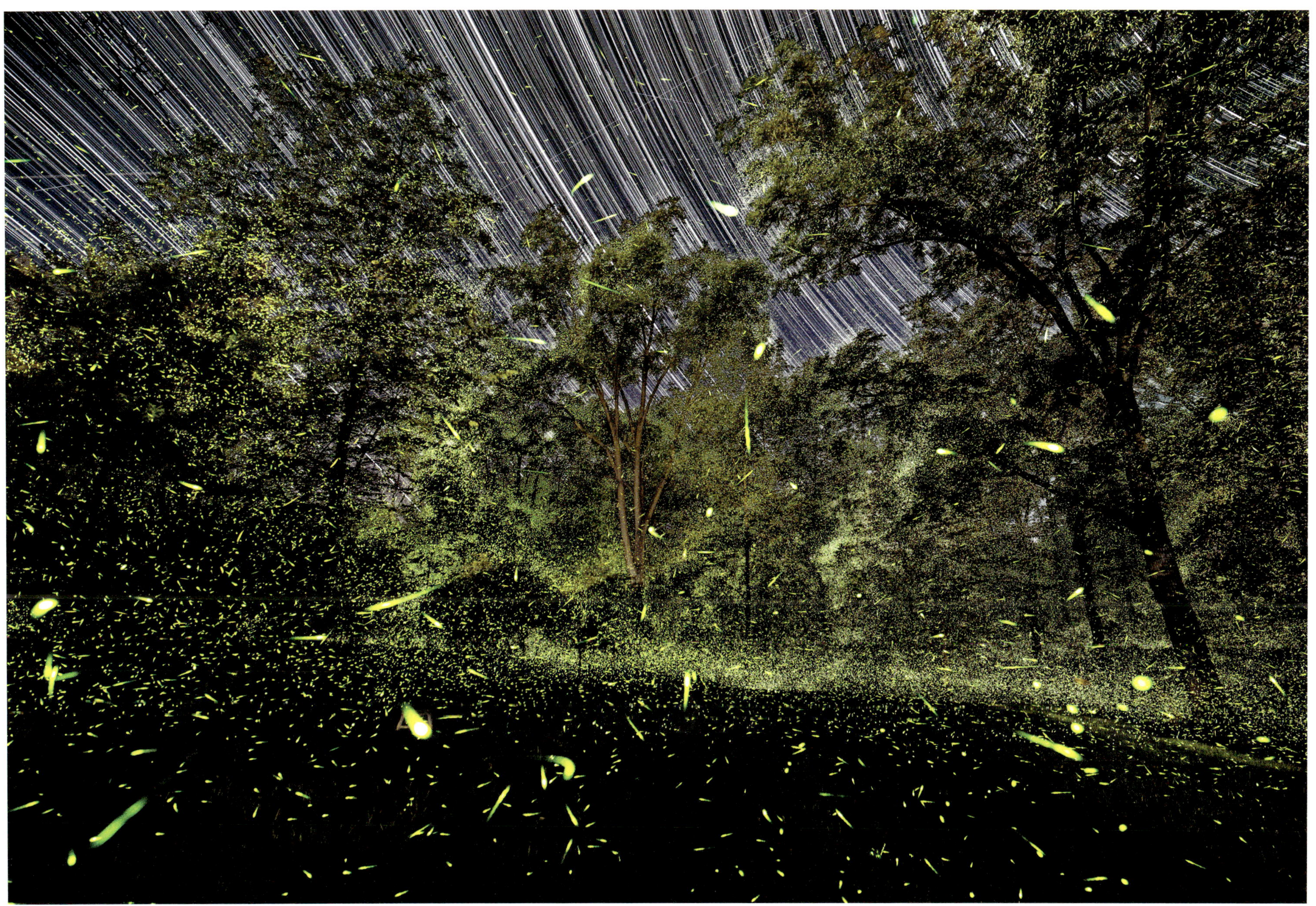

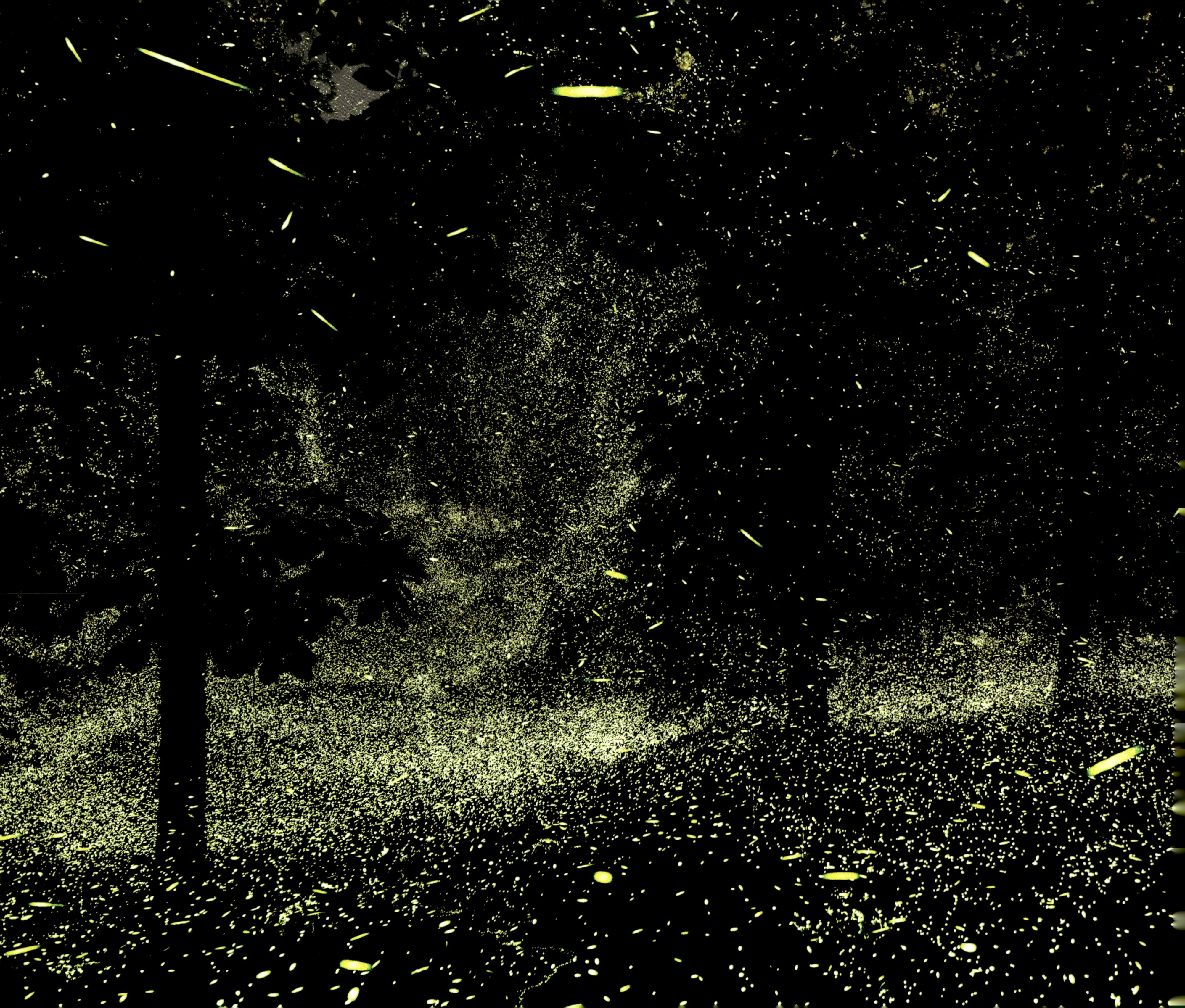

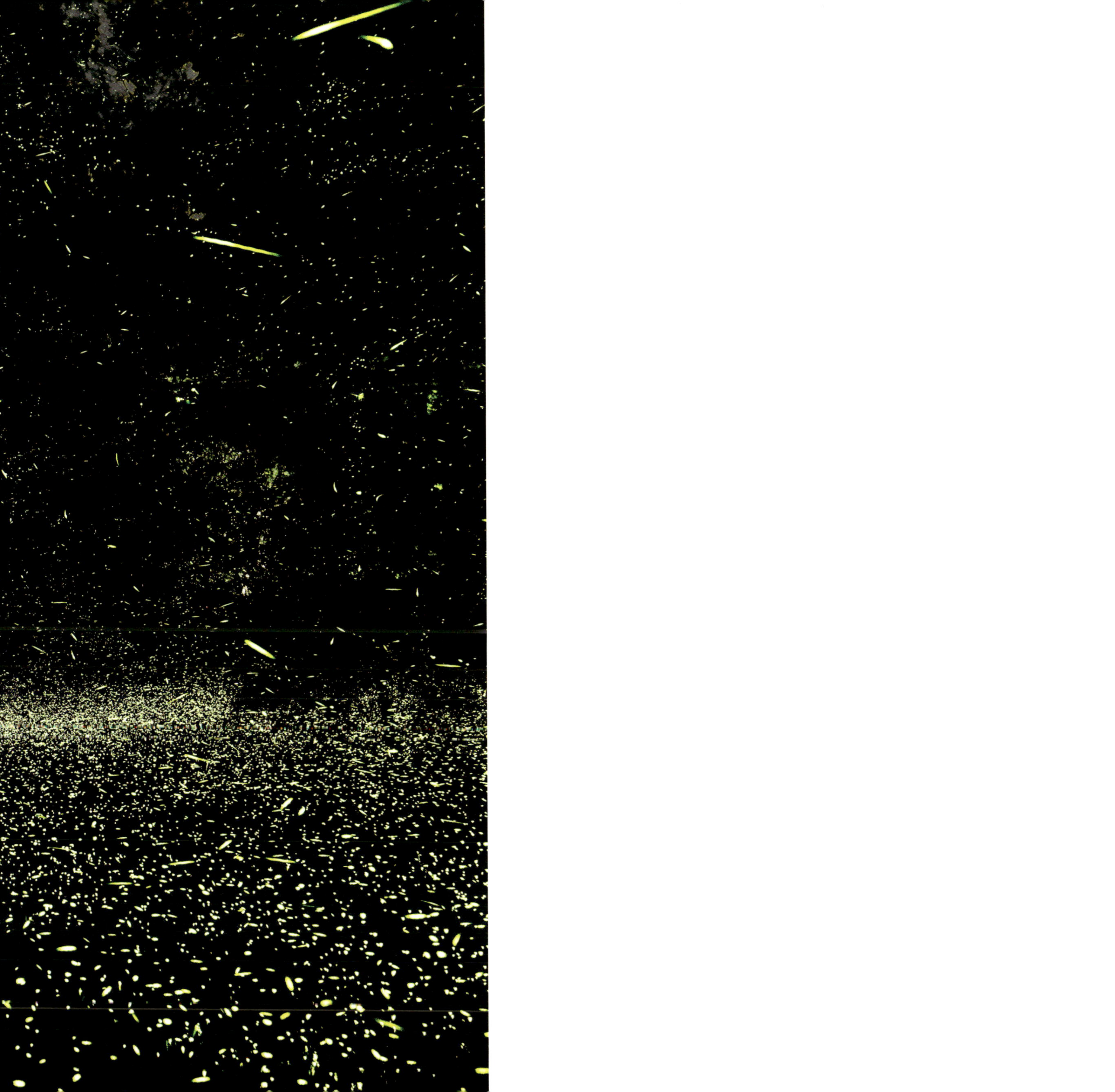

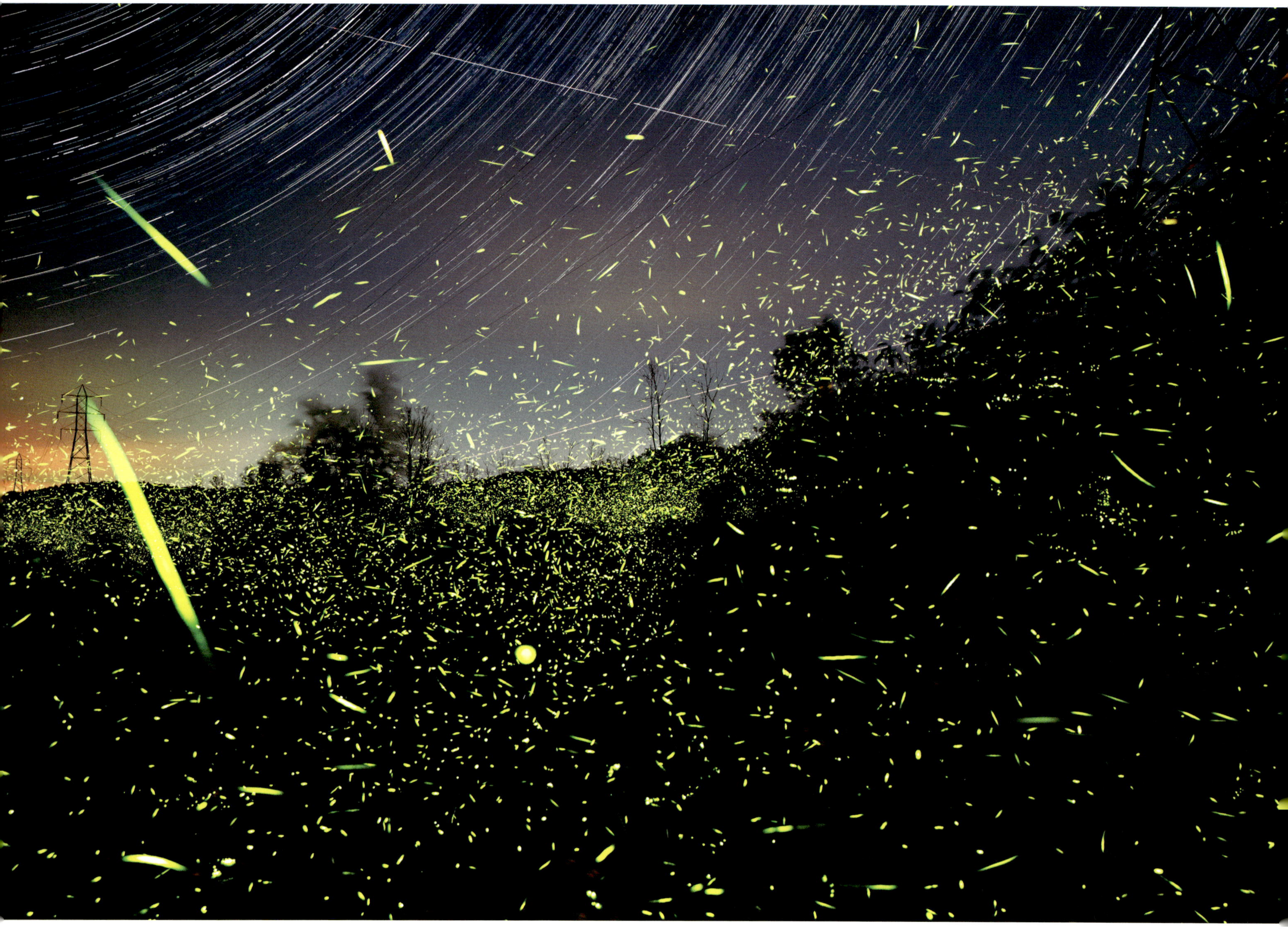

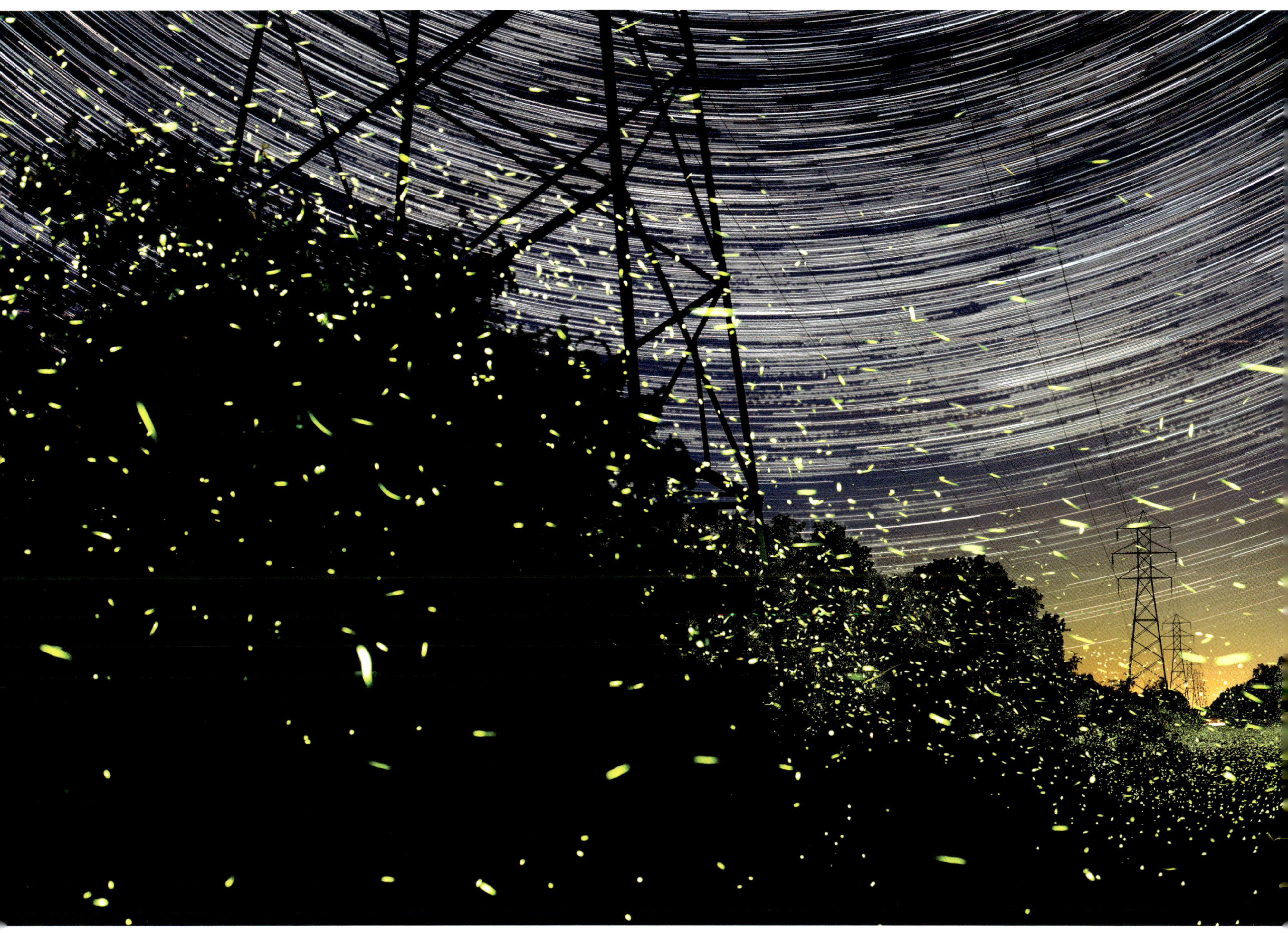

PETE MAUNEY AND JESSICA CHAPPE –
IN CONVERSATION

Why fireflies?

Honestly, fireflies chose me. As a night person I had come across them throughout my life and always found them beautiful because, of course, we all do. That being said, I had been photographing at night for decades before I considered taking them on as a subject. I used to see them on the edges of my film frames, but it wasn't until they started showing up in digital pictures I was already making at night in my small town that I saw the potential. For the first couple years, the fireflies did the heavy lifting, as it were, and I just followed them, making pictures and waiting to see what would happen.

It wasn't until I started to get really obsessed with them that I realized something. In order for the images to become something other than "pretty" or "cool," the work couldn't just be pictures of fireflies. It had to be more interactive, more intensive, more intentional, more revelatory. So I started being more methodical, trying to predict an eventual outcome to the composition. This can be a fool's errand when you're working with a subject you can't control. Over time, I learned to work with them. It became almost collaborative. For the first few years I felt like I was merely absorbing and getting to know them. Once we got through that introductory period, I was able to feel more photographically and artistically comfortable, both in terms of the approach and the outcome.

How do you attempt to control the composition?

I used to be more of a point-and-shoot photographer. More compulsive, more impulsive. Over-schooling tends to diminish that approach, for better and for worse.

Right after I graduated from college, for example, Wendy Ewald's[1] work was hugely influential for me. The children she worked with—without the so-called benefit of art school—knew what was important. They put it right in the center of the frame. That's the way I'd always seen photographs. I don't compose my photographs using the rule of thirds. Well, sometimes I do use that method of composition for day-job work, but in terms of my personal photography practice, I'm a centrally composed person. When I look back on all my work over the years, they've always been like that. Seeing Wendy's kids' pictures, particularly the Kentucky ones[2], the success and rawness of them, gave me a lot more confidence to follow my gut.

One of many things that attracts me to this process is that it's a puzzle, trying to get all of these different elements to interact. I am very much a control-oriented person. But I also think that being disrupted from your comfort zone is how good art gets made. For example, I know where north is, and I know what direction the stars are rotating. Those things are entirely predictable. You can semi-predict the weather, of course, but it's also subject to change. And the fireflies, again, aren't at all. So sometimes I get lucky and manage to get something good but more often than not the bugs determine the content.

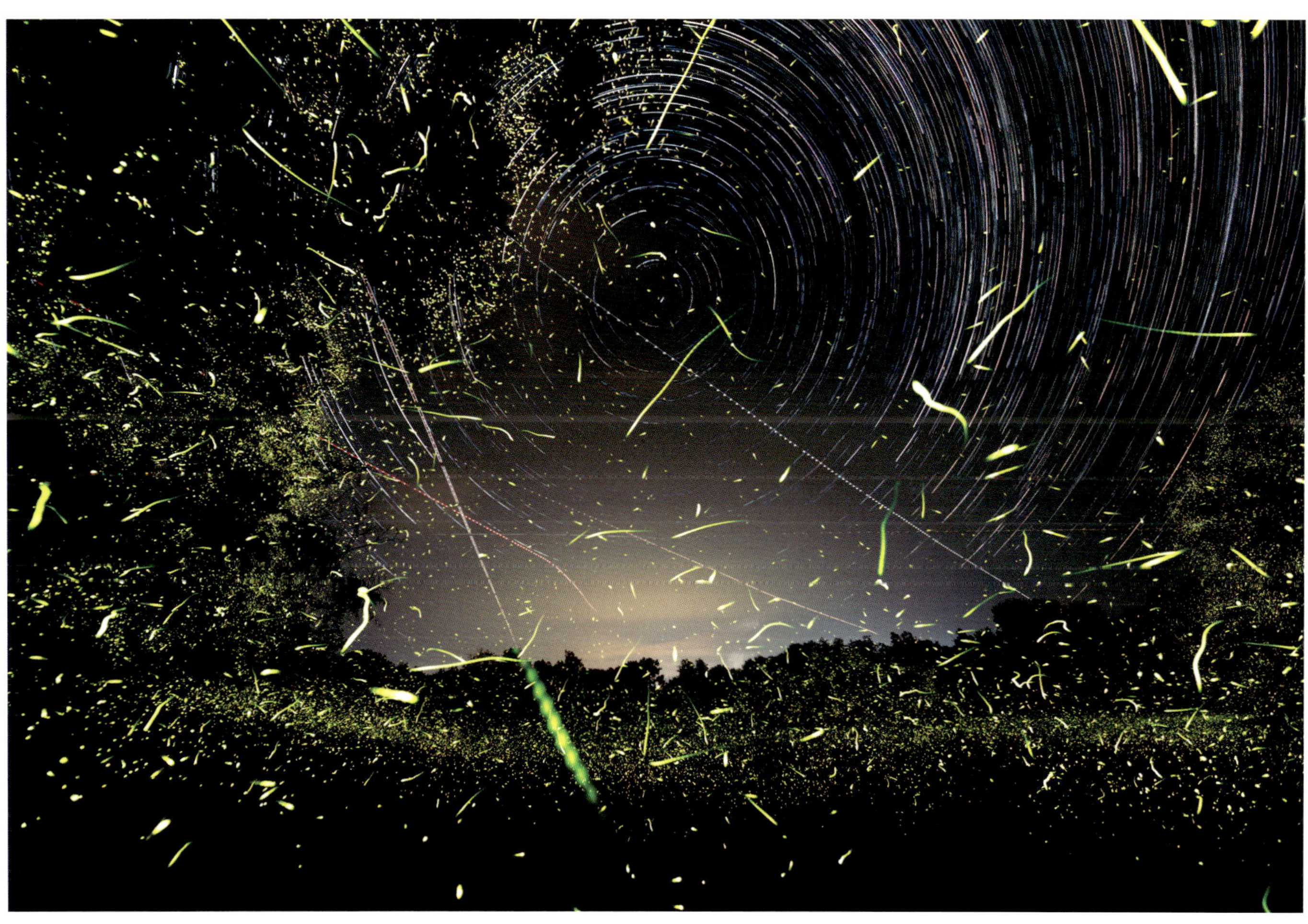

Because I have the freedom to set up the picture the way I want it to be, I can center Polaris in the frame, and I can put the trees on the edge, and I know that there are fucking fireflies everywhere. I have a pretty good idea that it's gonna work out, but I won't know if it works until I see it. And in the case of the picture that I'm thinking of, it's a magical one, one of the last ones I did this past summer.

What I learned the night before is often what I explore the next night. That photo, for example, was very controlled, very intentional. I first pondered this composition the previous night, and it worked despite the elements of total uncertainty and unpredictability of the fireflies, the clouds, the satellites, and the airplanes.

You mentioned that your process became more interactive, intensive, and complicated. Can you elaborate?

Once I'd started photographing fireflies regularly, I asked myself: How can I do more? How can I combine more fireflies into one picture without blowing out the background or sky from overexposure? That's a challenge, with single long exposures. Eventually, while searching online for a solution, I discovered image stacking, a technique that's been used for decades in astronomy and astrophotography with earth rotation tracking cameras. Image stacking is usually used to reduce noise in a final image. Instead of doing one long exposure with high sensitivity, and getting a lot of noise, you do a bunch of underexposed frames and add them together. The averaging out of the noise pixels across all the frames almost eliminates the noise, and then you can adjust the tones to get a much cleaner image. So, in each one of my final photos, there are between 100 and 2,000 photos taken over the course of one to five hours. Within that there are patterns.

When I discovered the possibilities of image stacking, it brought me back to the experience of processing black-and-white prints in the darkroom. Even though I've processed thousands of them, every time I see a picture come up in the chemicals, it's still magic. Until I began working with image stacking I'd never had that feeling when I was working with digital. You press the button, it activates a shutter and a sensor, which translates light into ones and zeros and outputs it to a memory card. It's completely separated from everything that makes analog photography seem like magic. There's so much more intervention in digital.

Image stacking is a very different kind of magic. It's a magic that is about the perception and the folding and the accumulation of time. Once the individual images are stacked, it's just one click of a button and everything is revealed. Everything happens all at once. The theoretical becomes the actual. It shows you a complete and accurate reality that's separate from your own.

A lot of my pictures don't work, but when they do, to me they're magic. What they do almost consistently blows my mind. I'm always wary of saying that my own pictures blow my mind, because I don't mean it as a narcissistic thing. It's more like, "Holy shit, I can't believe I was privileged enough to witness something like this, make this record, and to have been there."

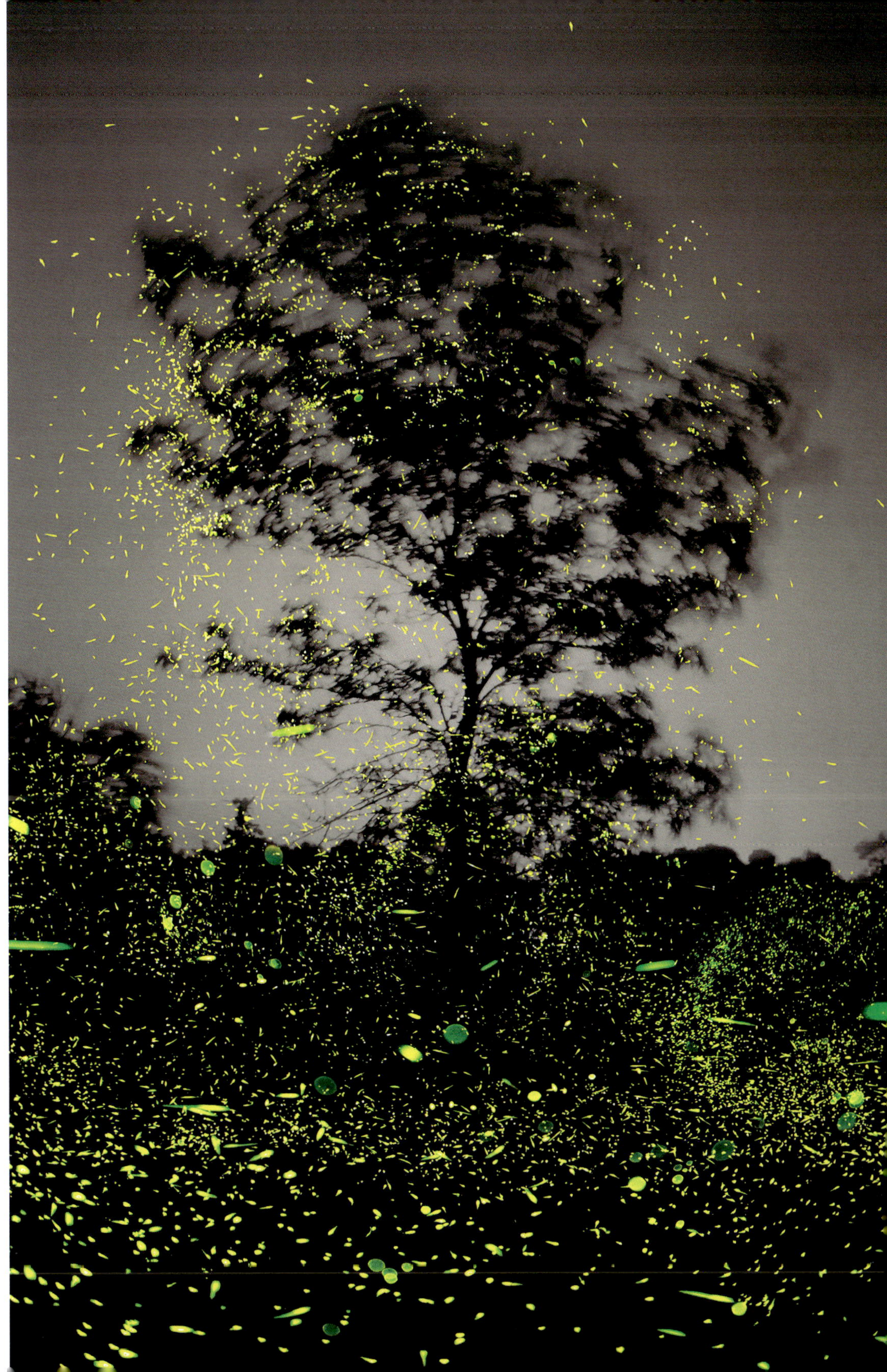

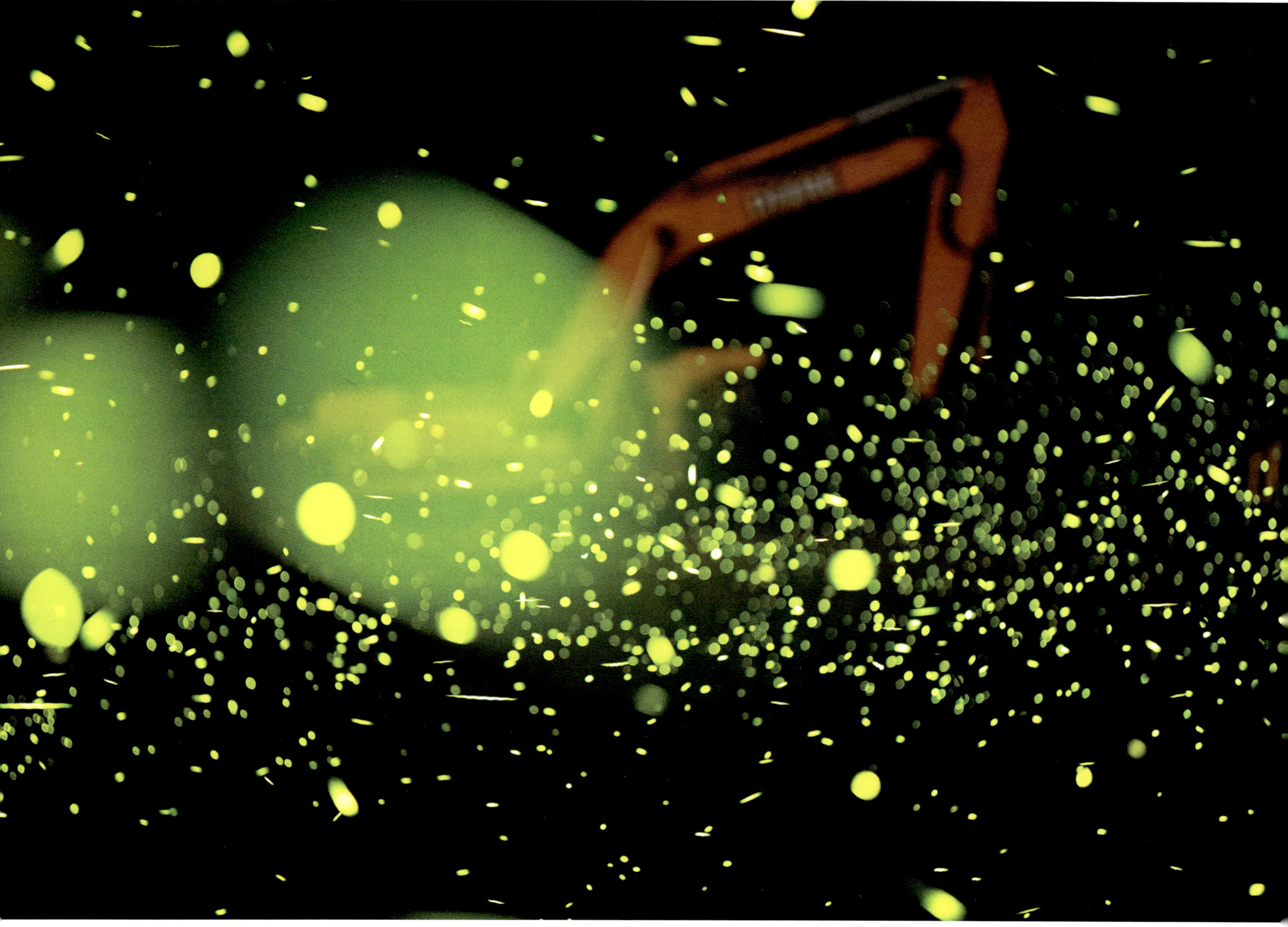

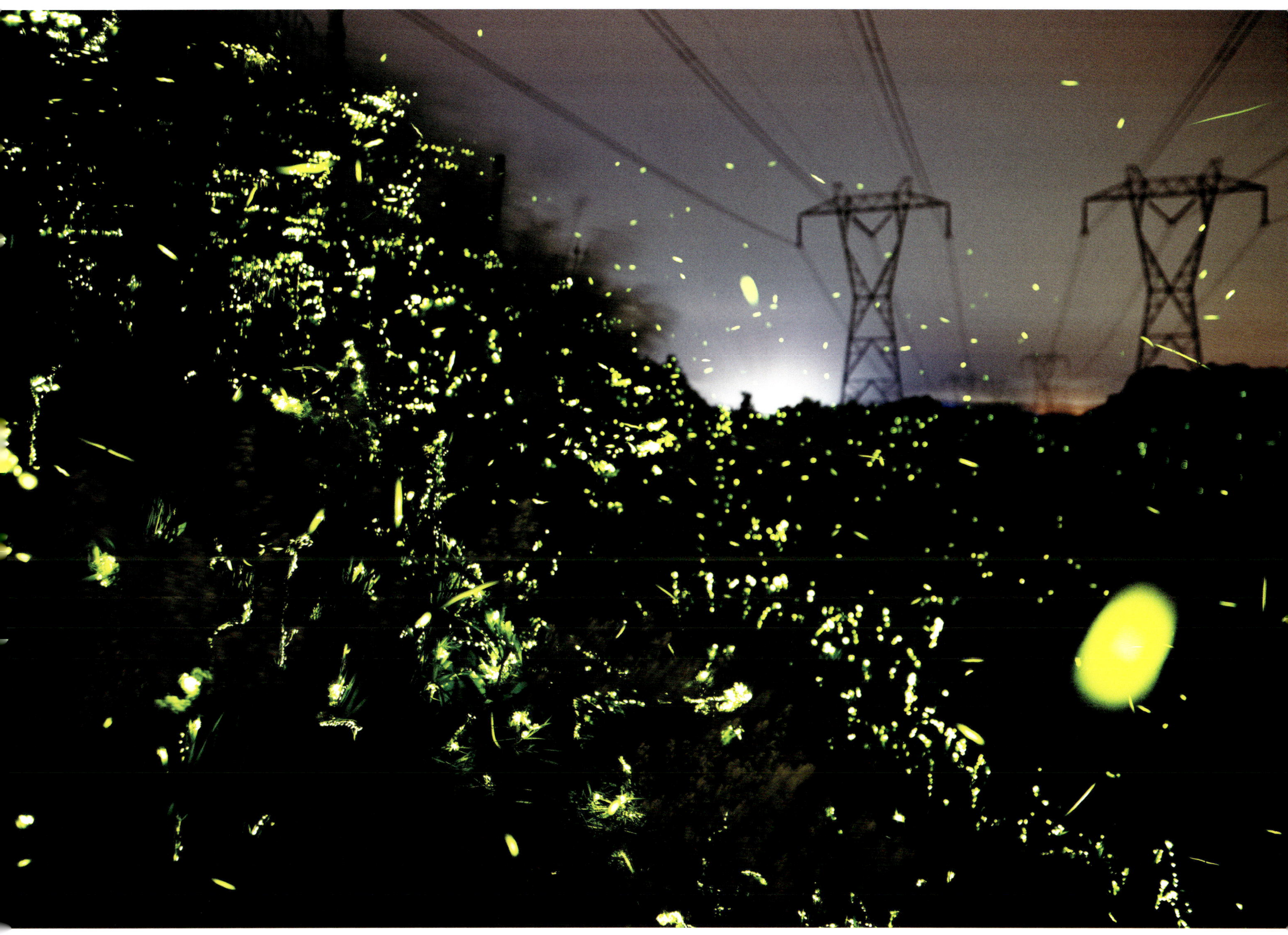

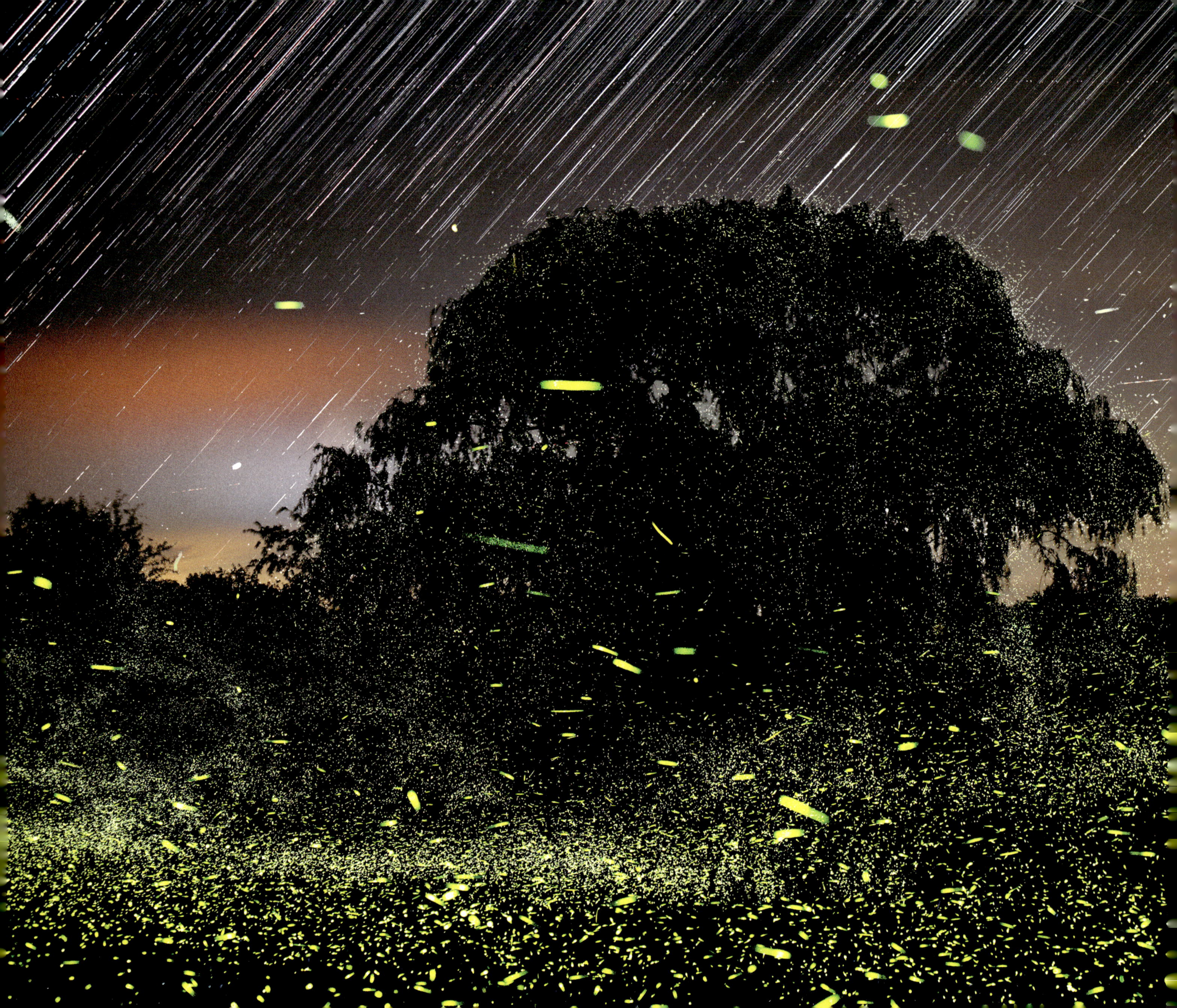

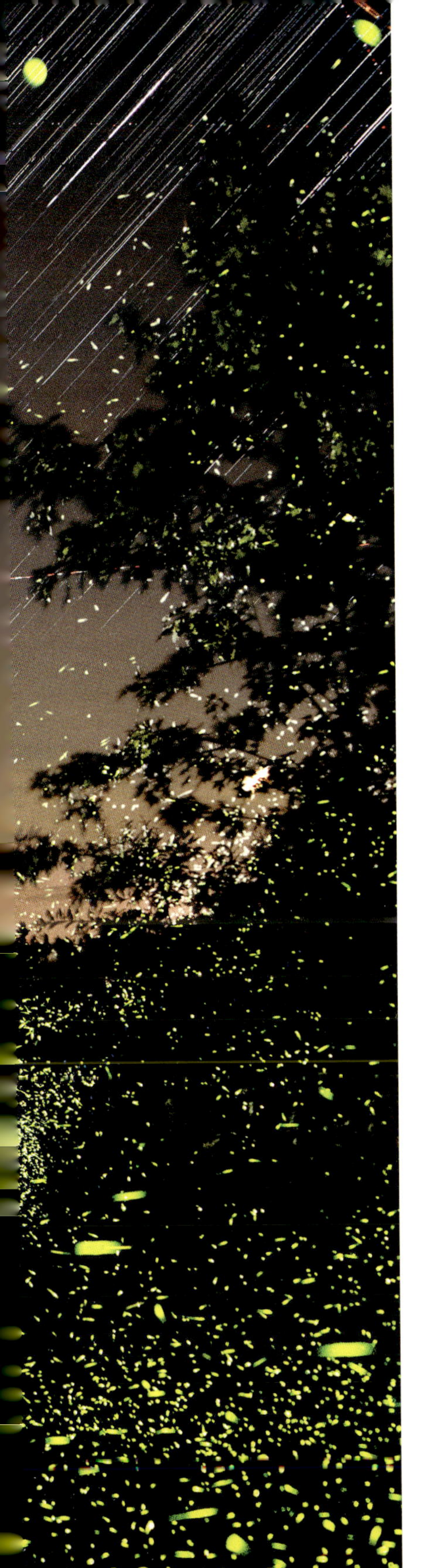

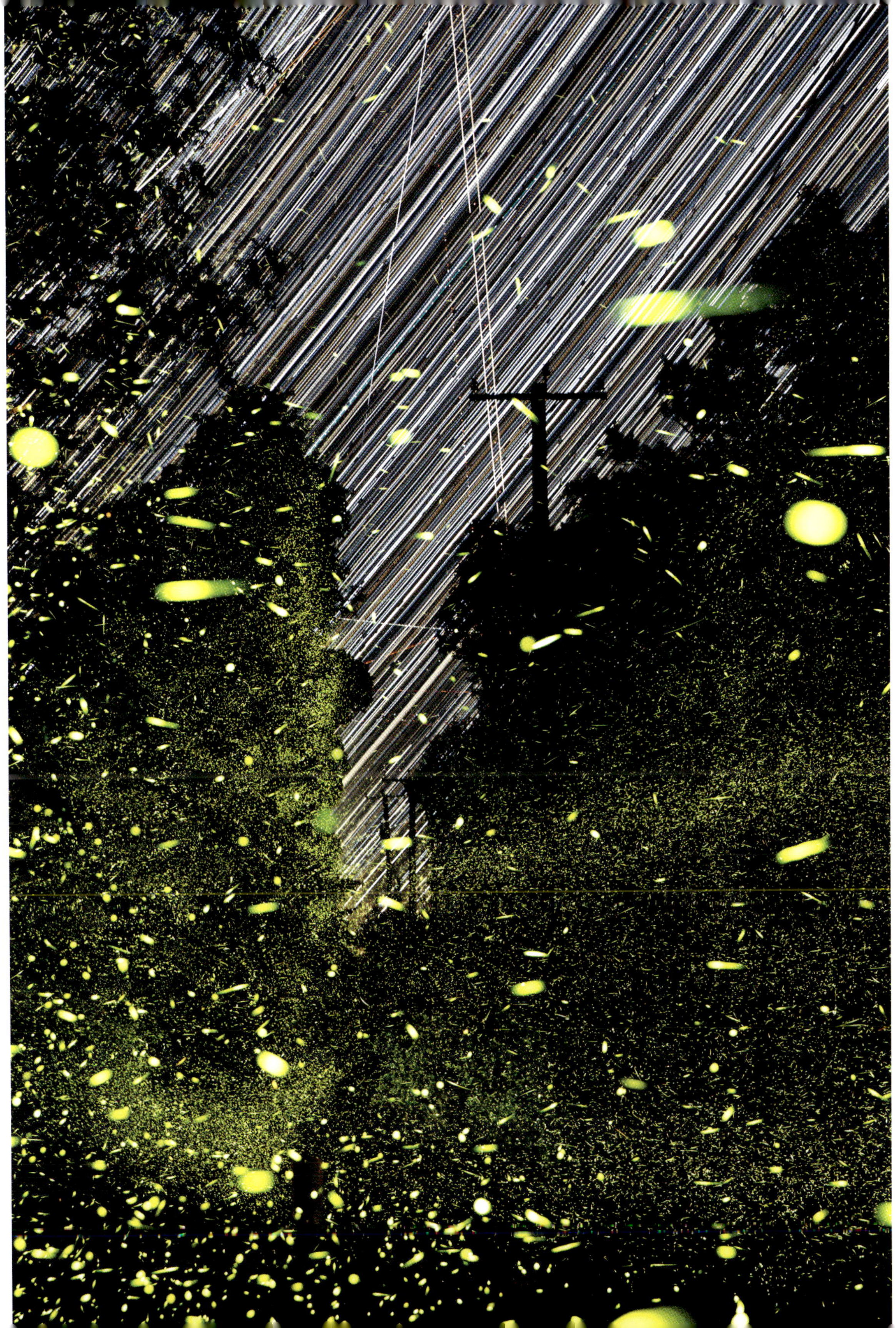

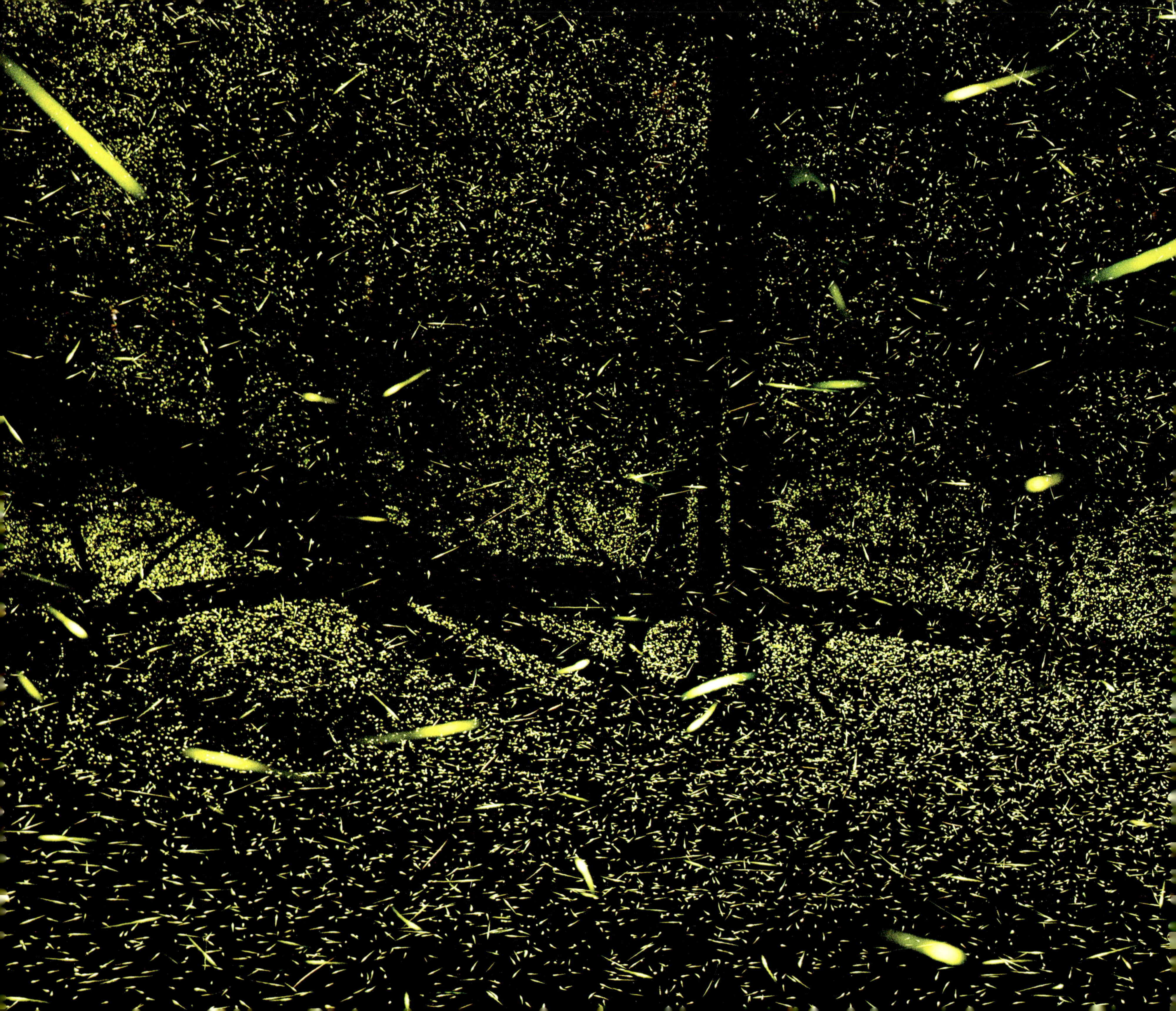

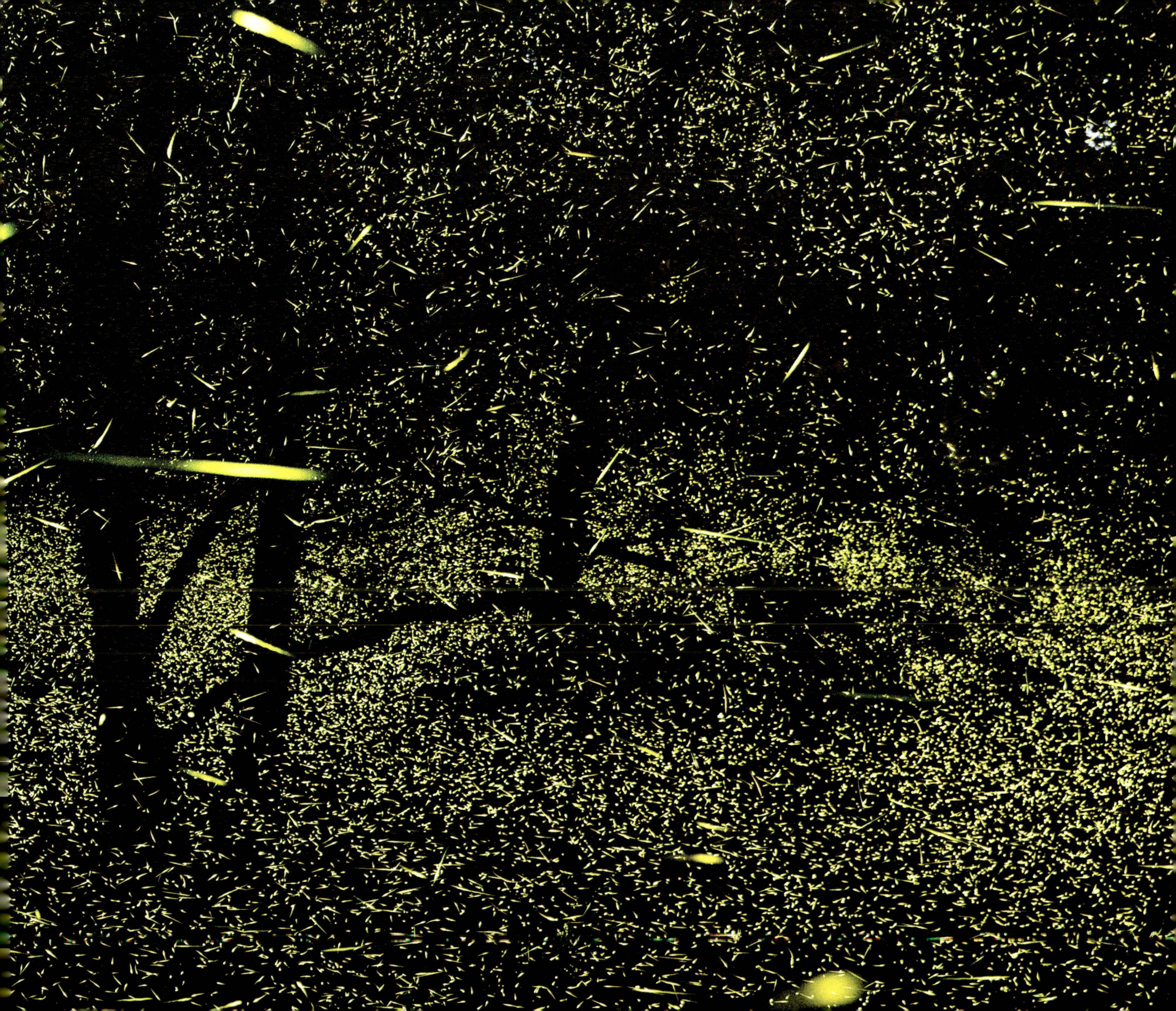

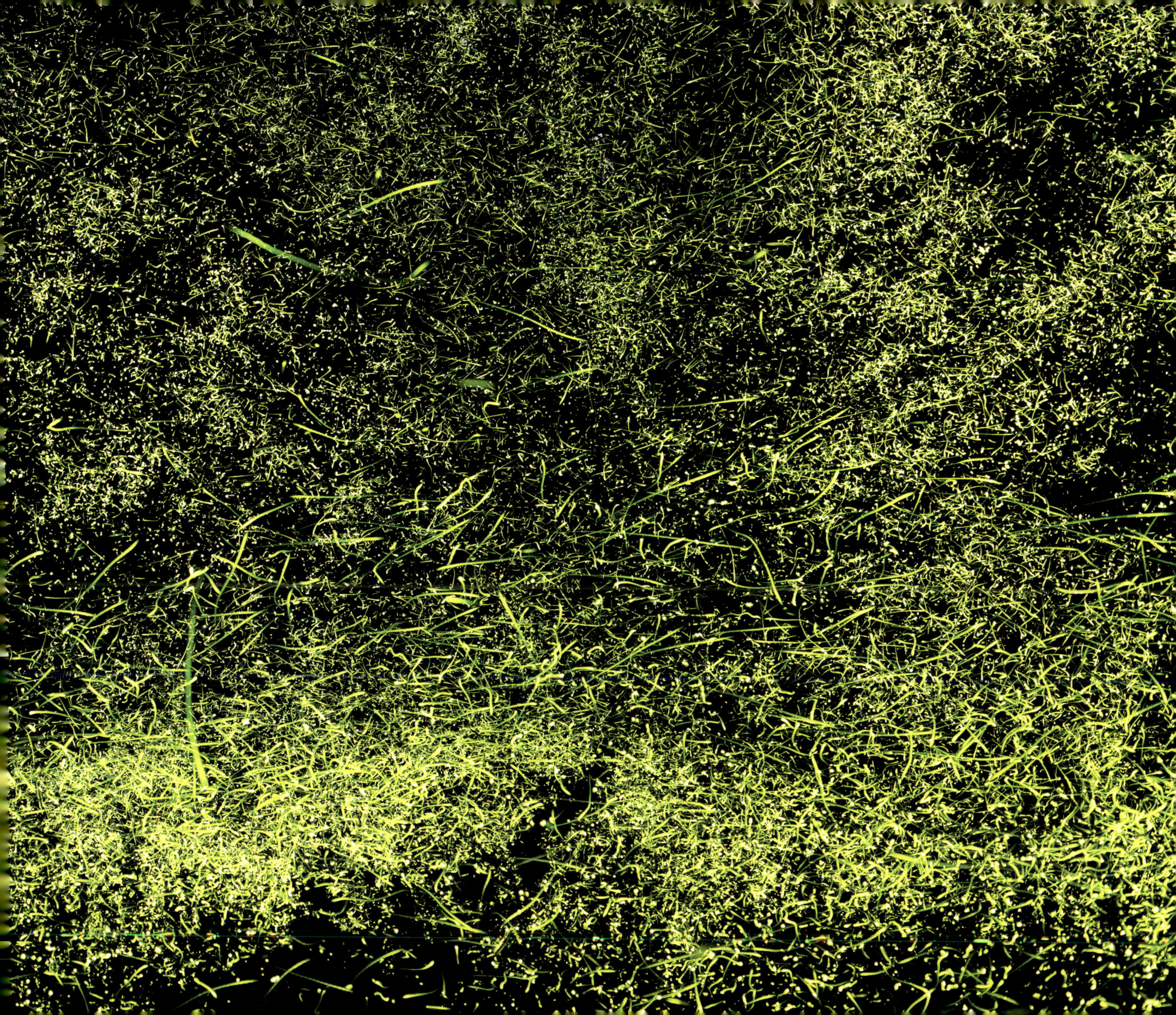

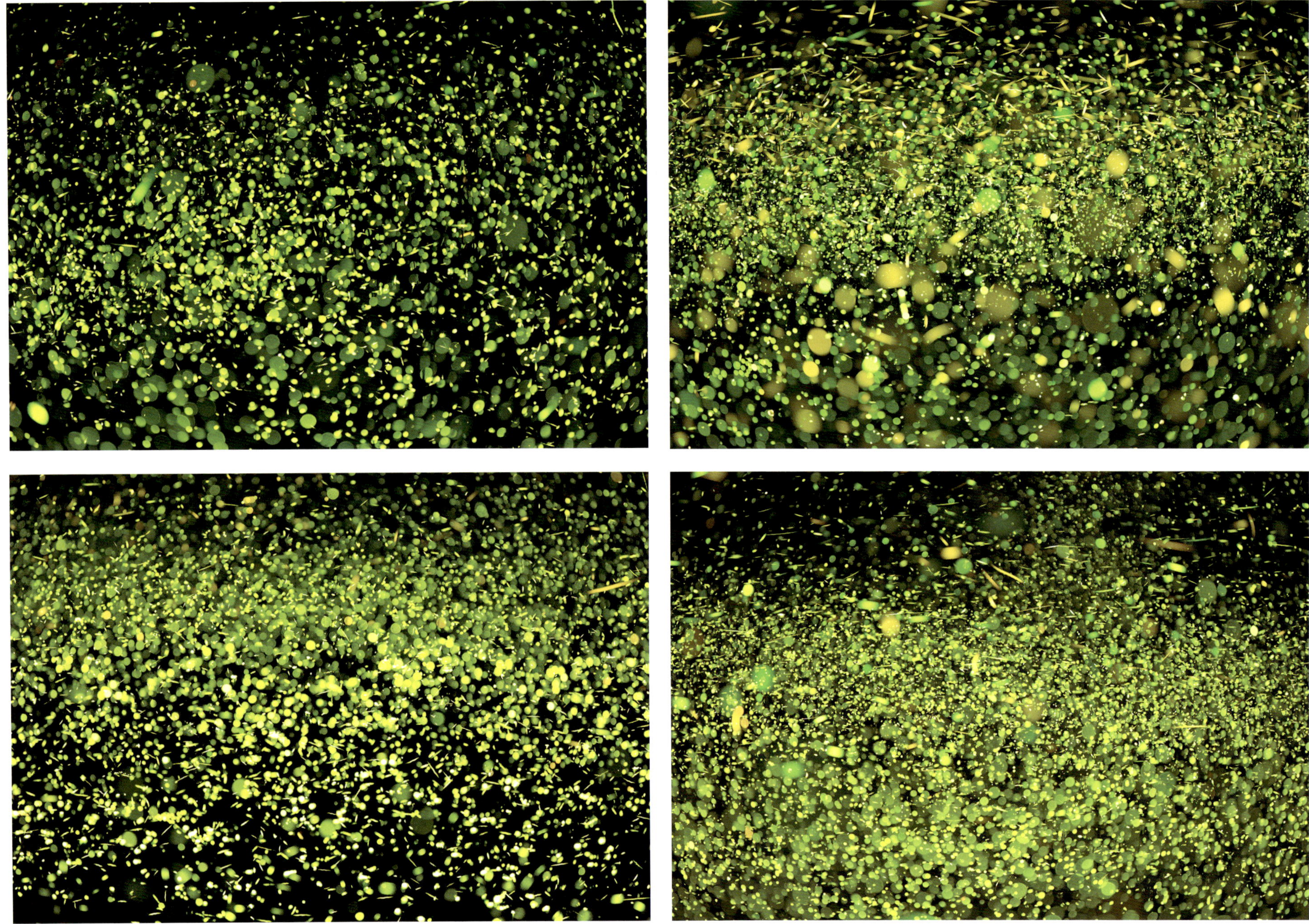

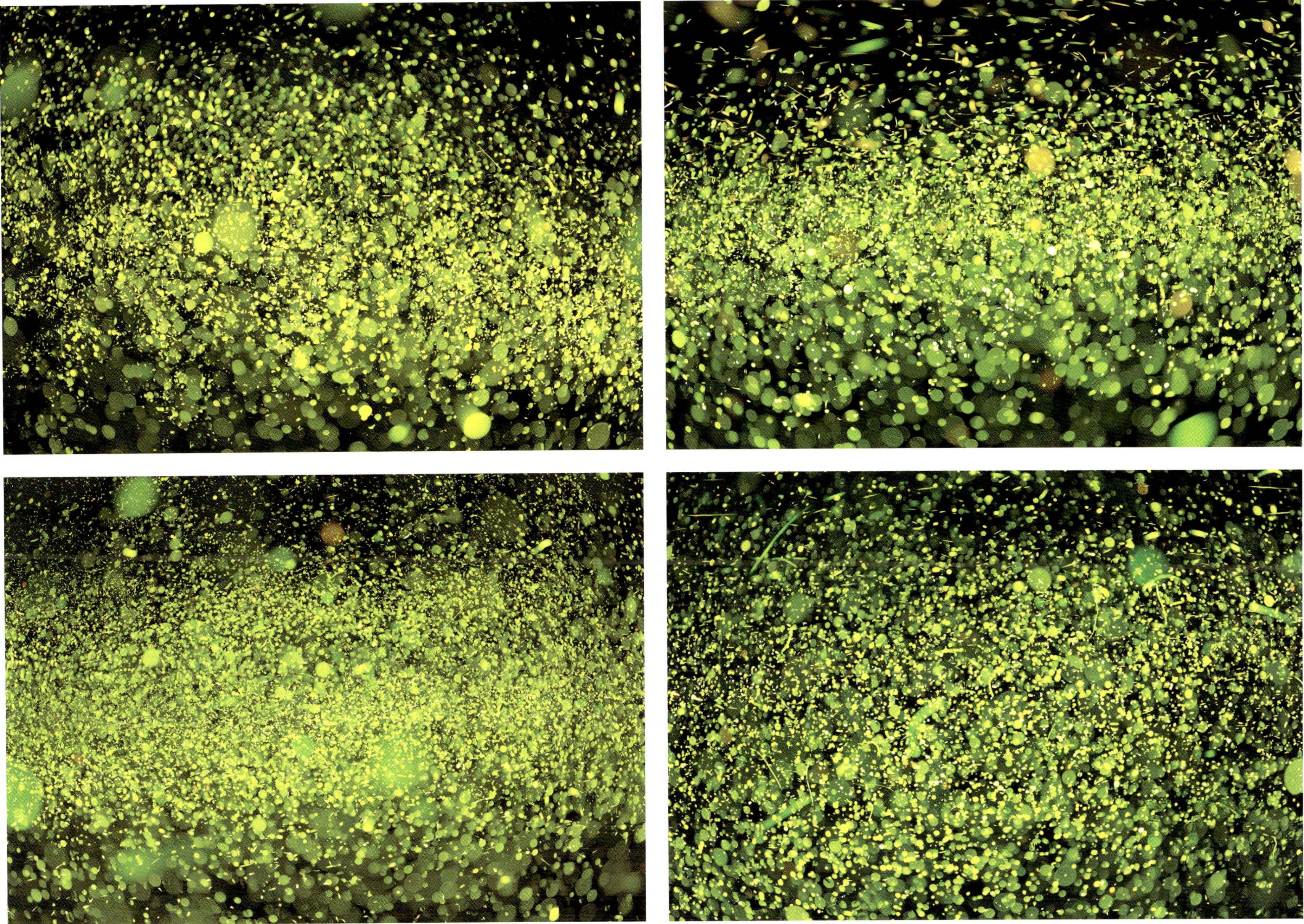

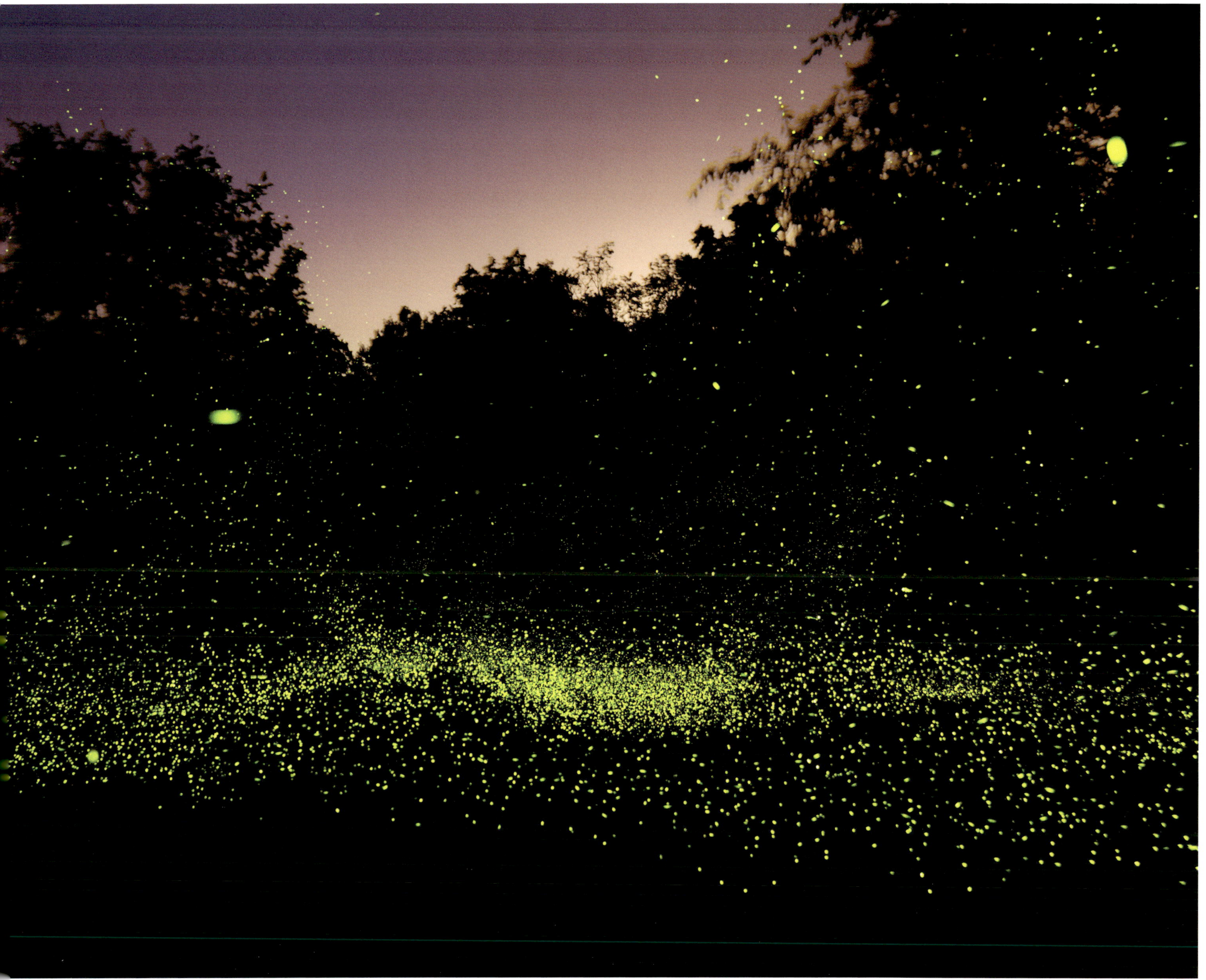

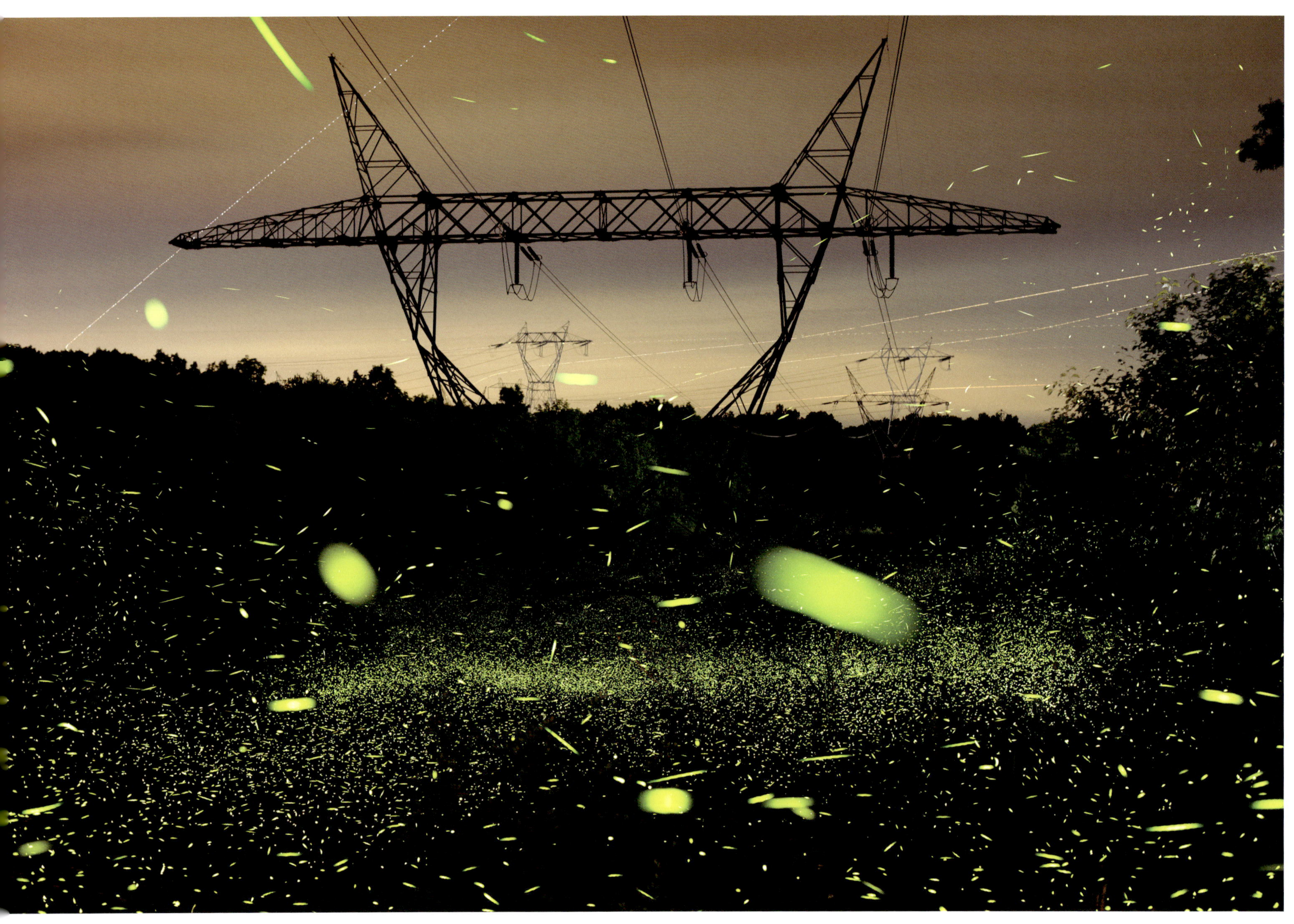

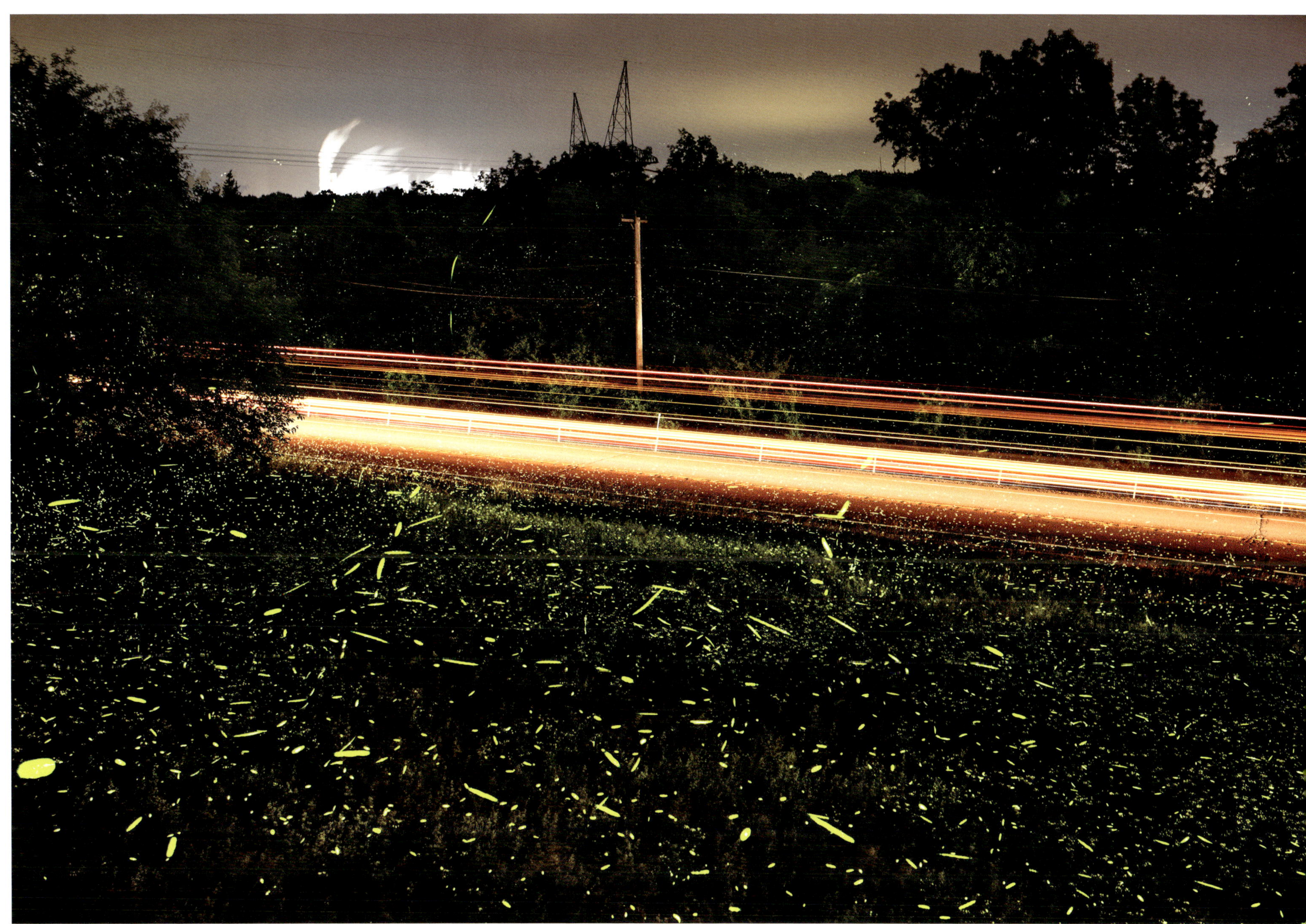

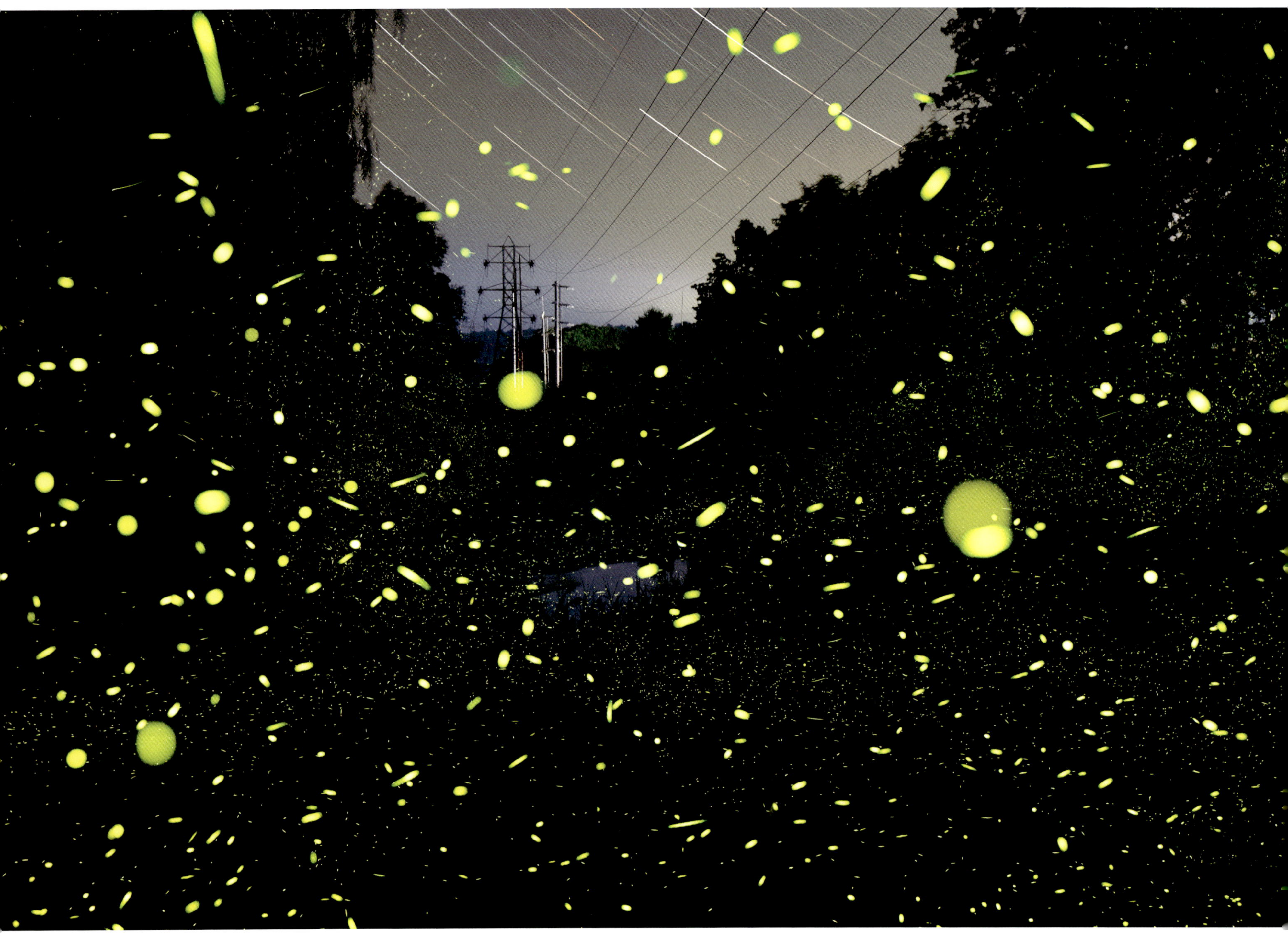

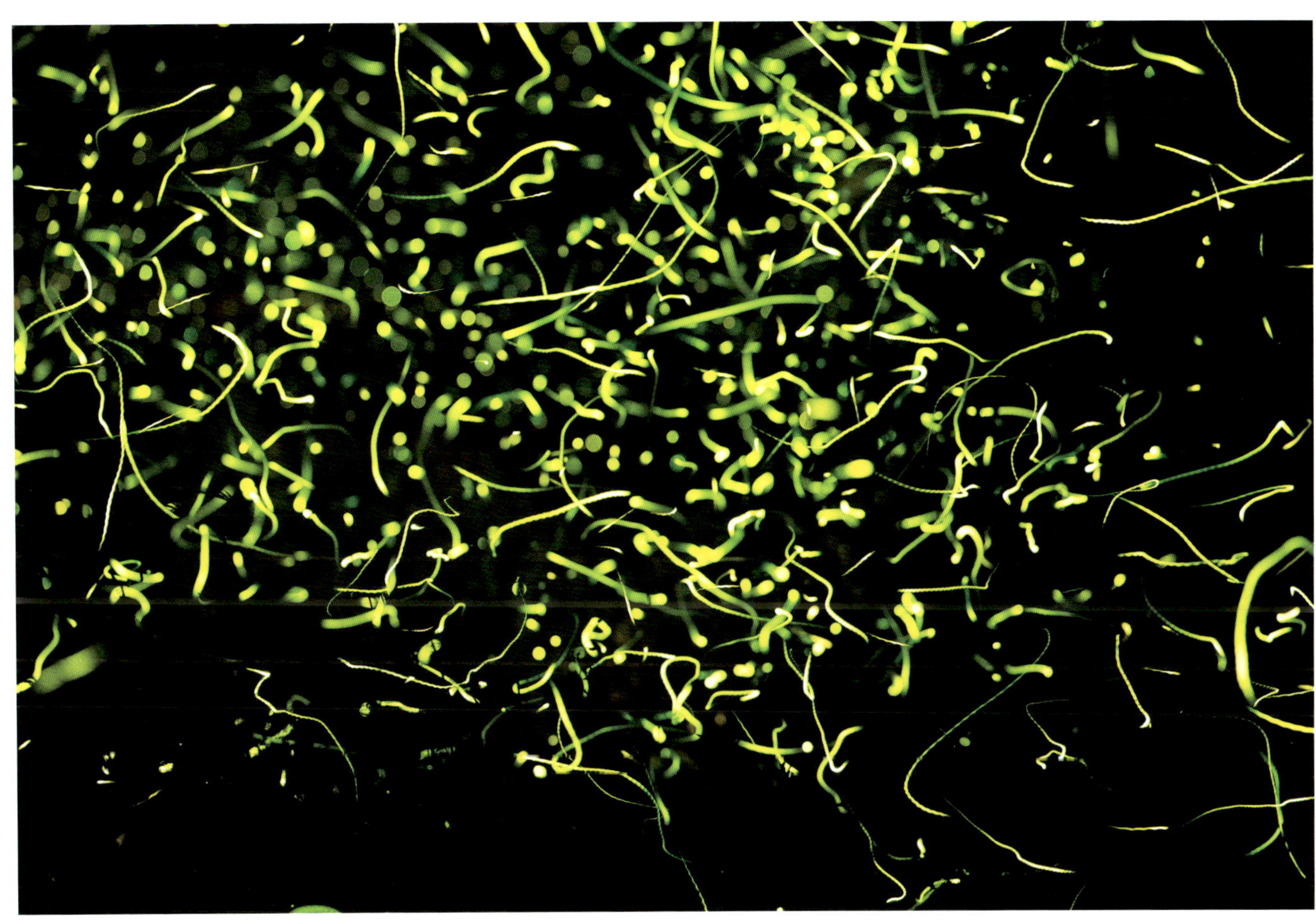

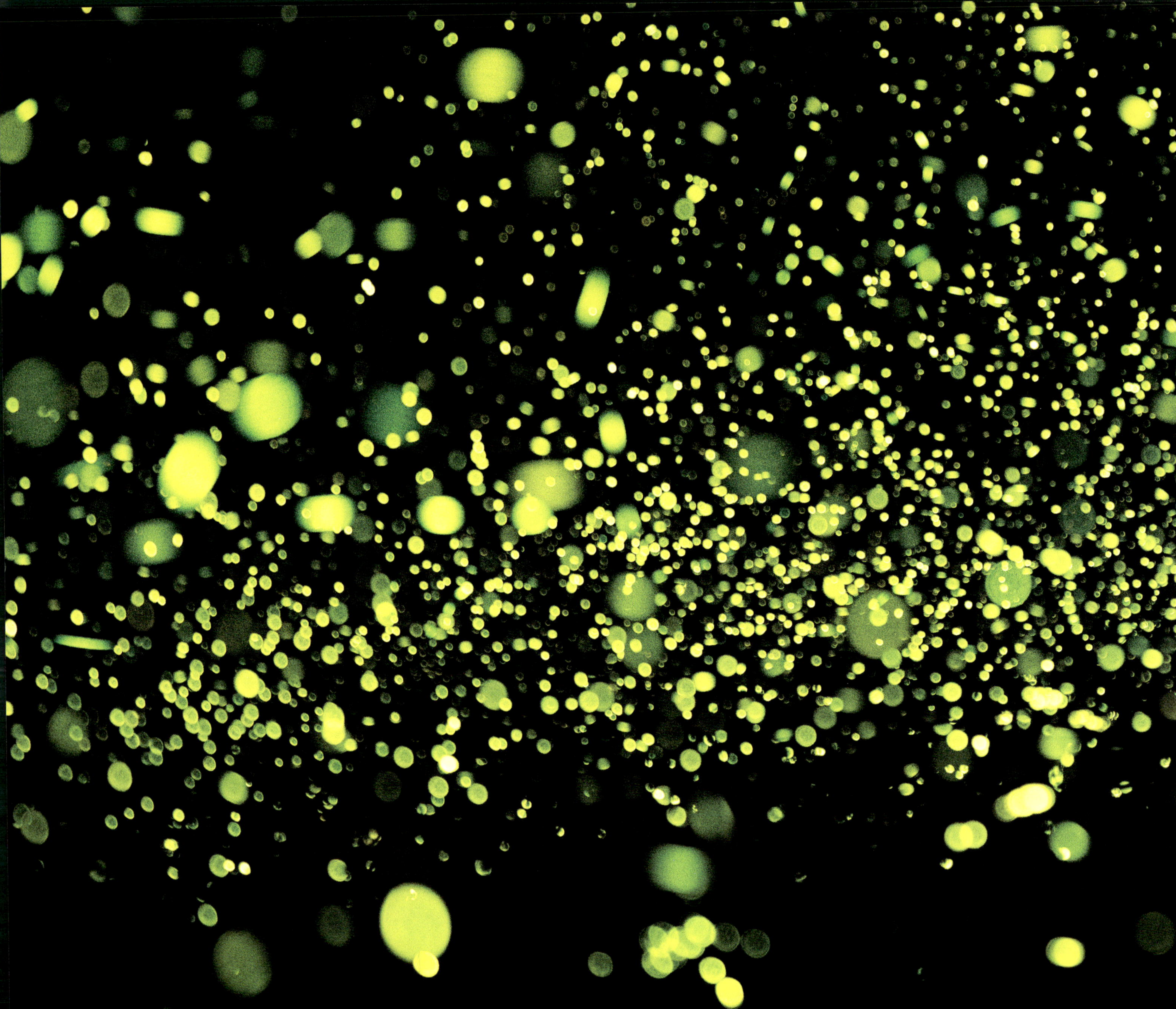

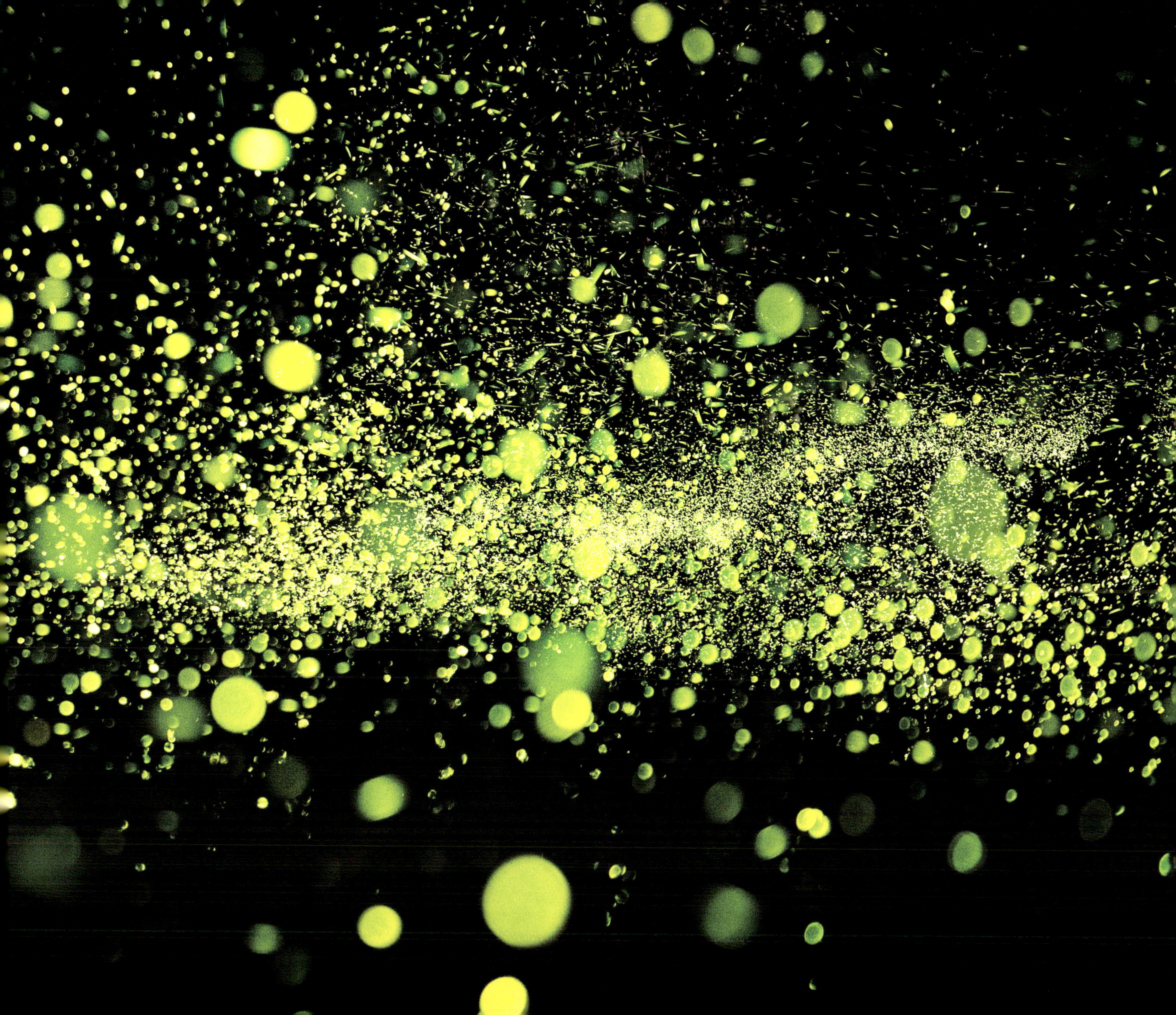

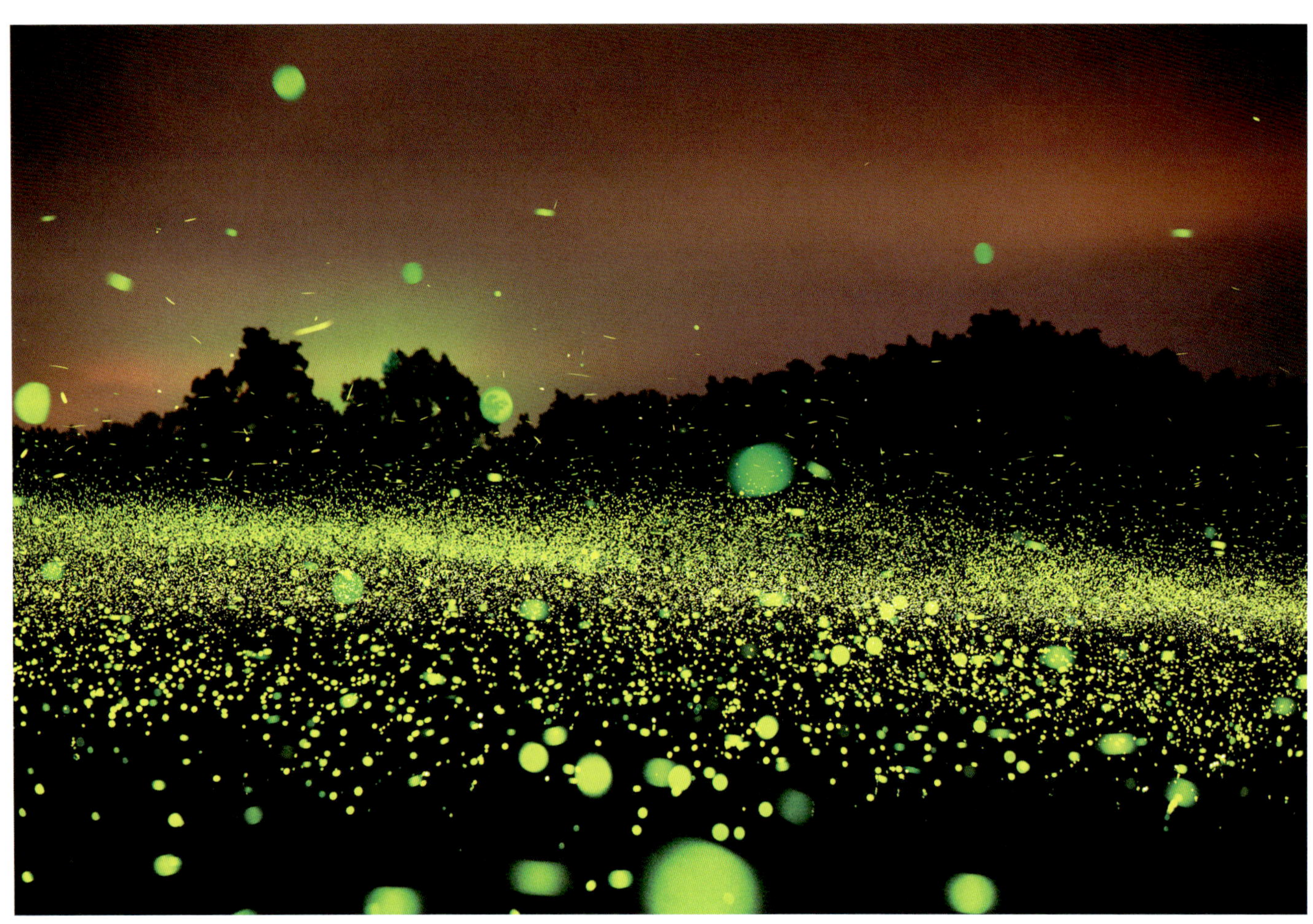

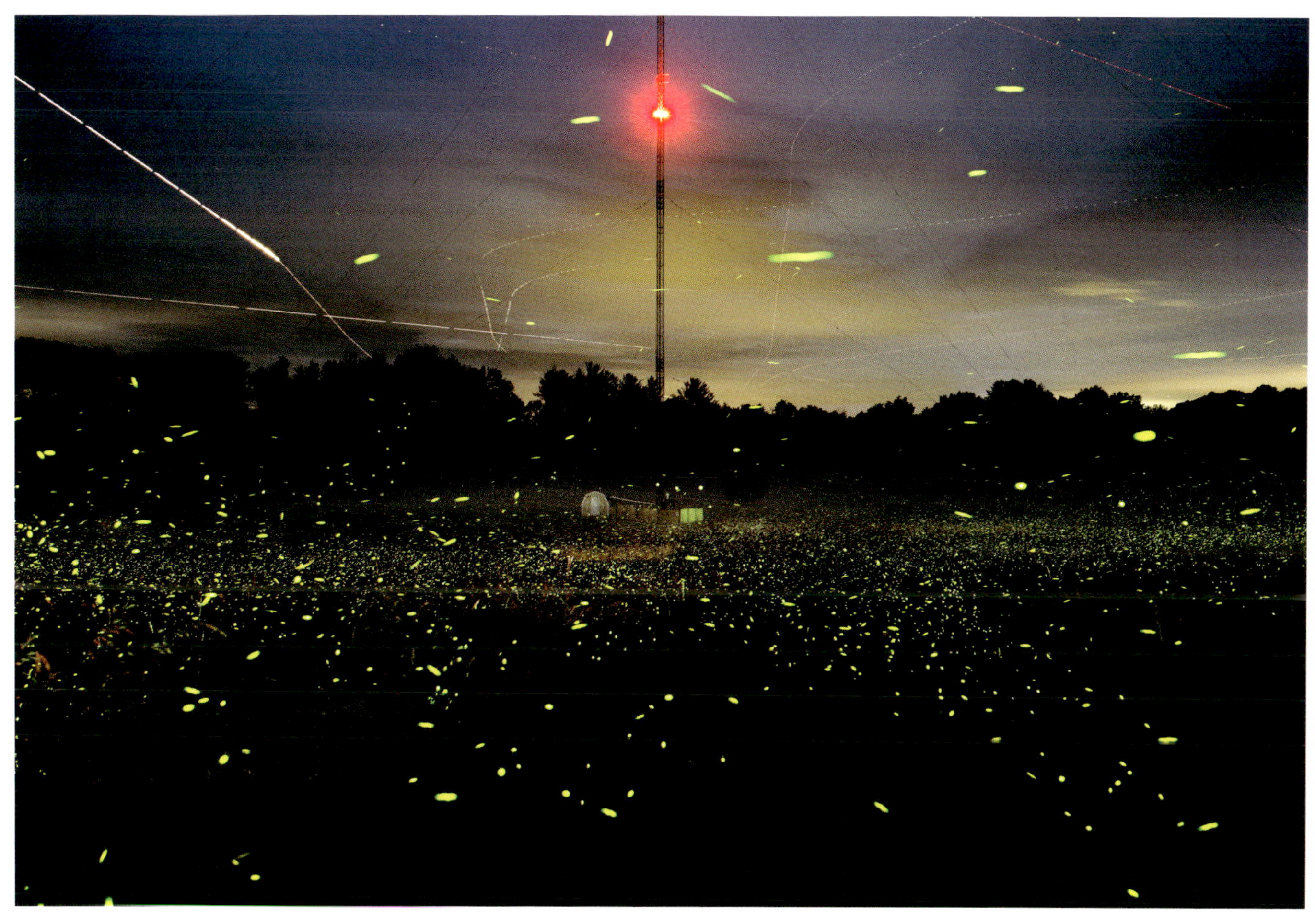

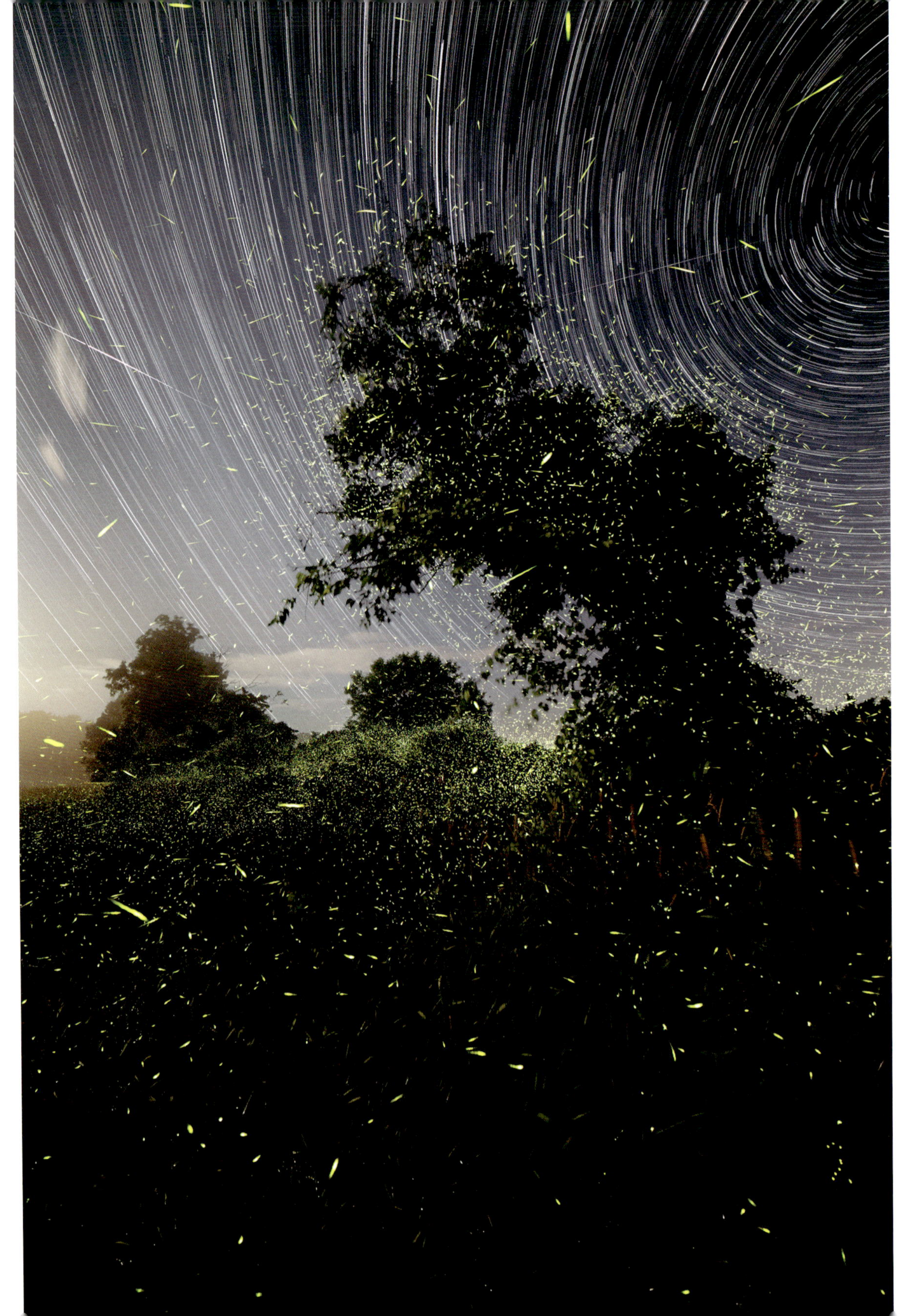

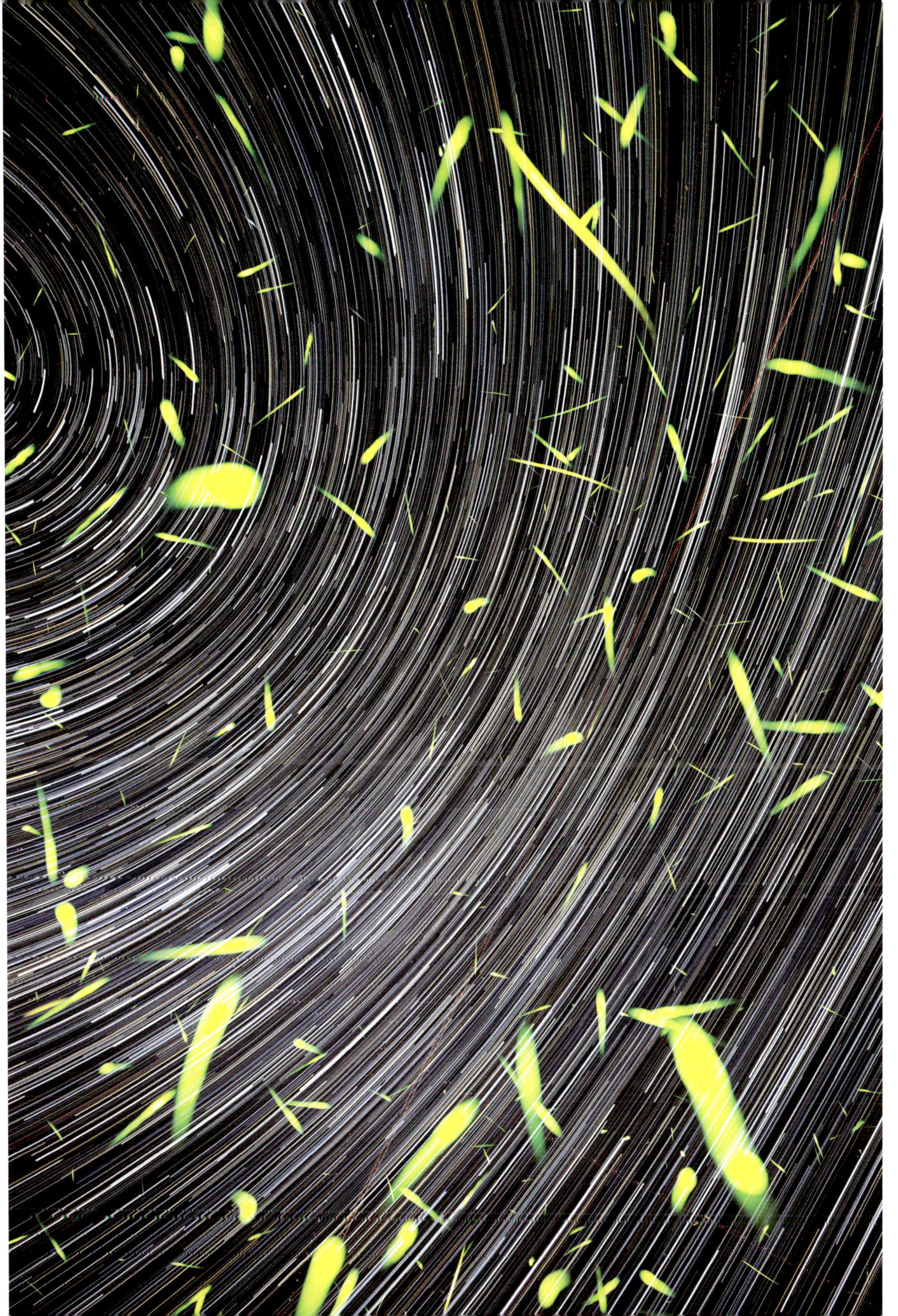

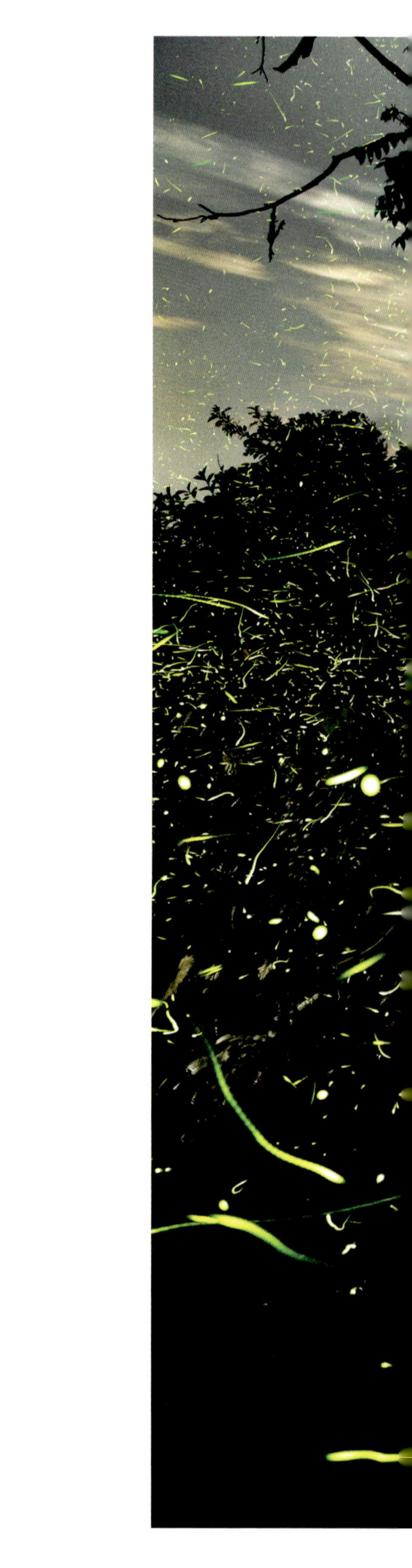

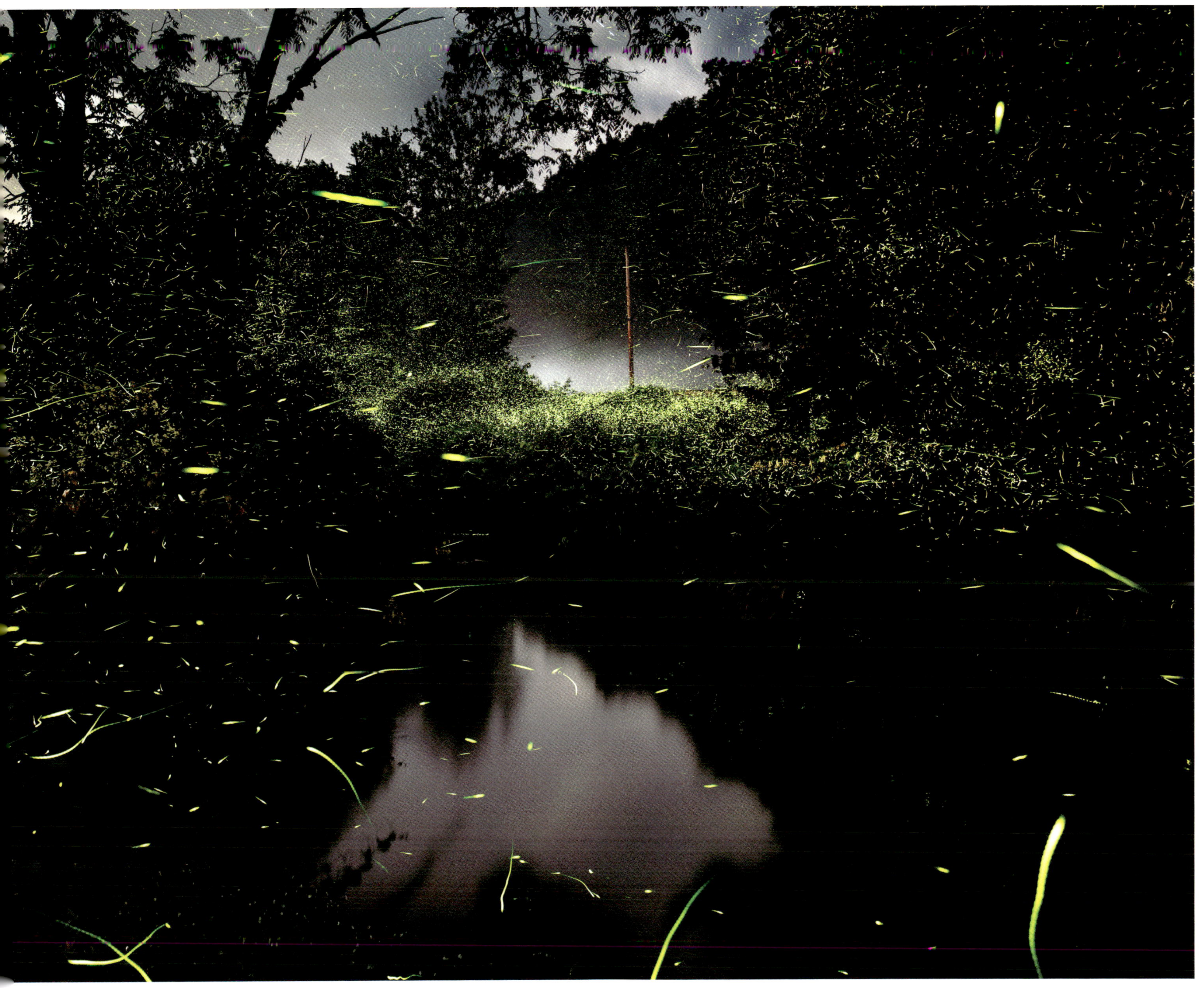

Can you talk about being out there in the field? How do you choose what to focus on?

I do test shots of locations to get an idea of what's happening, especially if it is my first time in a place. Sometimes I'll do short ones, like half-hour, 45-minute exposures. I call those "tasters." It's kind of like panning for gold. When you pan for gold, you take a small sample of dirt, and you swish it around in a pan of water and if you see any little gold flashes and then count them, you can get a general idea of what the payload might be. That's a lot like an approach I've used to find centers of density where the good shots exist. And that's also why, when I go to a new location, I generally start out with a very wide angle. One reason for that is because I want to try to capture everything I see in my peripheral vision. Which I can't. But it's also a tool to help me visualize what might be possible next time, what details I can come back to expand on a different night.

What do you do when you're waiting?

It varies. Mostly it's quiet contemplation, but it can also be pretty chaotic. I frequently work with up to five cameras, often separated by several miles, sometimes as much as 20 miles. On nights like that it can be pretty hectic. I don't slow down—I jump from place to place. So on those nights the vibe is about production and security patrols.

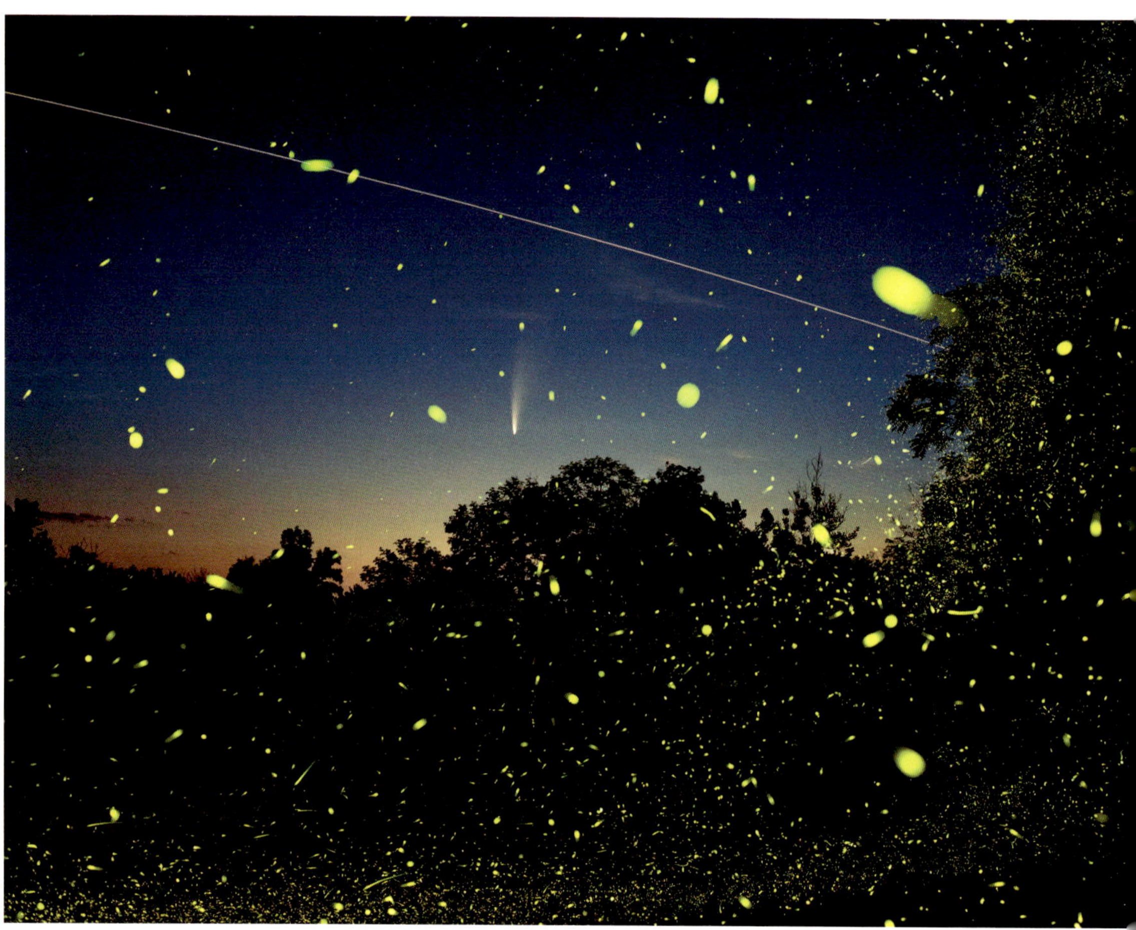

Field of Fireflies, Comet NEOWISE, and an unforeseen visit from the International Space Station. July 10, 2020.

The nights when I stay in one location are very different. Those nights I can just stay there and be there. I listen to the coyotes and the owls and the frogs. I'm not good at relaxing. When I need to move around, I check out the cameras while the exposure is still going, to make sure nothing has slipped and the tripod isn't messed up. But otherwise, I sit and stare and contemplate existence and the universe. It sounds cheesy, sure, but I also plan shots, I plan for the next night, I plan for the next summer.

When I am deeply engaged in photography, everything else fades away. Anxiety, tinnitus, an annoying day-job thing that's bothering me. All of it. It's better than any drug and amazingly therapeutic and stimulating. I don't mind a little bit of serenity every now and then, but that is not what most of my pictures are about. I am generally not a photographer of the pastoral, of the scenic. I want my pictures to elevate the heart rate a bit. Or a lot. Maybe even destabilize the viewer. Many of them aren't traditionally beautiful.

You mentioned that you used to work in a more impulsive way. When did that change?

Starting in about 2015 my entire work process and approach throughout this body of work changed largely as a result of, well, drugs. Another layer to this work, maybe part of its obsessive nature, is that it is also helping me recover from a series of traumas. At a certain point I had to make the difficult choice of starting medications to attenuate severe anxiety and depression. It was difficult because, well, artist types like me are often wary of fucking with whatever the thing is that is making us work right by trying to fix the things that maybe aren't.

The result? For my photography it was… interesting. Now, instead of frequent and impulsive rapid-fire sessions that may or may not have coherence as a whole, I work in a much more structured, patient, self-forgiving way. For example, I haven't made an intentional photograph in two months, except casually with my phone. There were decades in the past when that would have made me feel nervous or depressed or doomed for eternity. Now that's not so much the case because I work more project-based. Between what I call the Before and the After, there's a substantial difference in terms of how I work.

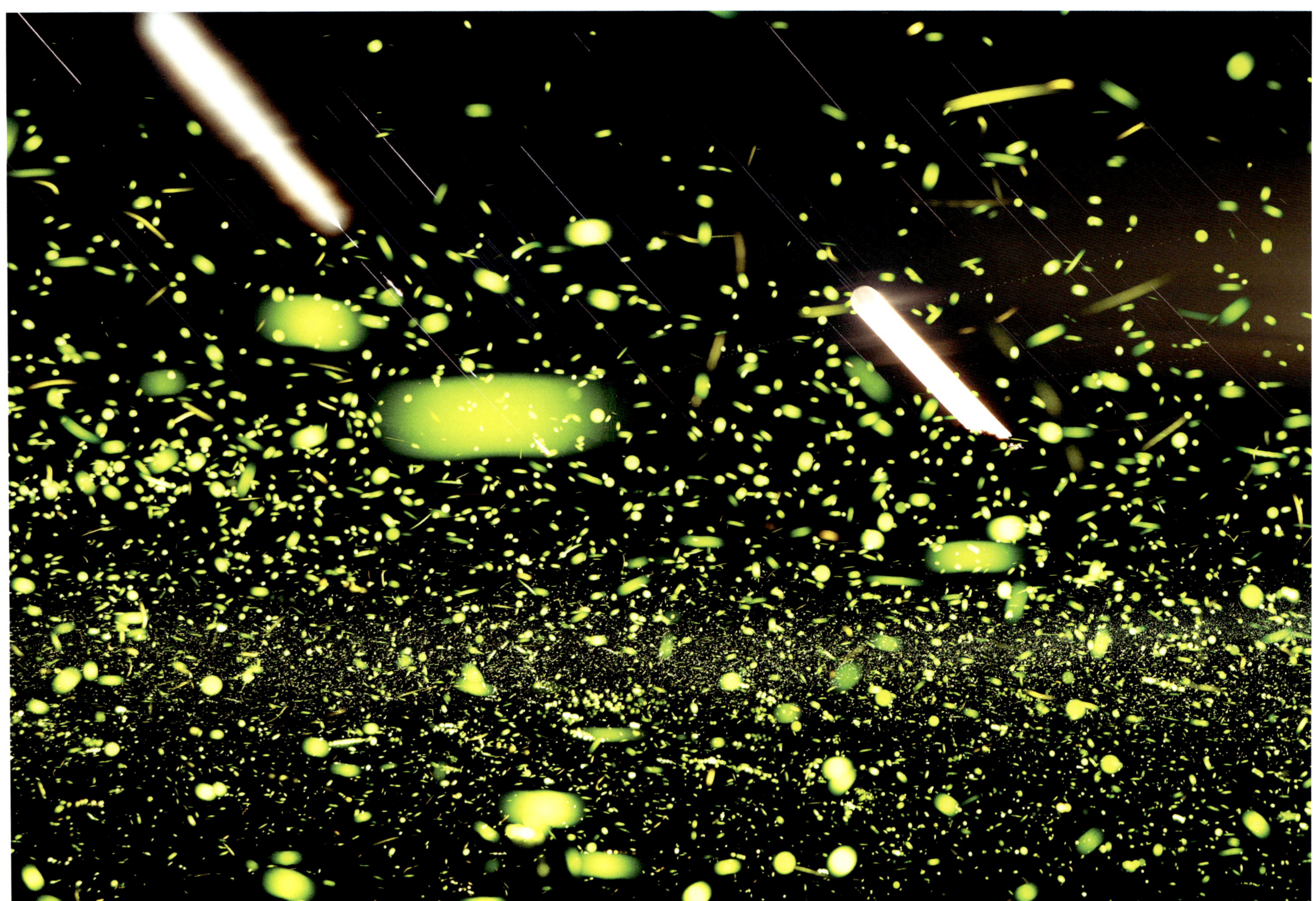

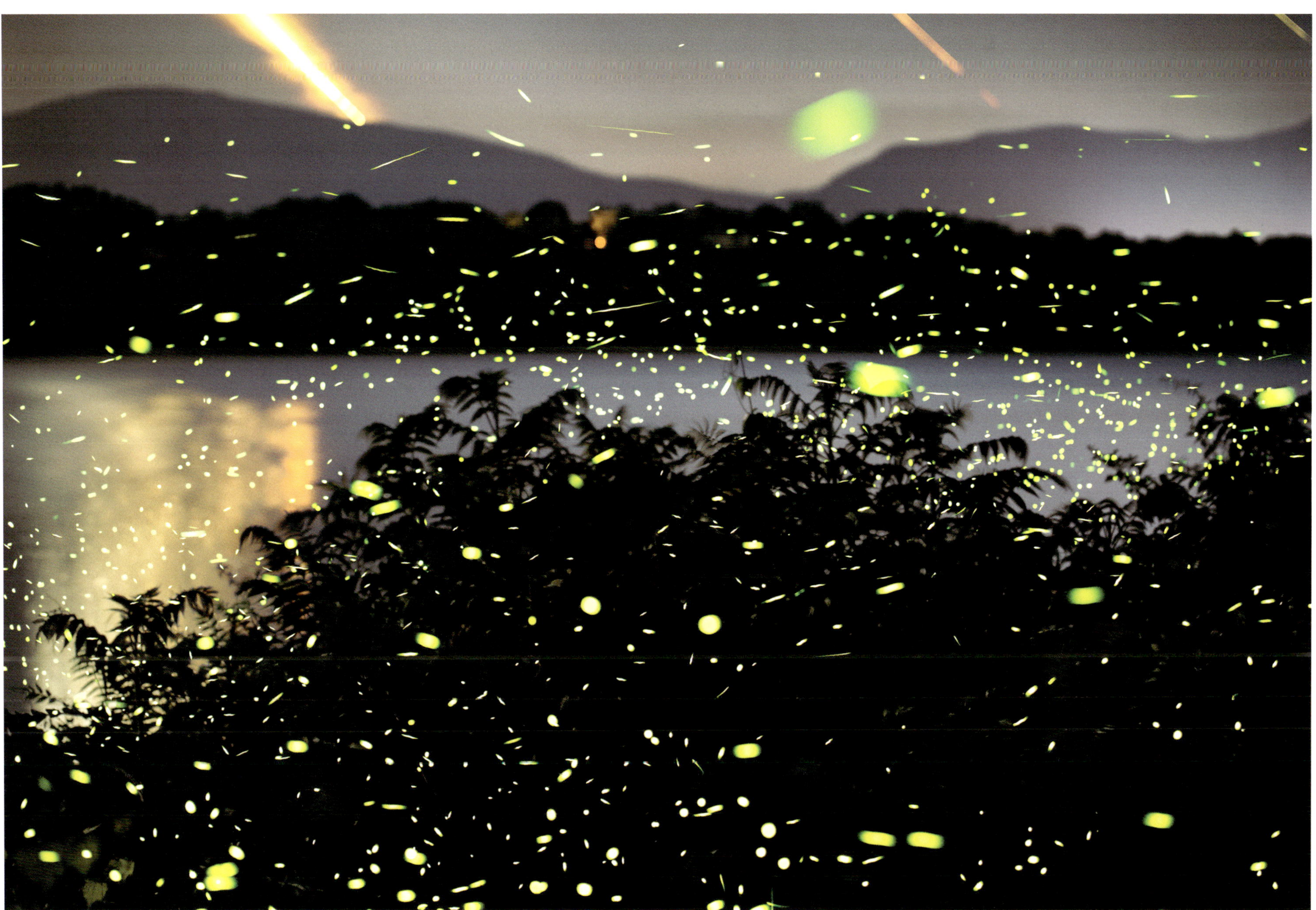

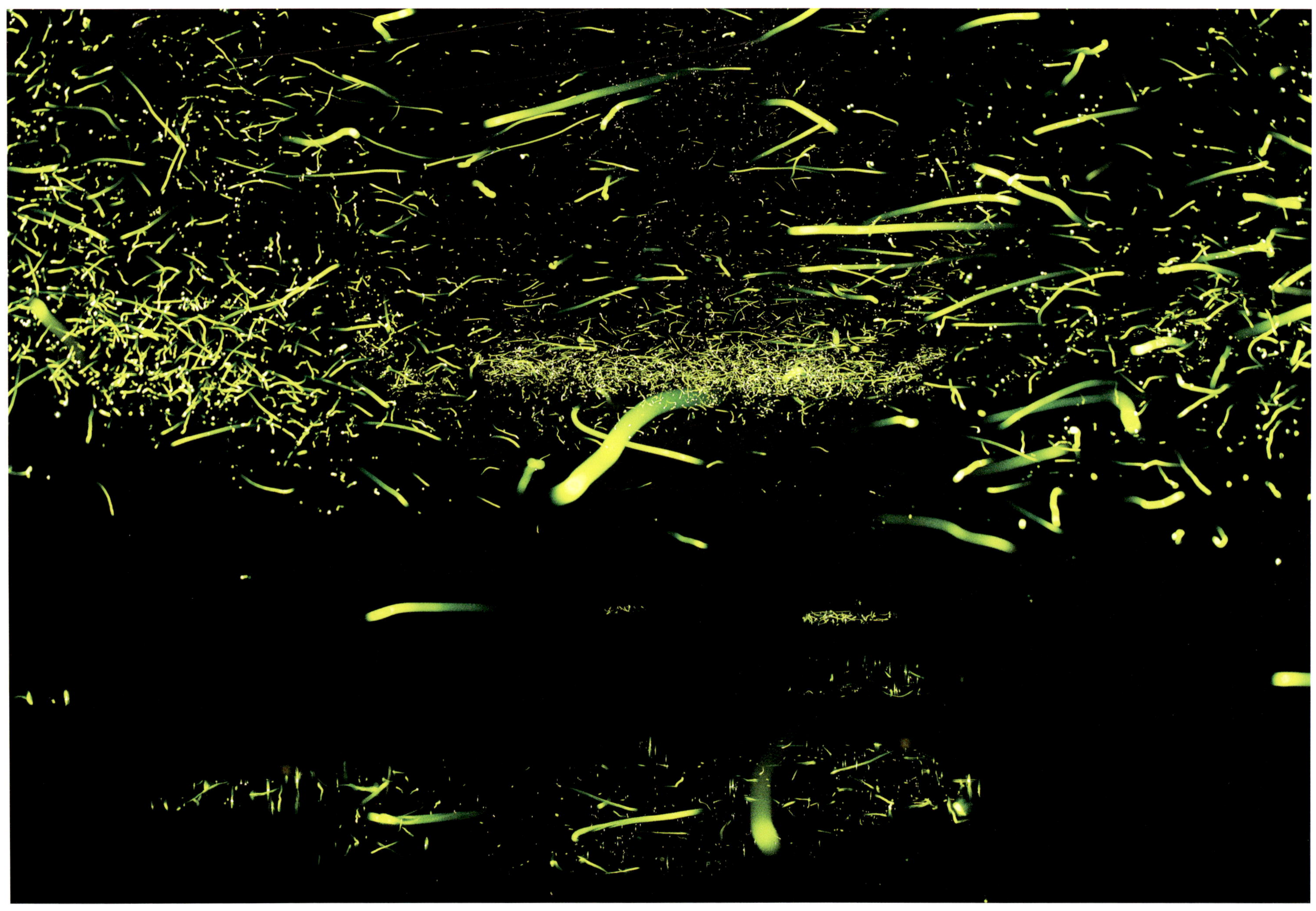

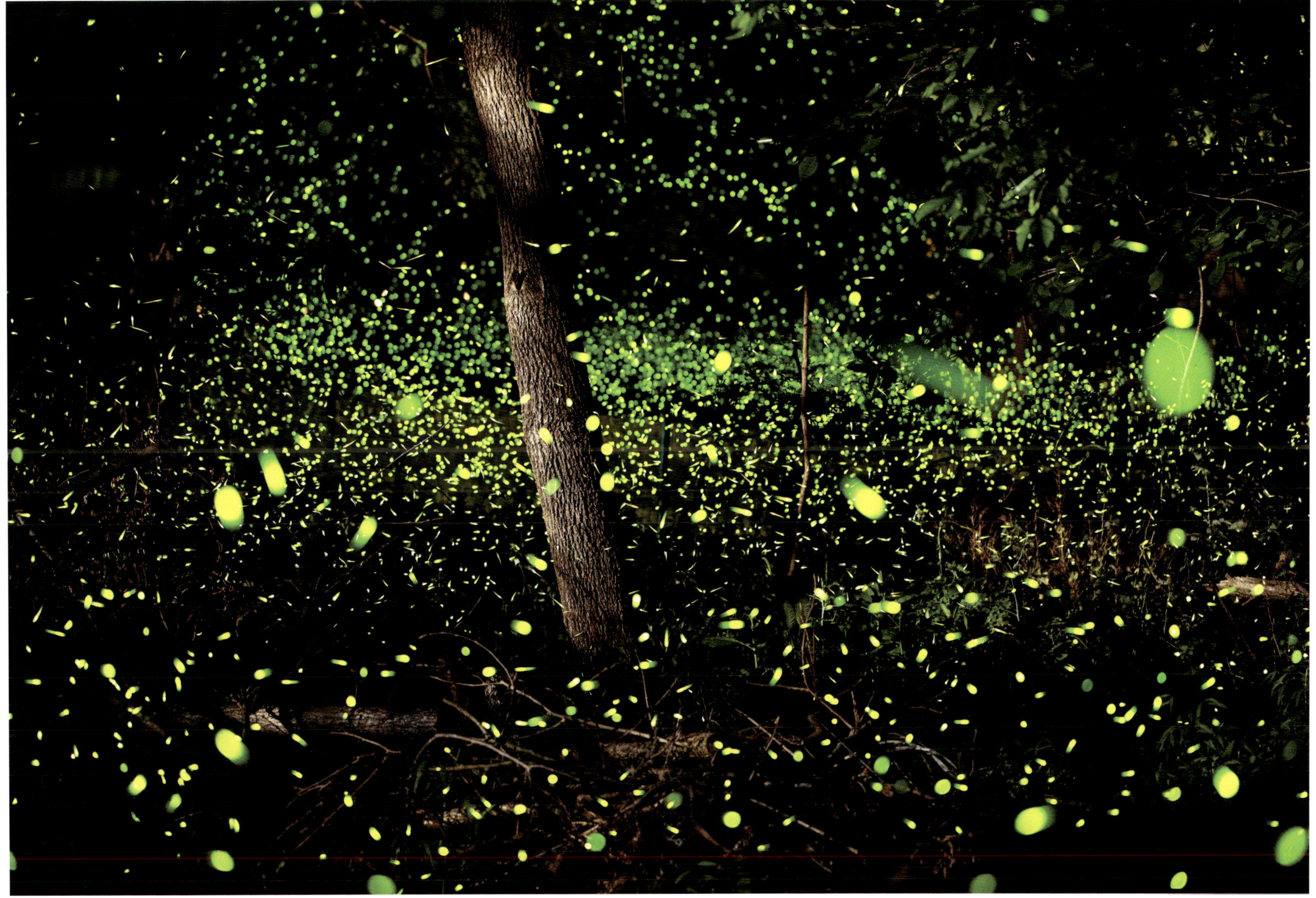

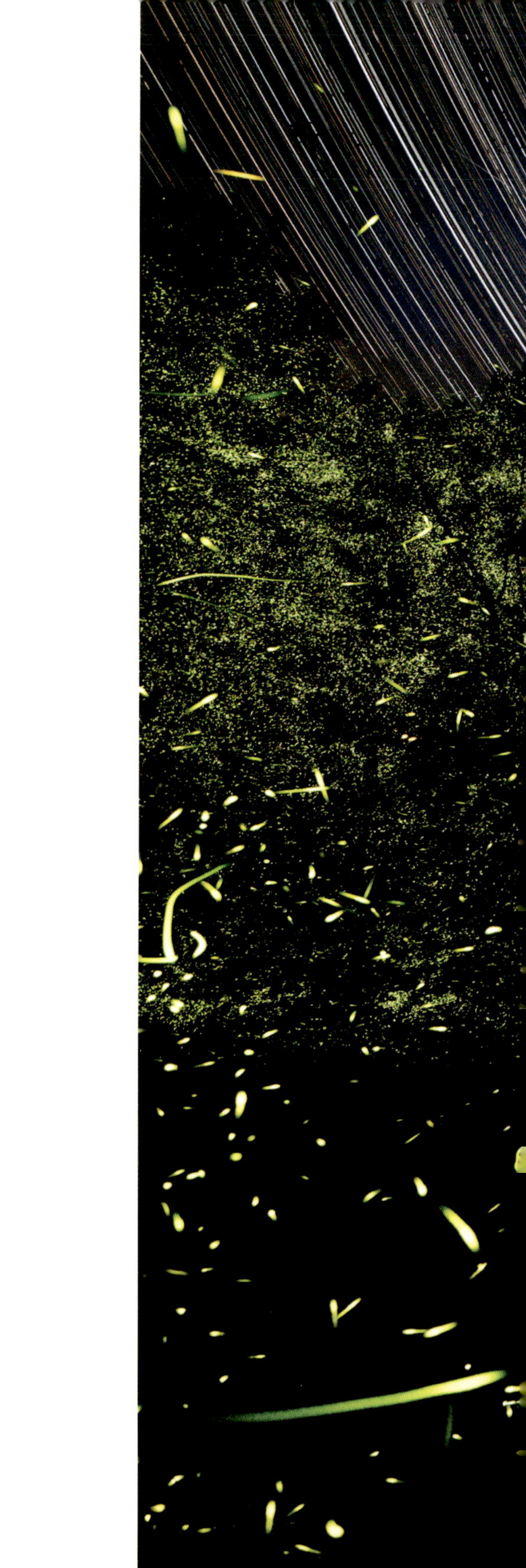

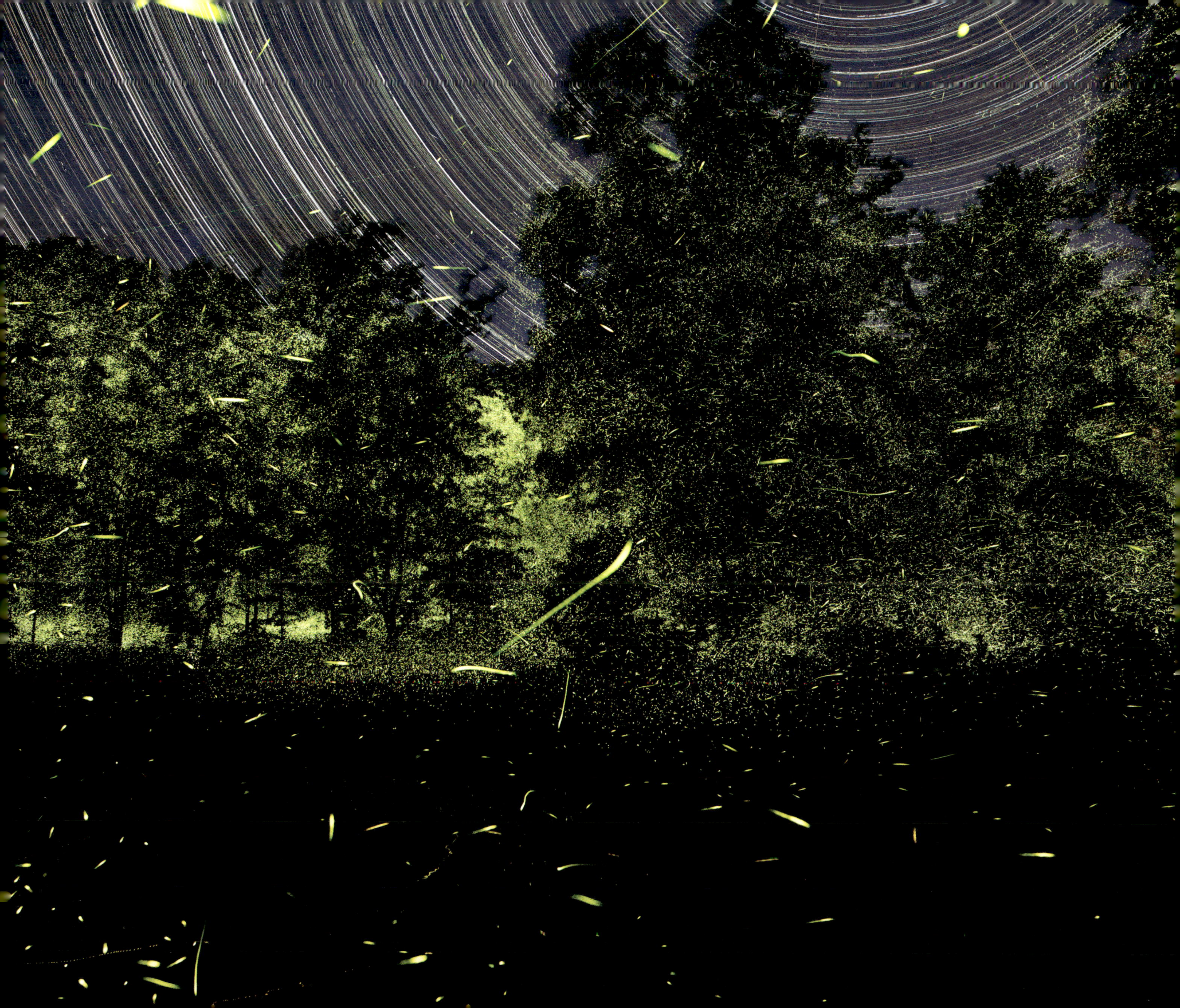

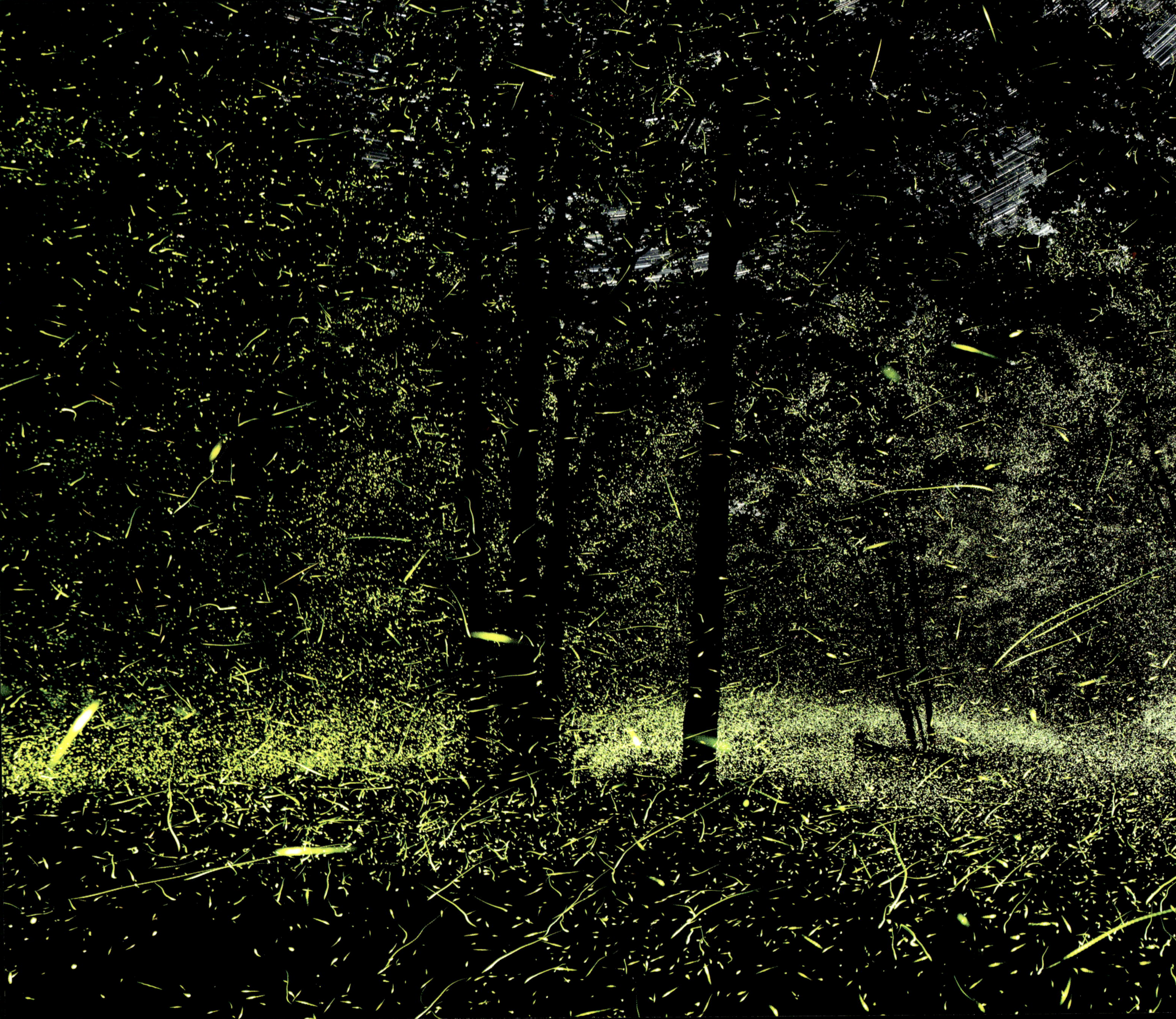

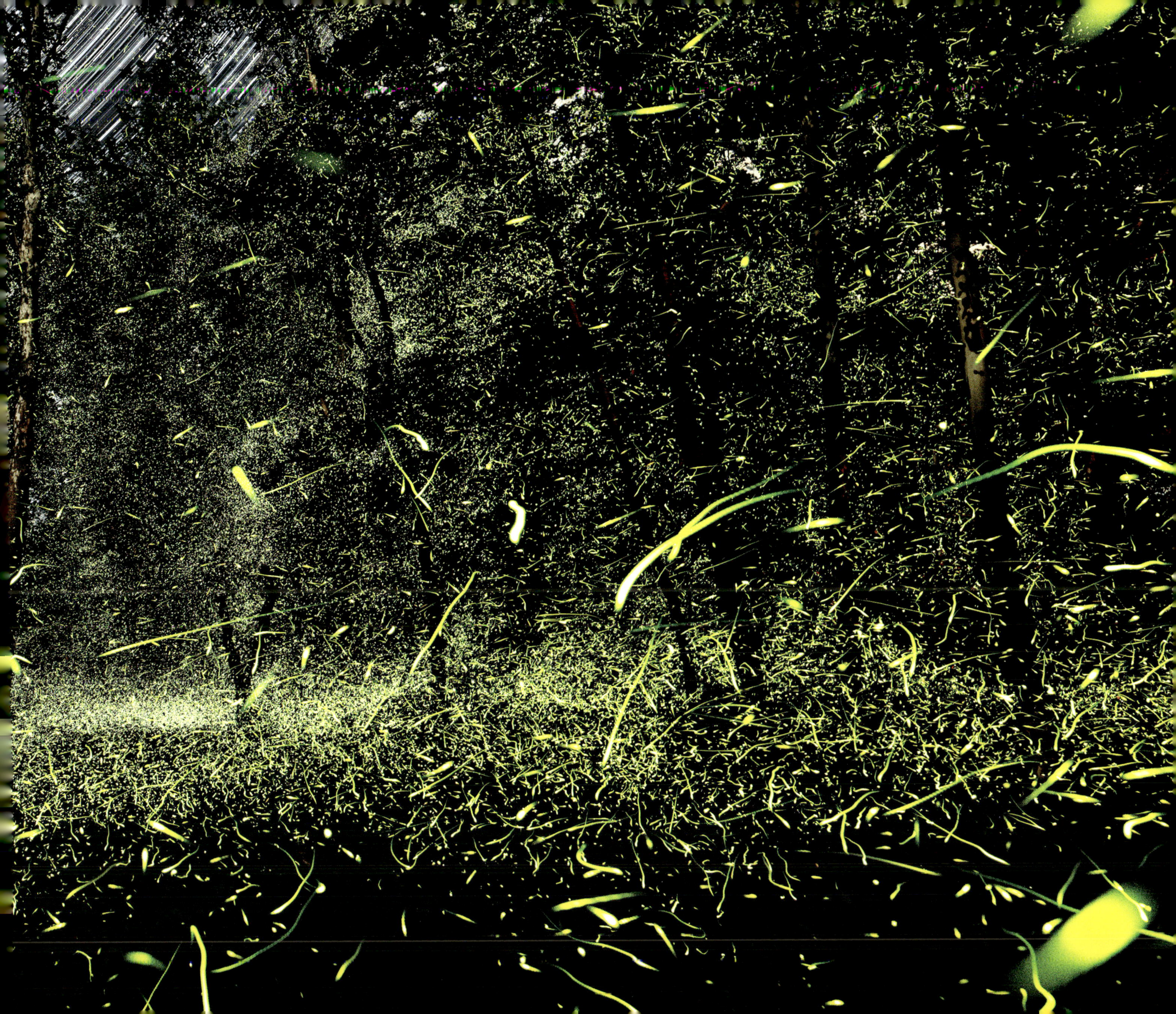

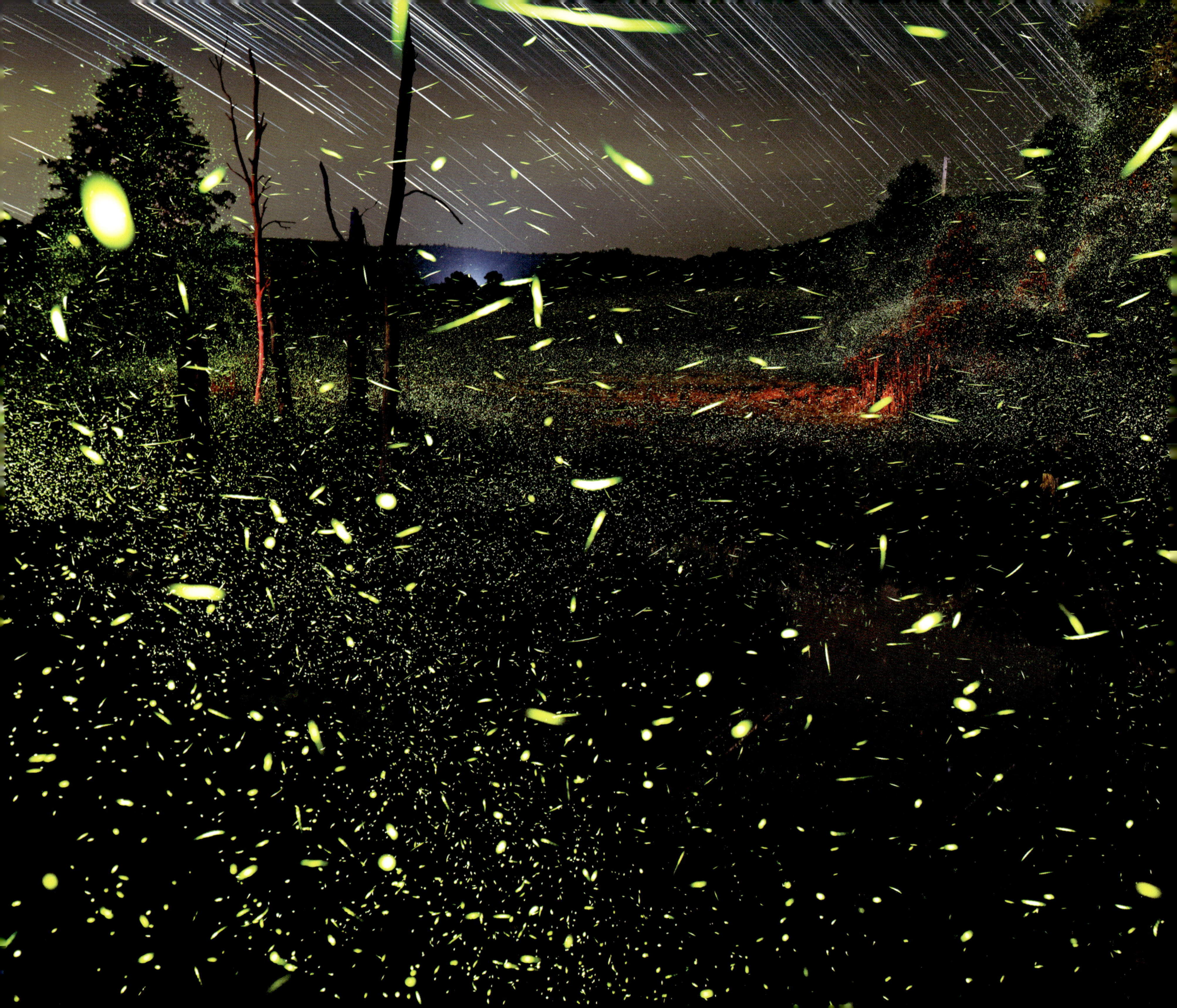

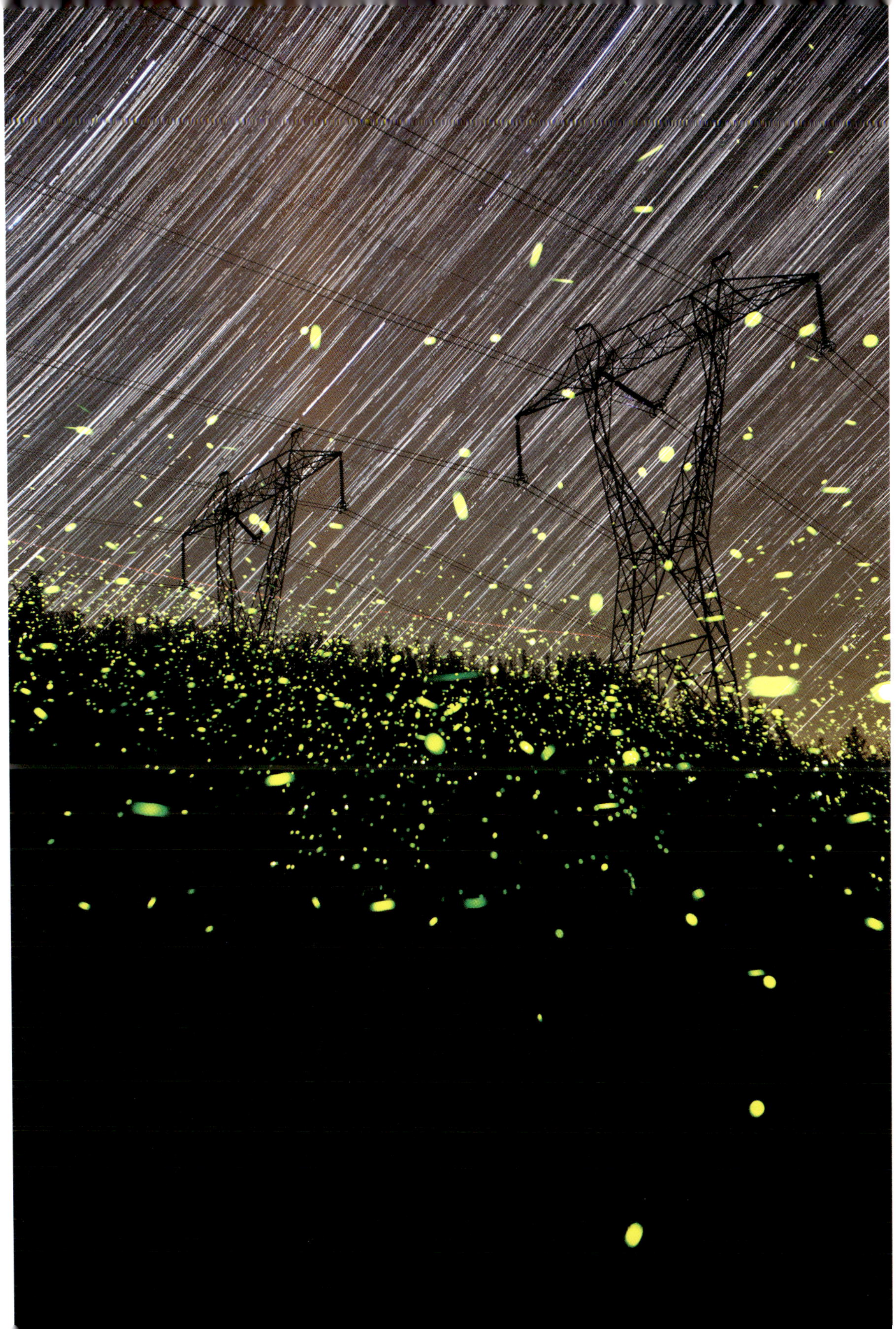

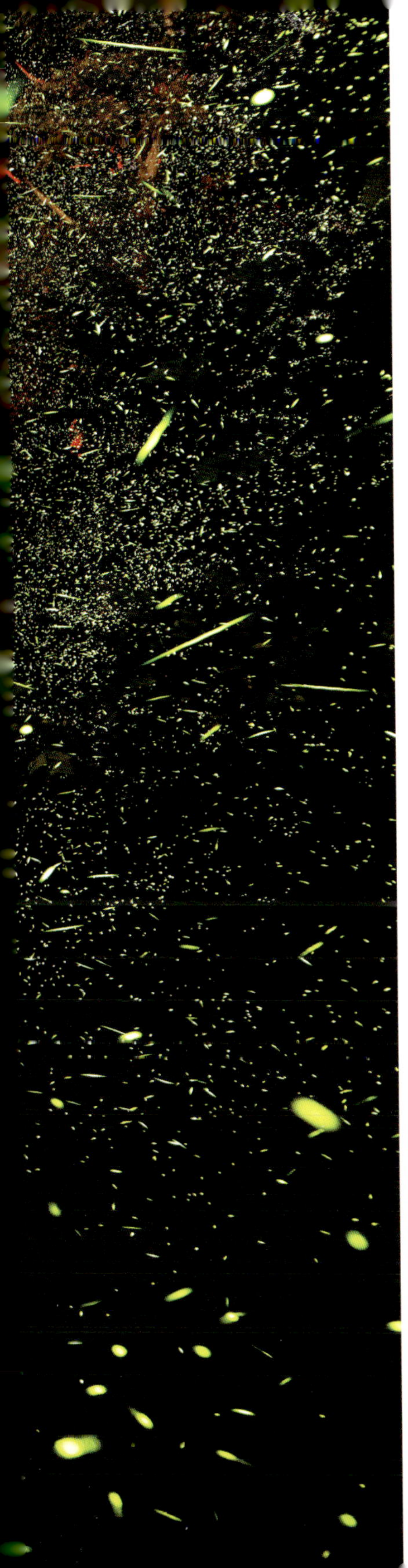

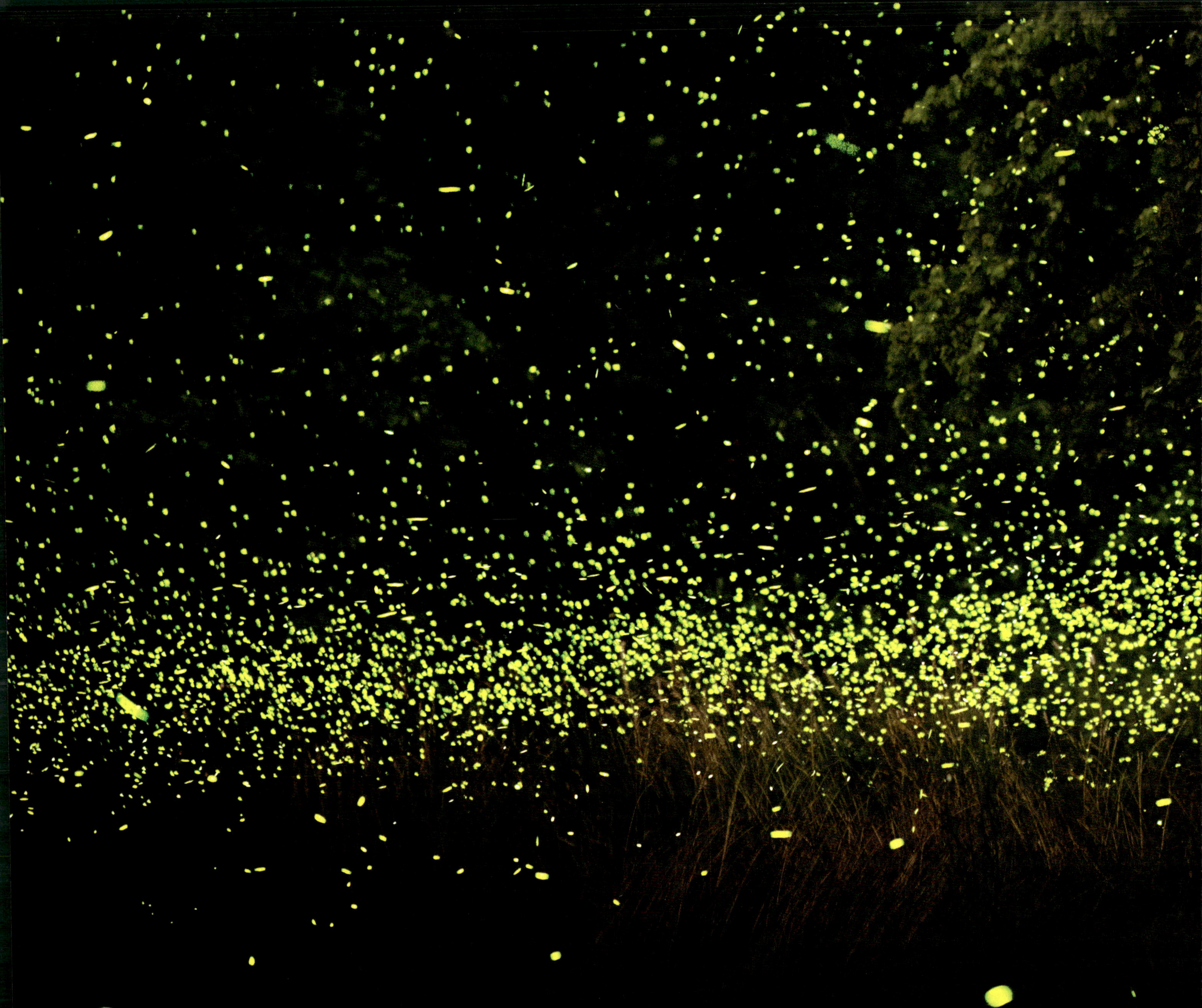

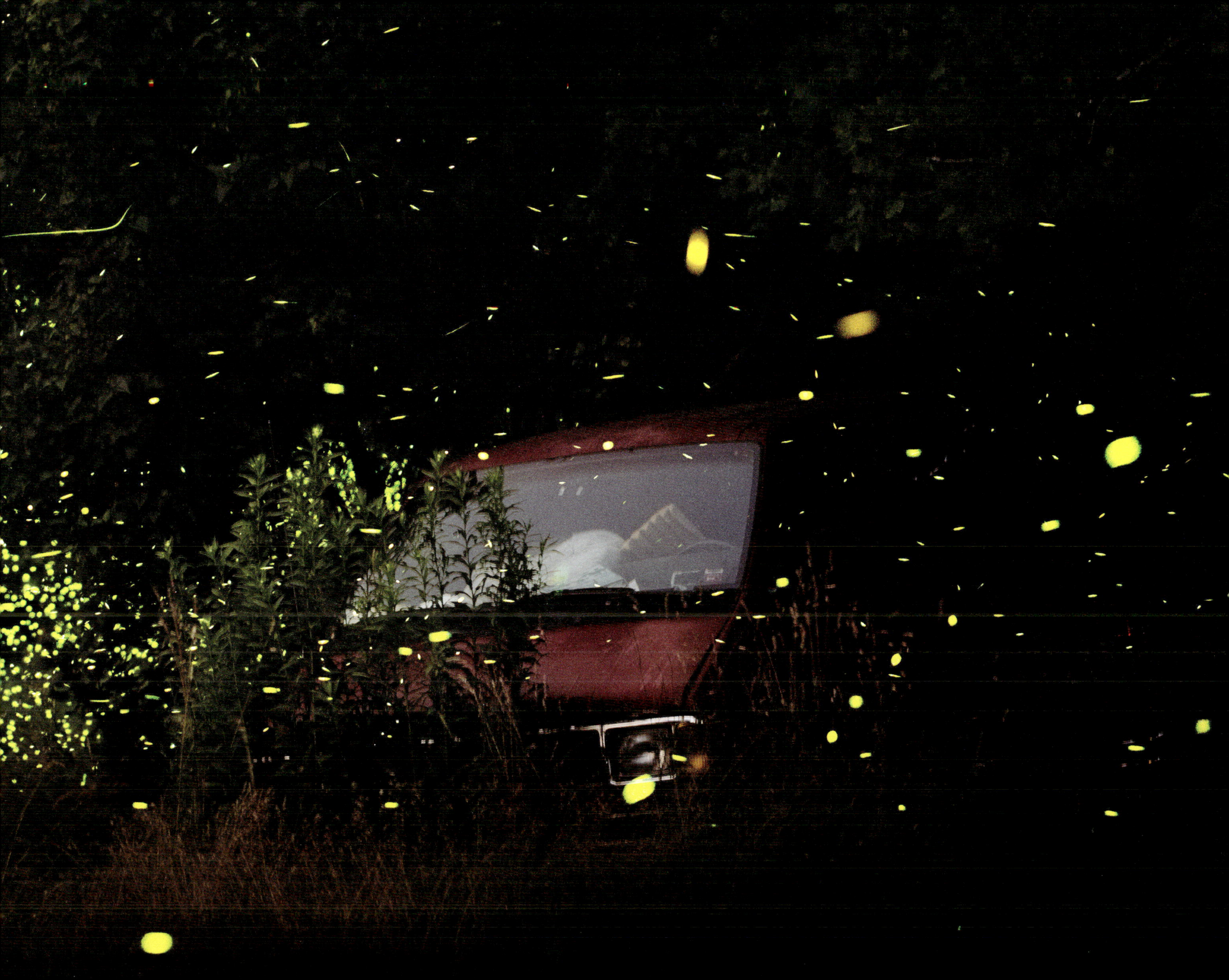

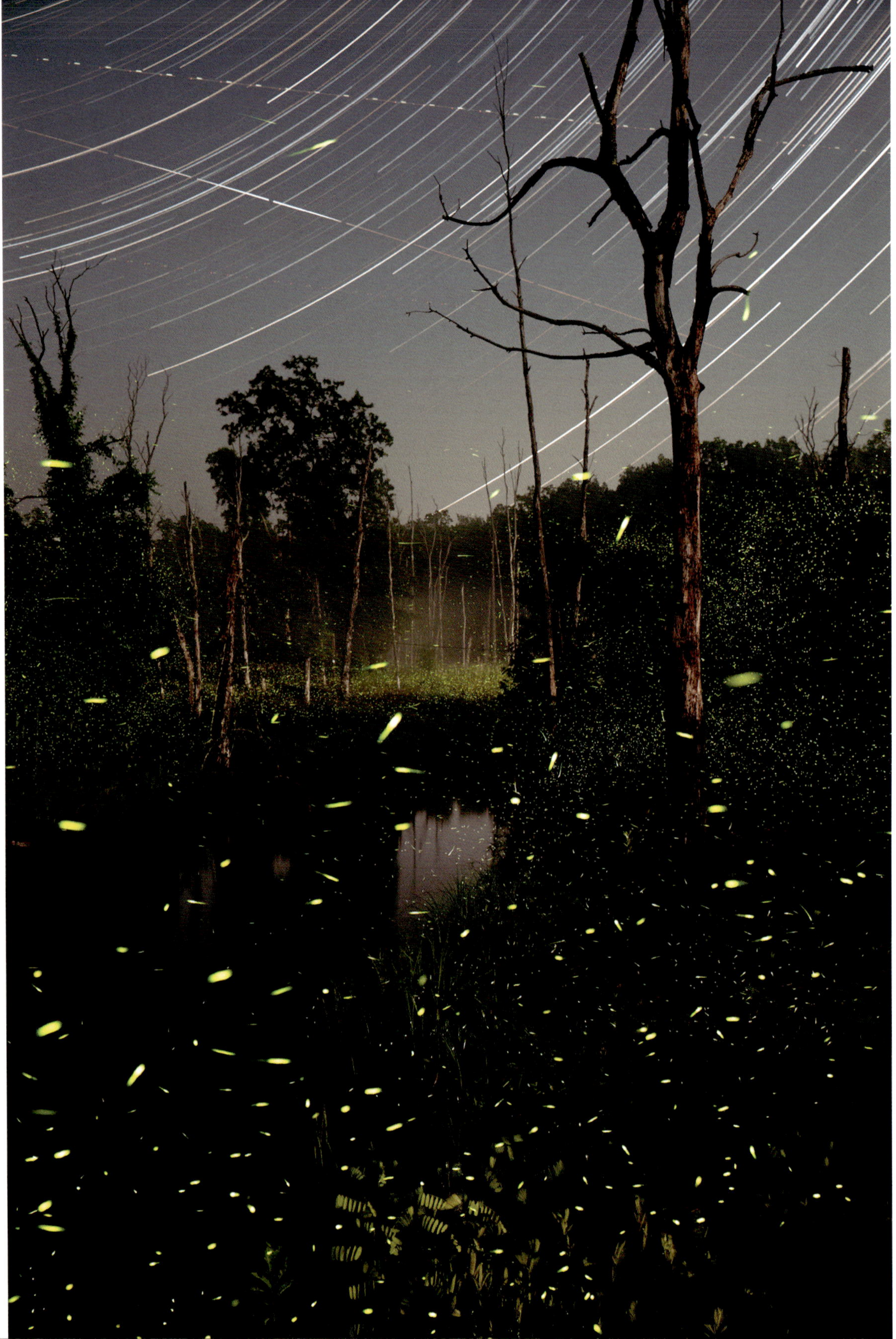

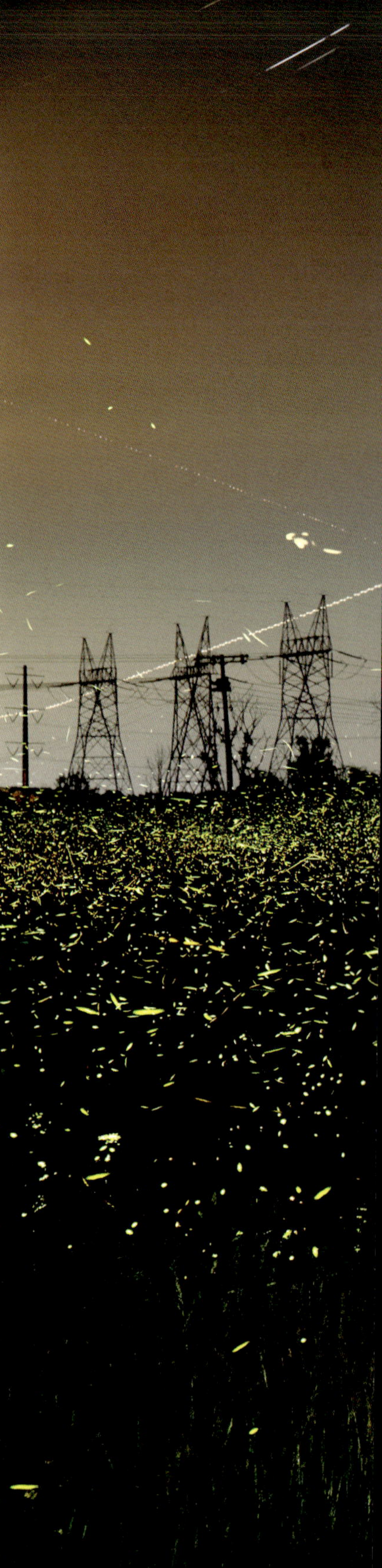

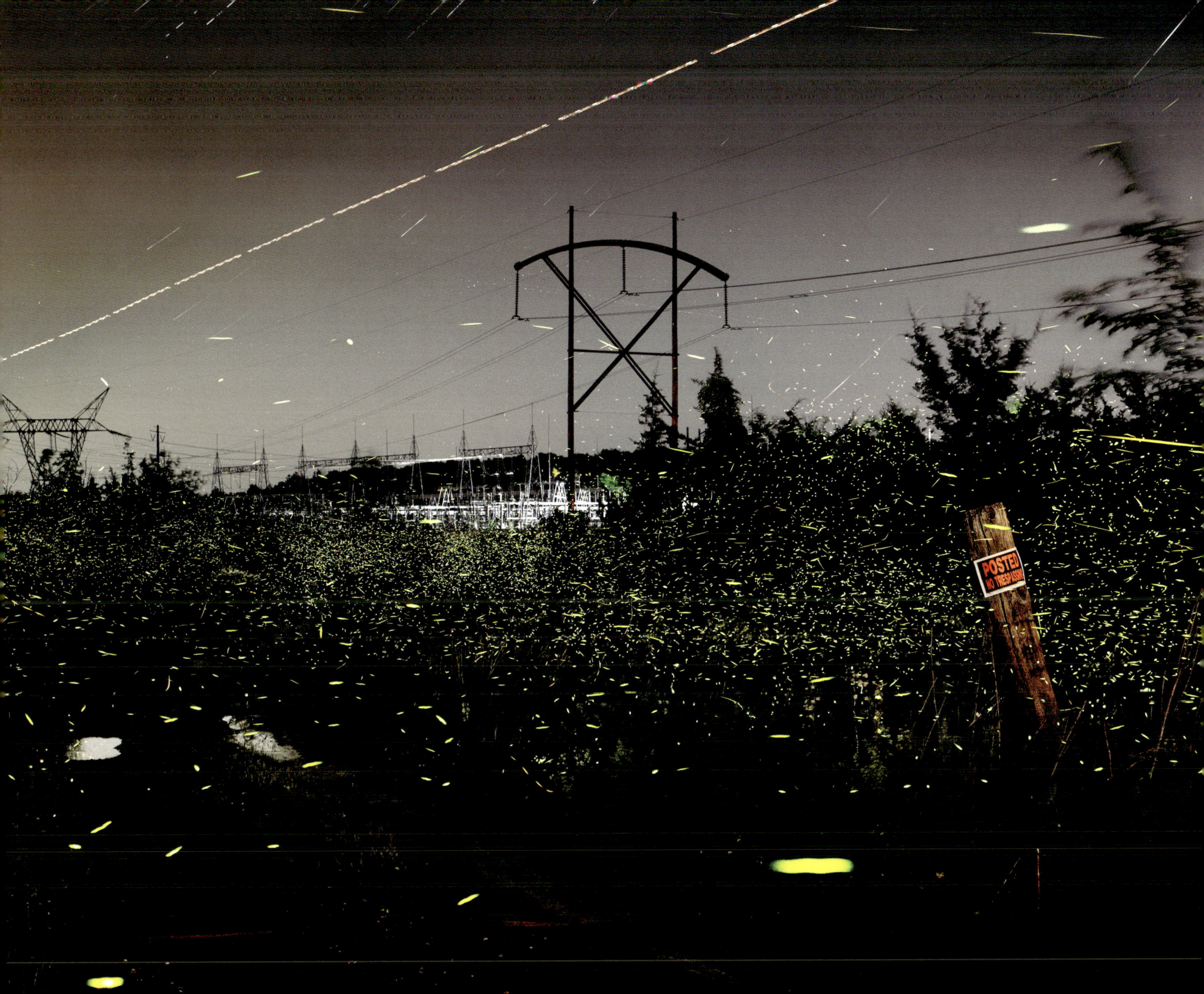
POSTED
NO TRESPASSING

How do you find fireflies?

At first I would just look around. I'd either find some or I wouldn't. It was very hit-or-miss. I'm not a biologist or a scientist, so I don't have any technical understanding of how these wonderful insects work. Also, they all seemed to be a little bit different. Some I would find in trees and some I would find in swampy areas. At first, as an outsider, it seemed almost random where they were, because I didn't see any commonalities. Then I started realizing there's usually a stream or a pond nearby.

And then I began using Google Maps. I would start by searching near known spots and as I became aware of terrains that they were attracted to, I was unknowingly training myself. I can now find them based on particular textures or water features in satellite photos. I don't know if I could write it down, or teach it to someone else, but it's something I've grown to know more or less intuitively. It's not always correct, by any stretch, but I have a much better success rate now at finding viable places. And more importantly, to me, as an impatient, production-oriented person, I waste a lot less time randomly driving around.

Have you trespassed before?

I plead the Fifth. No and yes. I rarely trespass. The way the laws in New York State work, and I'm sure in other places as well, is that there is a roadside right-of-way that varies by community. If you're walking down a road, for example, you don't have to walk in the road. You're allowed to walk on the side of the road, even if it's private property. I can usually guess it, based on how far back the grass has been mowed or the location of a utility pole, so I have a pretty good amount of latitude.

I do not go into people's front yards. I always err on the side of being respectful. If I'm photographing a house that I know to be abandoned I might get a little closer. But if a house is or might be occupied I tend to not get very close. Partly because I don't want to cause anyone distress or anxiety, and partly because I don't want to get shot at, because around where I live that's how people get shot.

I find it especially interesting that you stay mostly near a road when most of your photos look like they were taken in the middle of a field.

Sometimes I am in the middle of the woods or a field, but that's rare now. I'll tell you something else: getting a wicked bad case of Lyme disease a few years ago really changed the cost/benefit analysis of going out into a farm field. Sometimes I have to ask myself, is this picture worth another lumbar puncture? I'm guessing it's also part of getting older.

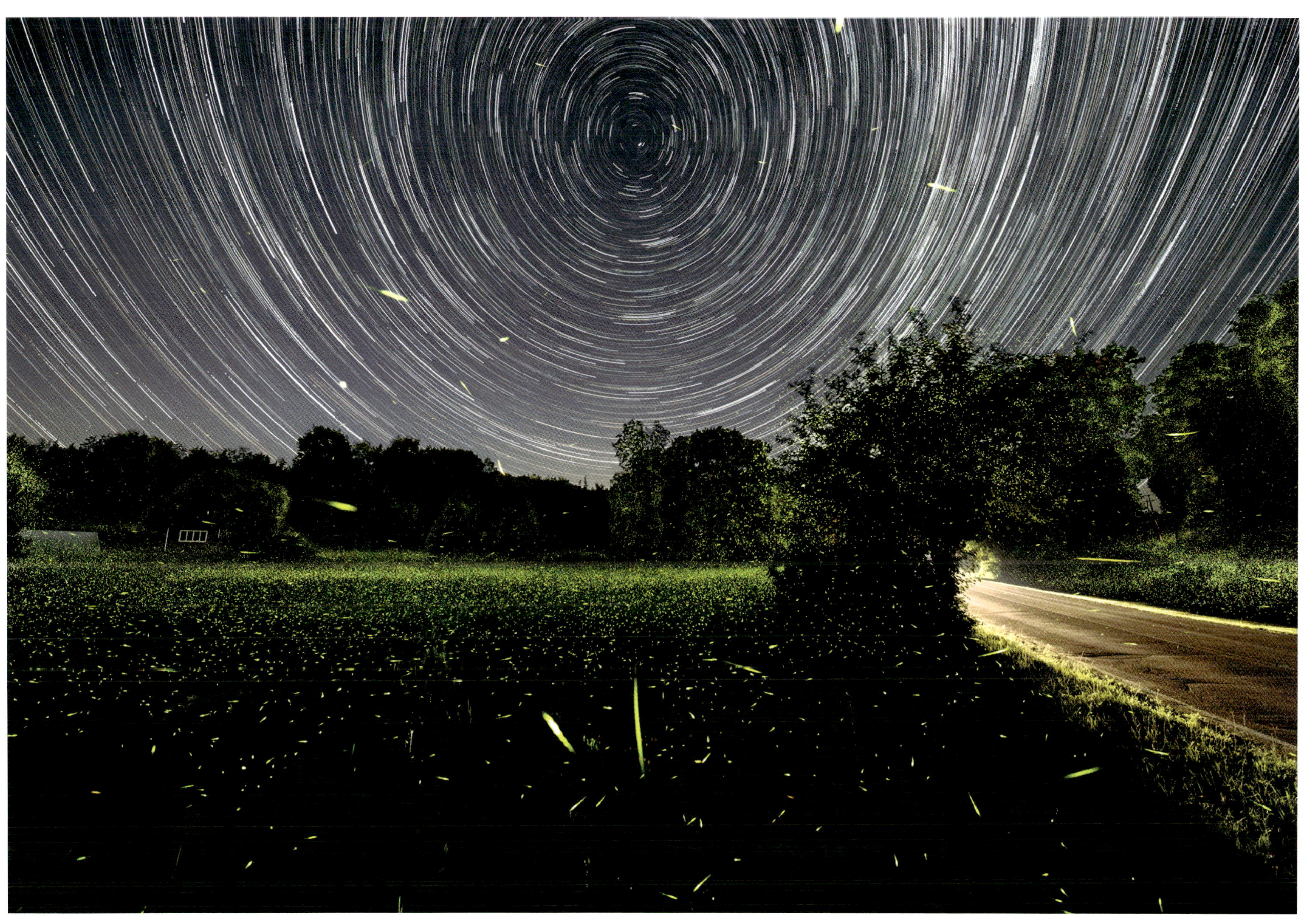

Self portrait driving, Milan Hill Rd. July 8, 2020.

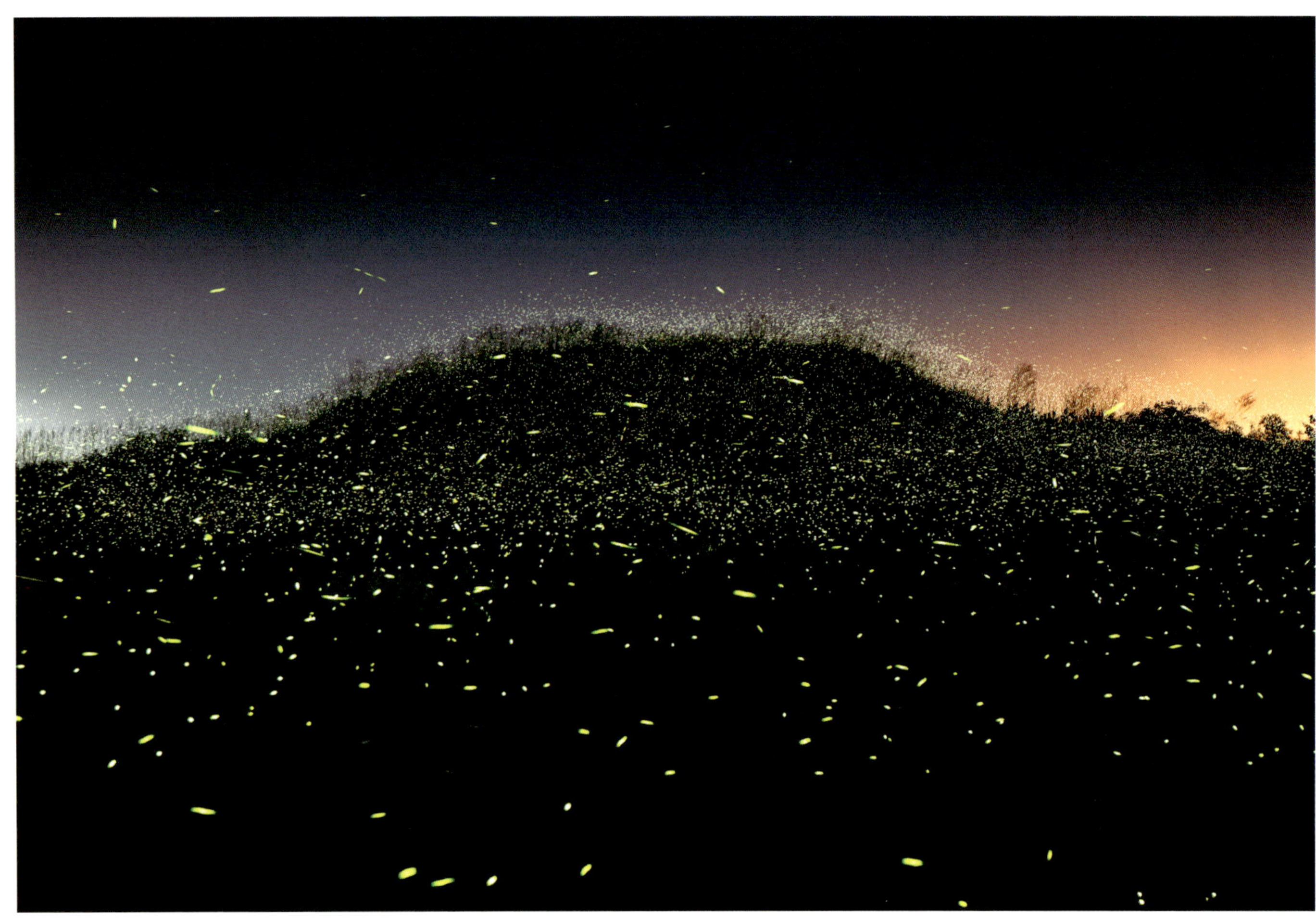

LED light pollution (left) and sodium vapor (right). June 18, 2019.

Do you share your locations with other people? Or do you take a more private approach?

I take a hybrid approach to that. It depends on who the person is. If the person is a friend of mine, fuck yeah, I'm gonna tell them where to find some great-ass fireflies. But if it's some random human DMing me on Instagram, I'm not. There are a couple of spots that are my favorites, and I am reserved about telling people about those places because, for me, they're precious and unique. I don't want to bring attention to them. Not so much because I need to keep it for myself, but because I want to keep it private for them.

My favorite stretch of road ever, which I discovered pretty early on, is a fantastic display, even in the off years. It's not very long and it doesn't go to or come from anywhere. It's a compact range of geographies, histories, topographies, and water, plus the widest range of firefly species I have ever seen in such a small area. It's also old farmland that is ripe for development and has changed hands several times over the past few years by, per my guess, wealthy city investors. Another thing about these special places is that the experience of witnessing the fireflies in person is completely different from looking at photographs of them. In fact, it's almost the opposite. It's actually considerably more wondrous and mind-bending. And very quiet. I have shown a few people some of those spots.

I'm not a religious person. In fact, I'm a pretty solid atheist. But those experiences I've had out in the fields with the fireflies are about as close to a religious or spiritual experience I've ever had. So, I do feel proprietary about some particular coordinates. But depending on who you are, and how you ask, I may bring you to a prime firefly spot.

You return to the same locations again and again. I'm curious to know what you, as a very intentional observer of land, have experienced in terms of space regulation and infrastructure shifts?

I have a depressing answer to that question. I have lost a lot of locations. And that's also happening to many of the locations I've used for my winter work (which is photographing airplane traffic at night). Development. Many places I used to be able to access have been developed or gated and I can't get in there anymore. Or now they have too much light, even if I could access them.

With the fireflies there are a few things that happen. Like on that favorite stretch of road, for example, a couple photographs in this book were made on what is now the driveway to a new house. That magic spot will never be the same again. The vegetation has been cleared from one side of the old farm road and the road itself has been paved. Development in and of itself takes space away from the fireflies—literal space.

And there's also the addition of outdoor lighting, especially these horrible LED floodlights that people now put everywhere. I've probably lost more locations to so-called updated farm floodlights than I have to new houses.

The general idea about fireflies is if you install outdoor lighting they disappear. That's not entirely true. There are actual firefly species that don't give a shit about light pollution. Some of them will leave, and some will stick around.

I'm thinking of one photo that I've always thought is particularly interesting because it shows a contemporary, slow-motion, societal transition. I took a photo of a hill. You can see different shades of light on both sides. The source of the light pollution on the left is a town a couple miles away, across the Hudson, that had already started a shift to LED outdoor lighting. The closer-by town polluting the night sky on the right is still using orange sodium vapor lighting. I have noticed this in many places and contexts, but this photo shows it nicely. It'd be interesting to attempt to remake this image now and see where we are on that curve.

I've also witnessed things that I didn't think were possible, such as firefly populations coming back. One spot I found when I first started doing this got hit by a microburst storm in 2017, and most of the trees that the fireflies liked were ripped down. Over the next three to four years I kept going back to scout that spot and almost never saw any. That goes along with another generally accepted narrative about fireflies: once you remove a population from somewhere, it's very difficult for them to reestablish themselves. In this case, I've been pleasantly surprised to find that they did in fact recover pretty well, but only over the past couple of years. I'm not sure about the reasons behind that—the area had been pretty heavily damaged. That storm was so destructive, it might have physically killed the active DNA transfer mechanisms at the time. But the population is back. I made three or four pictures there this past year and was just thrilled by that rebound.

You mentioned in a previous conversation that pesticides also affect firefly populations.

Yeah, it's quite obvious when you see houses and neighborhoods where pesticides have been used on lawns. There's a good example of that near where I live. Some friends bought a house on a property that seemed promising, so I asked for access. This place was glorious, with fireflies everywhere, but the place next door is one of those neatly kept properties. They have this huge, perfectly maintained yard. They also have an outdoor floodlight, and there are signs all over the yard about lawn maintenance. That pesticide shit kills fireflies, too. You can stand on the border between these two properties, but not too close because the guy's a bit, uh, temperamental, and I don't want to, you know, get shot. When you look left, there's a shitload of fireflies. On the right, there's none. That's from pesticides and things like it. Pesticides are not intended to hit fireflies. But they do.

A lot of the time when I post pictures and people start commenting on them I hear, "When I was a kid there were so many fireflies, and I live in the same place now, but I never see any in my yard." I'm like, "Well, do you use chemically based lawn products?" That'll do it. Maybe it's not that society has killed off the fireflies in your backyard. Maybe it was you? That's really a no-brainer, rather than something I've noticed gradually over time.

What does an off year look like to you?

Fireflies have a flashing period of two to three weeks. There's a spot that I got to know early on. The spot was the earliest to activate and the latest to shut down in the season, which told me that it has a large range of overlapping species. Photographically, it wasn't very interesting, but it was so close to home that I would use it on my way out to photograph every night as a barometer. This past year, for a range of reasons, that location was disrupted from normal years. The timing was different than any other year. That was generally across the board, along with a significant decline in

activity from years previous, which affects how much time a camera is left collecting data. Fewer fireflies, longer exposure.

How did you come to choose the title, *While We Slept*?

The night is as active as the day is, just not for us. Because we're diurnal creatures, and can't see below certain light thresholds, we have this bias that everything else composes itself according to our behaviors and needs. But that's not true. I chose the title *While We Slept* to reflect that unnoticed reality.

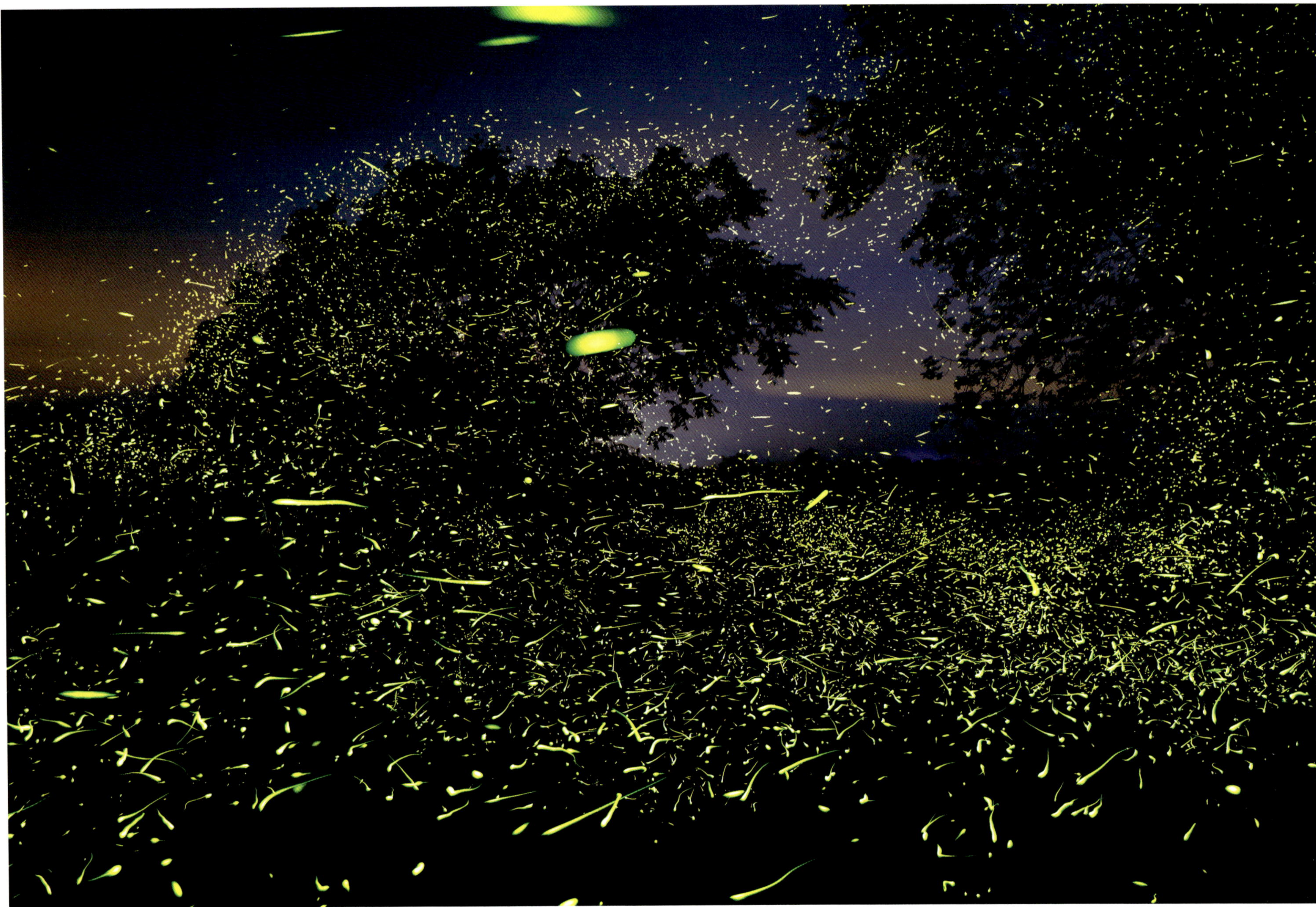

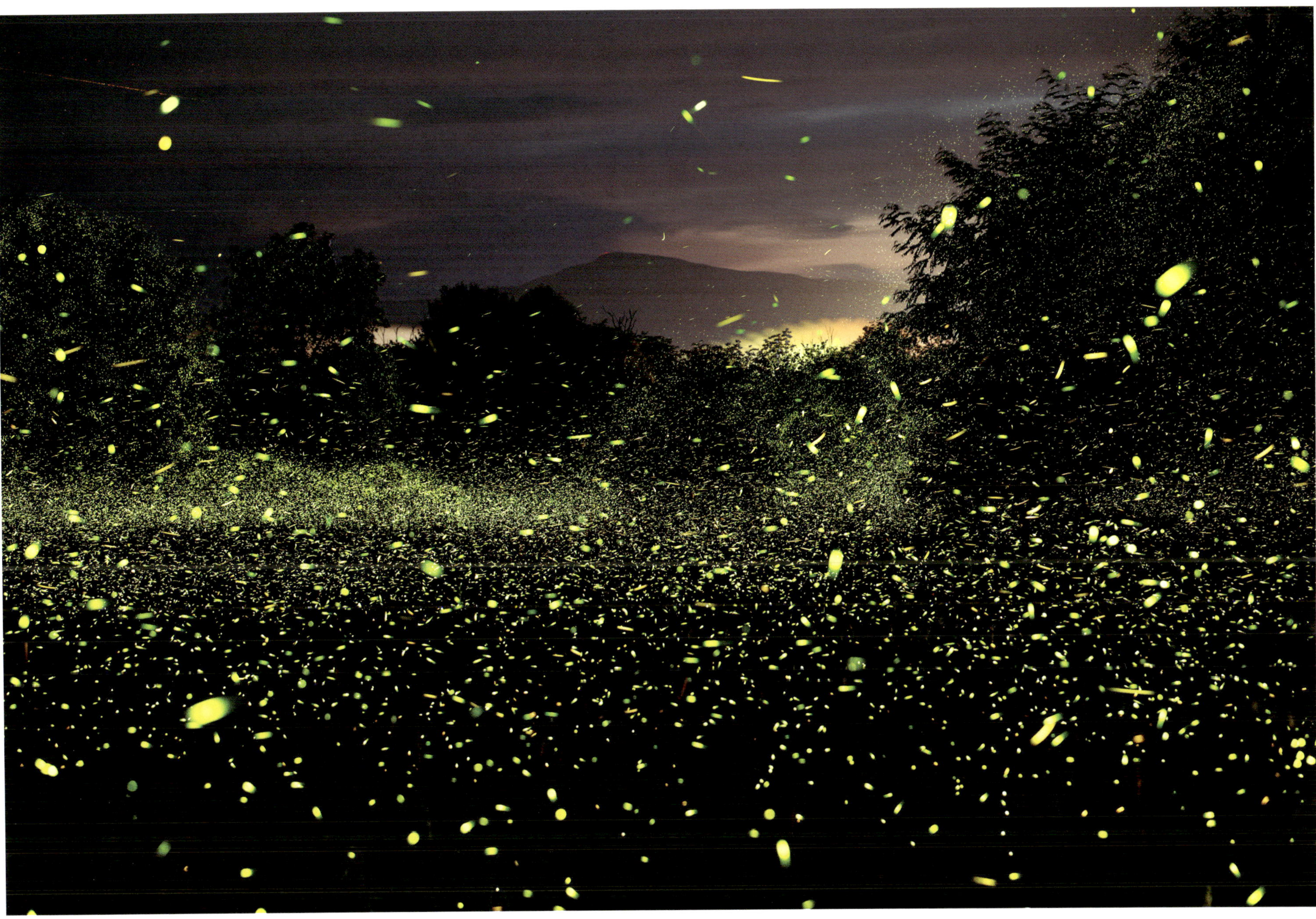

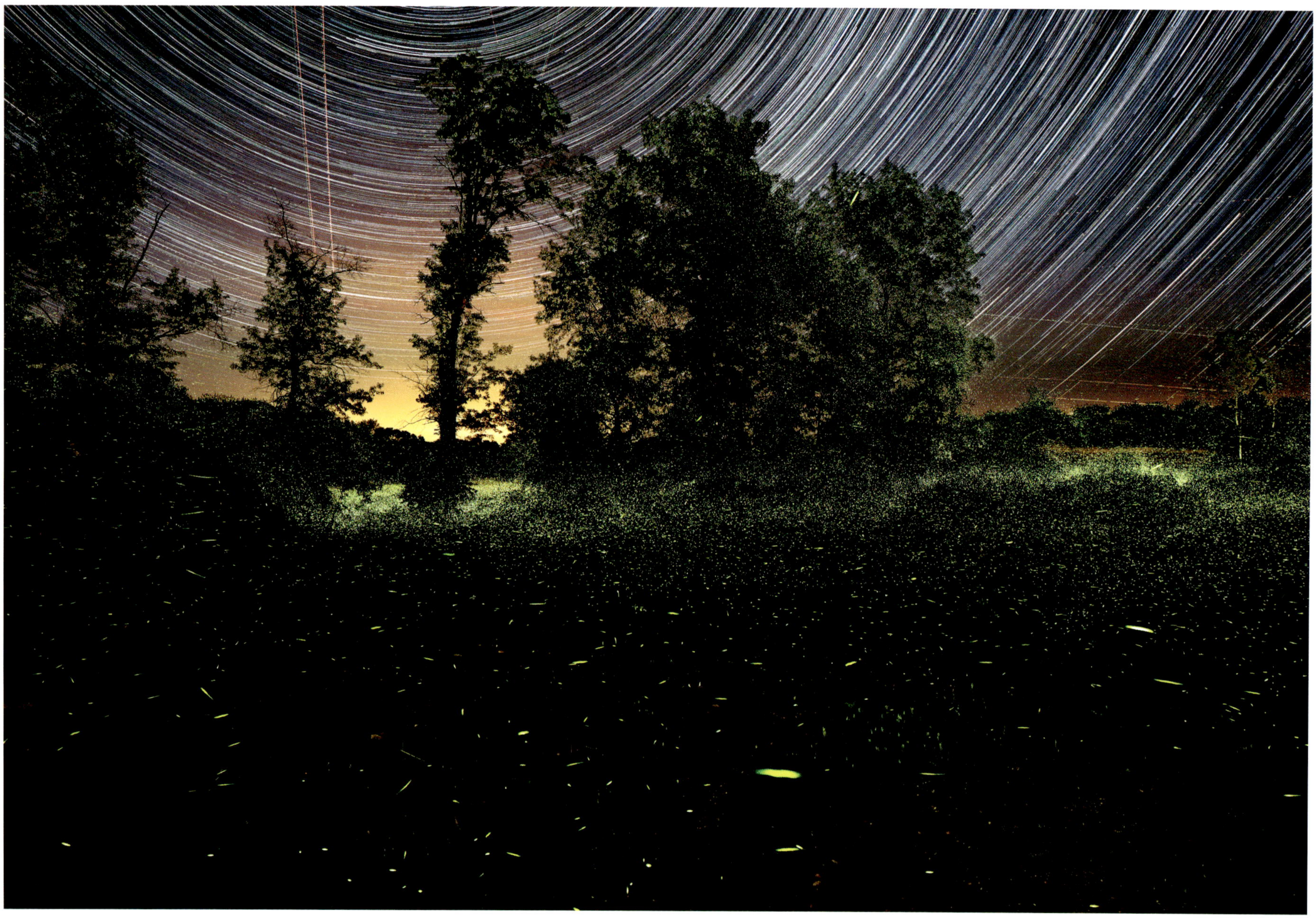

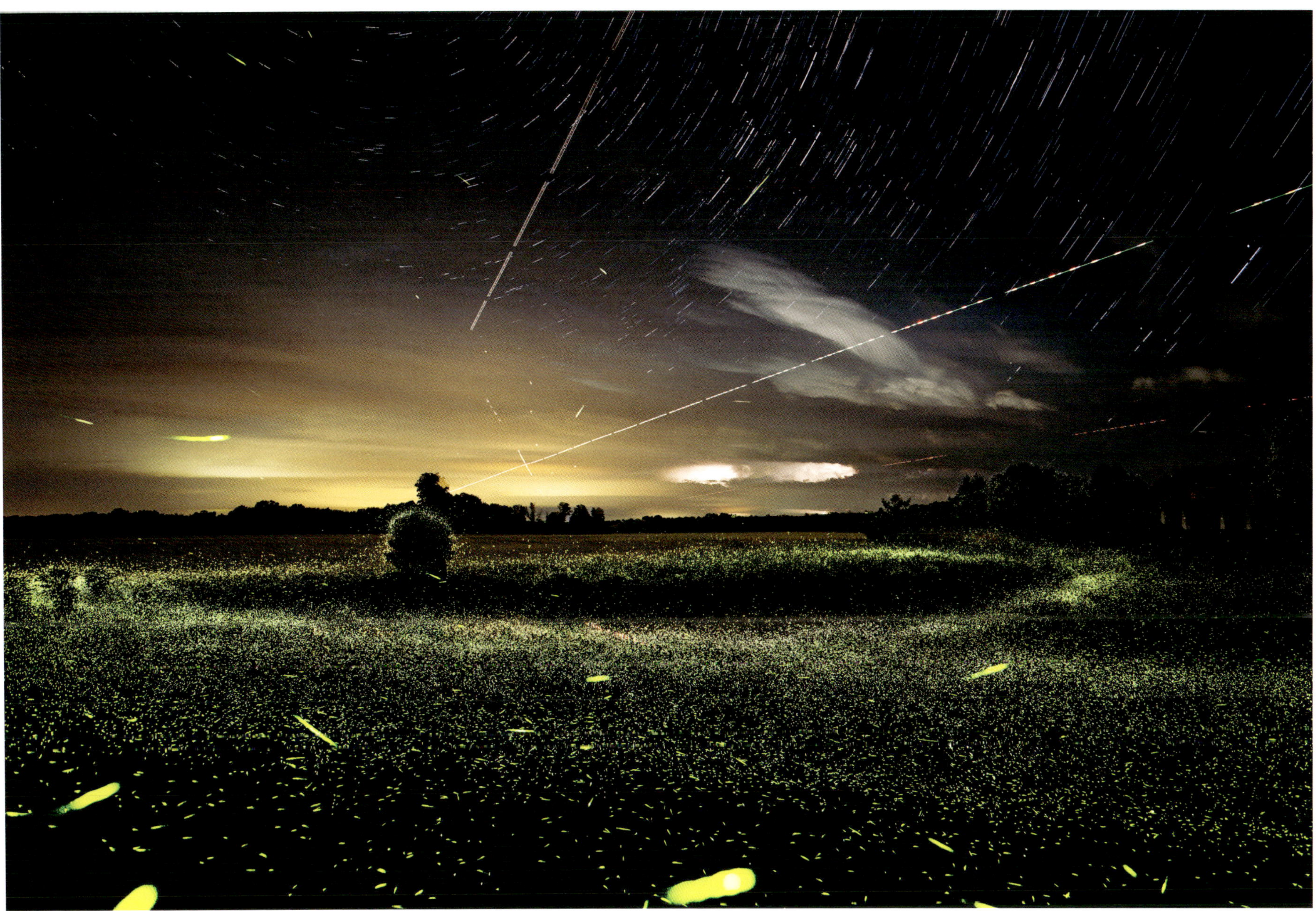

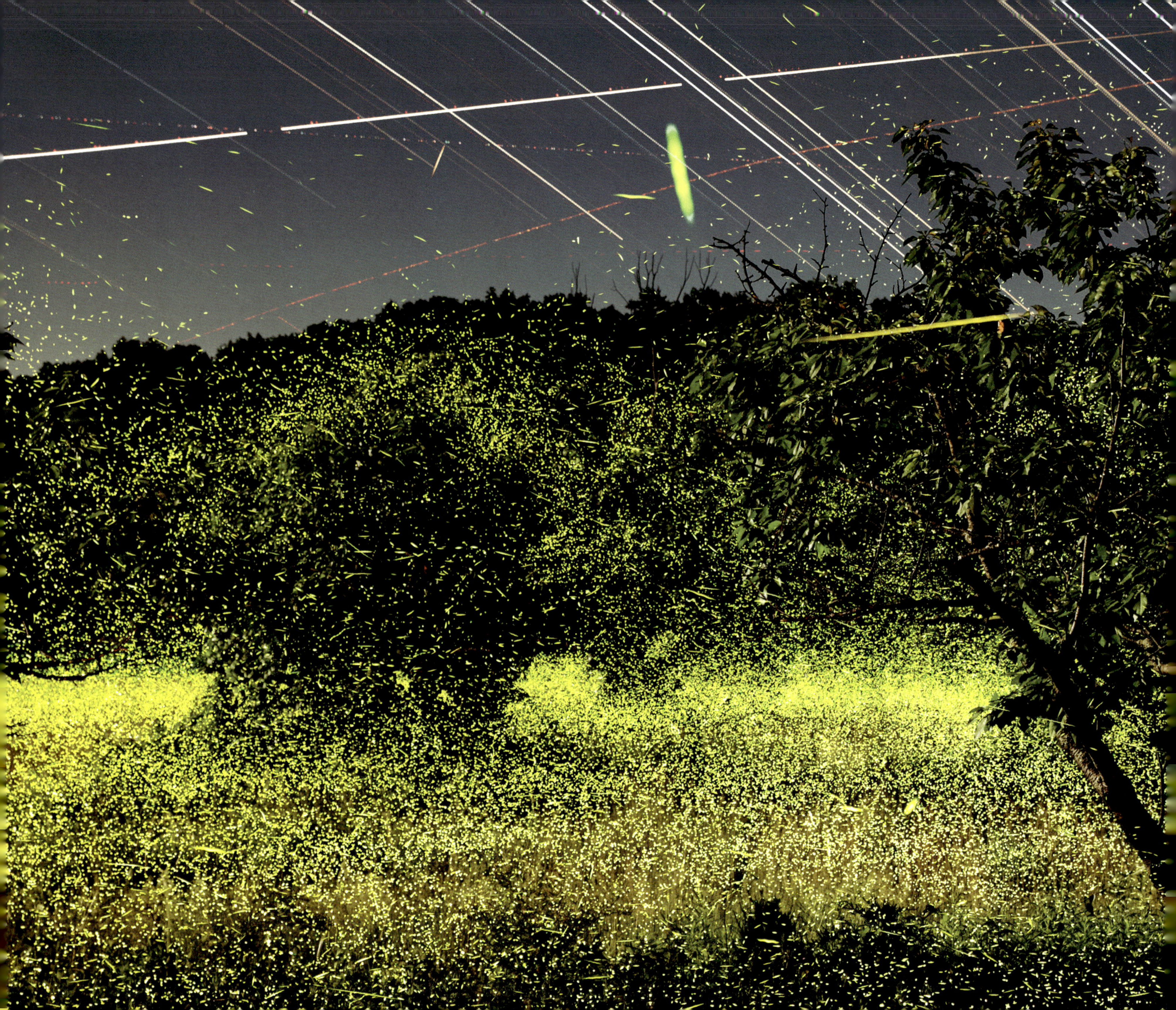

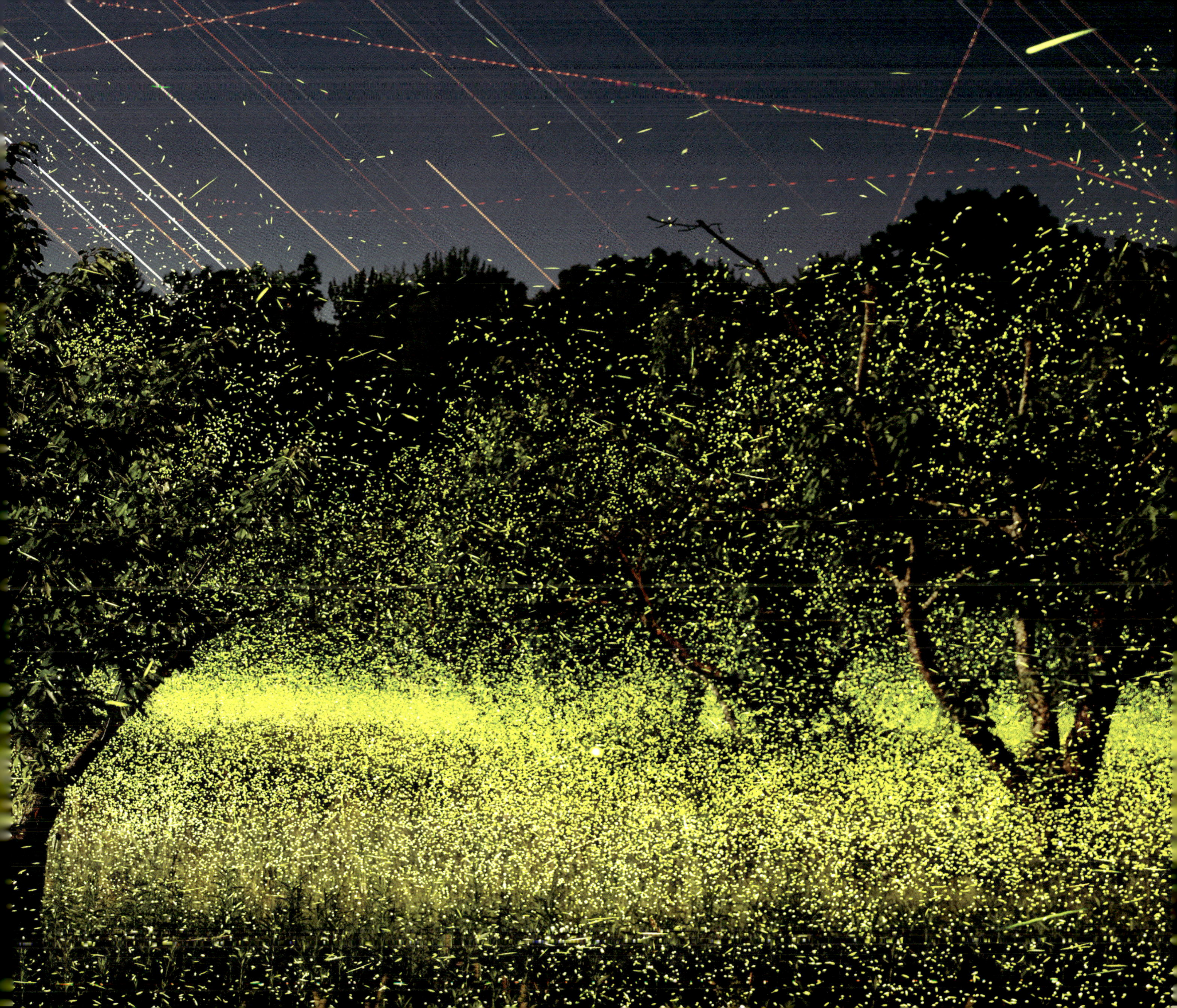

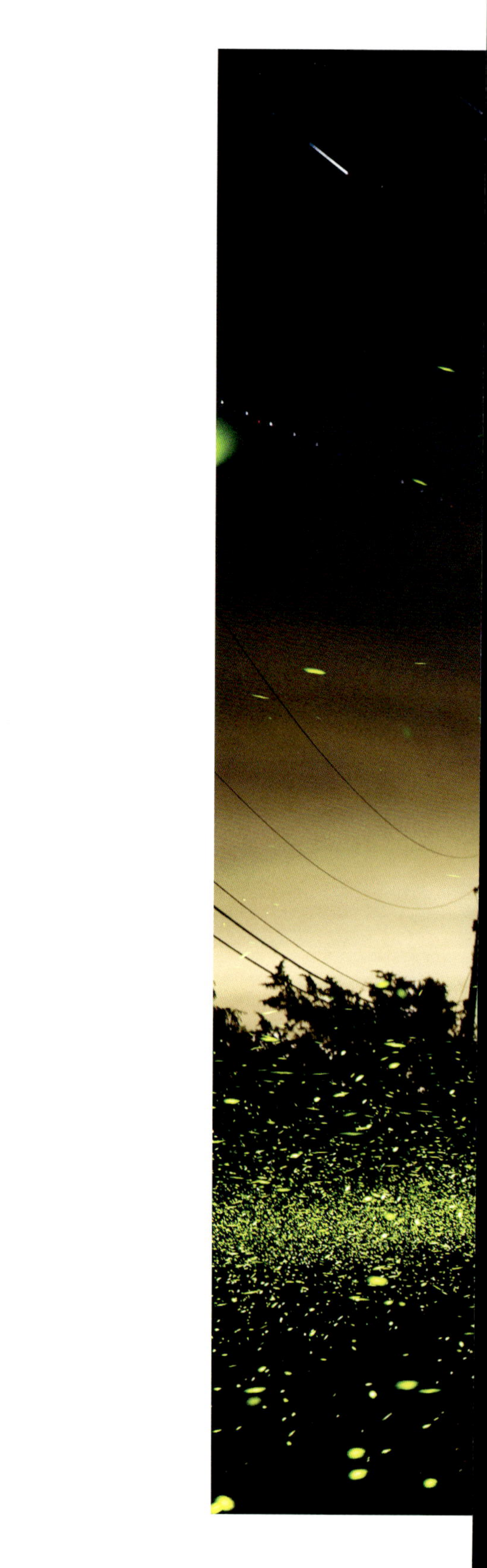

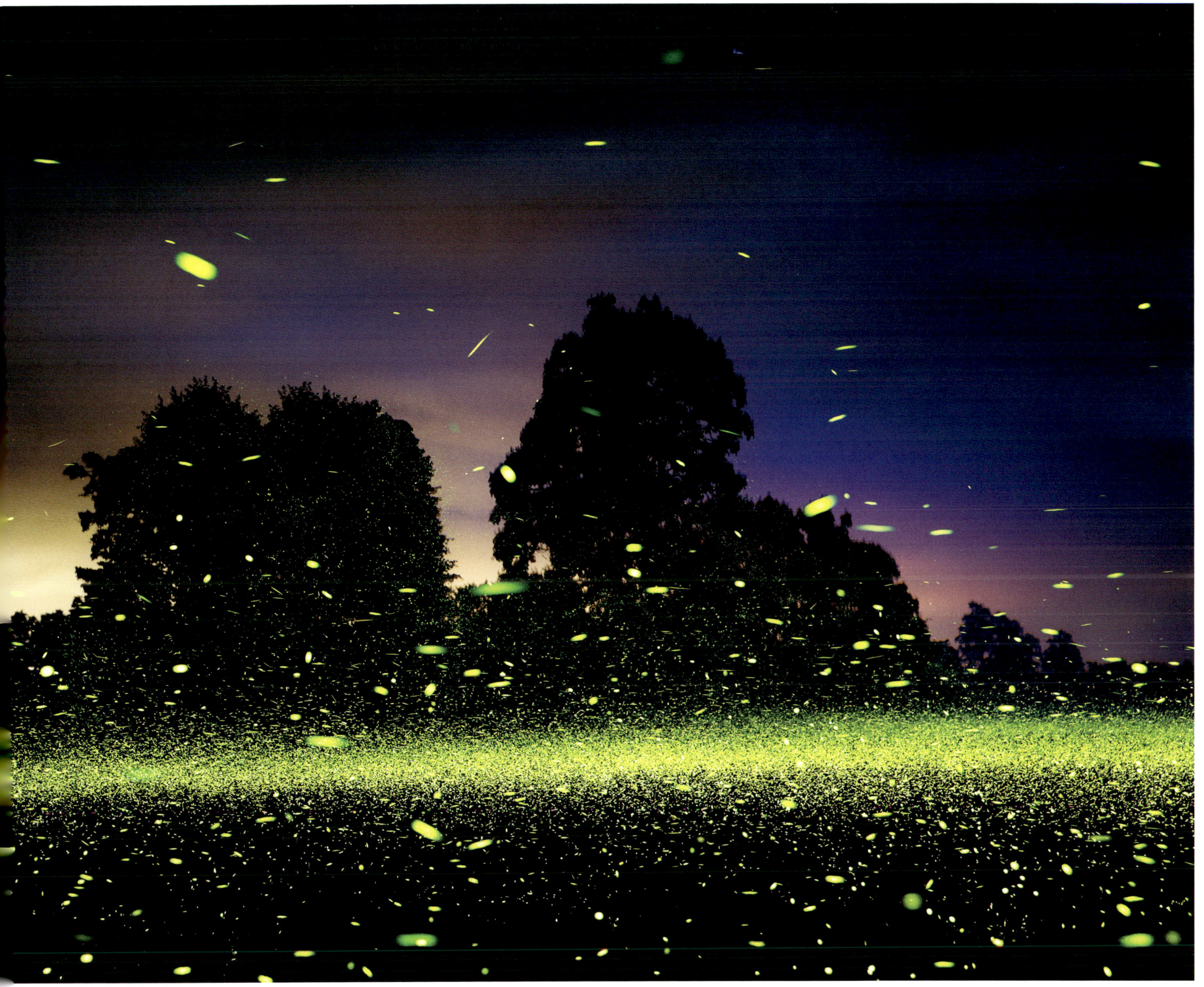

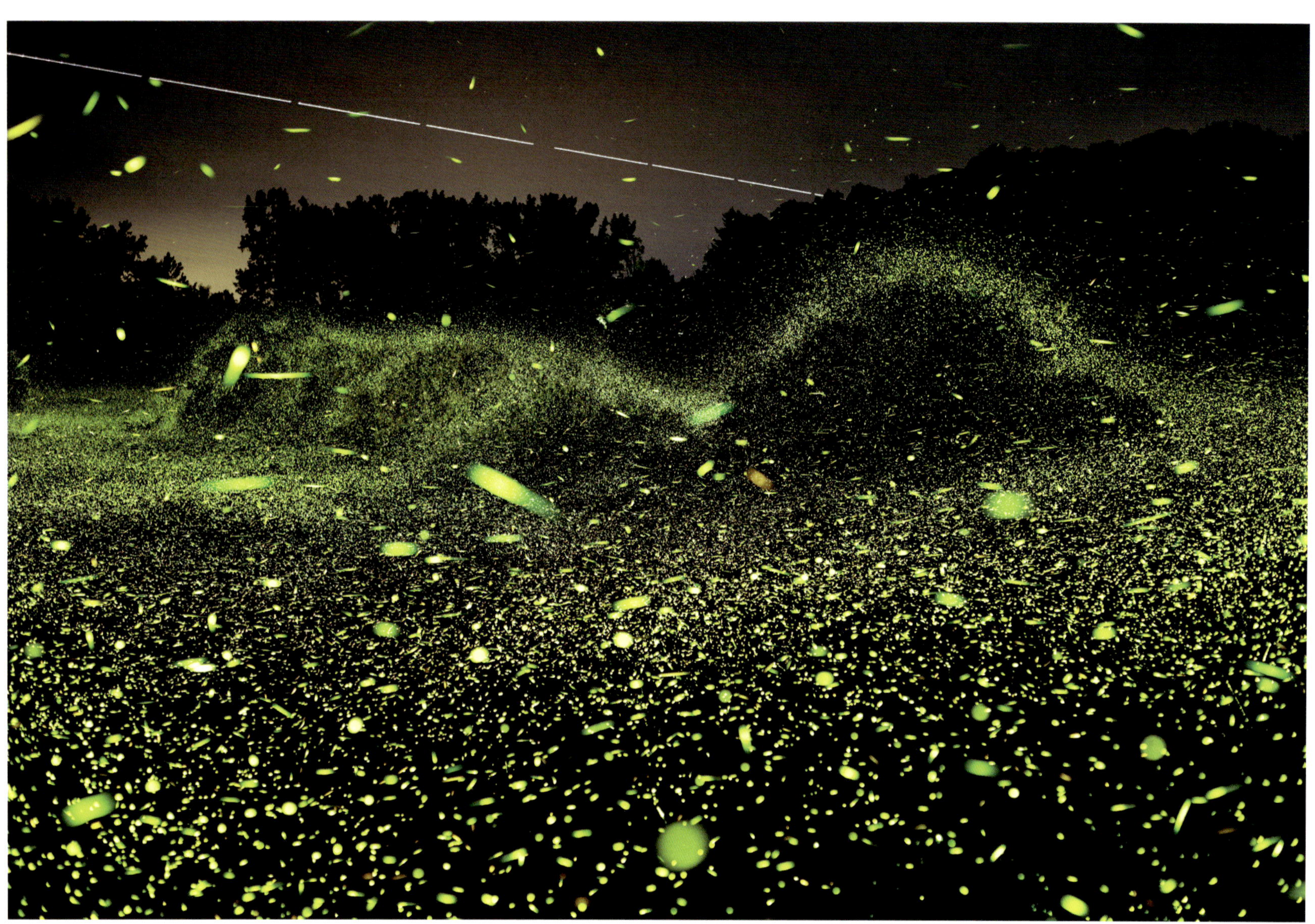

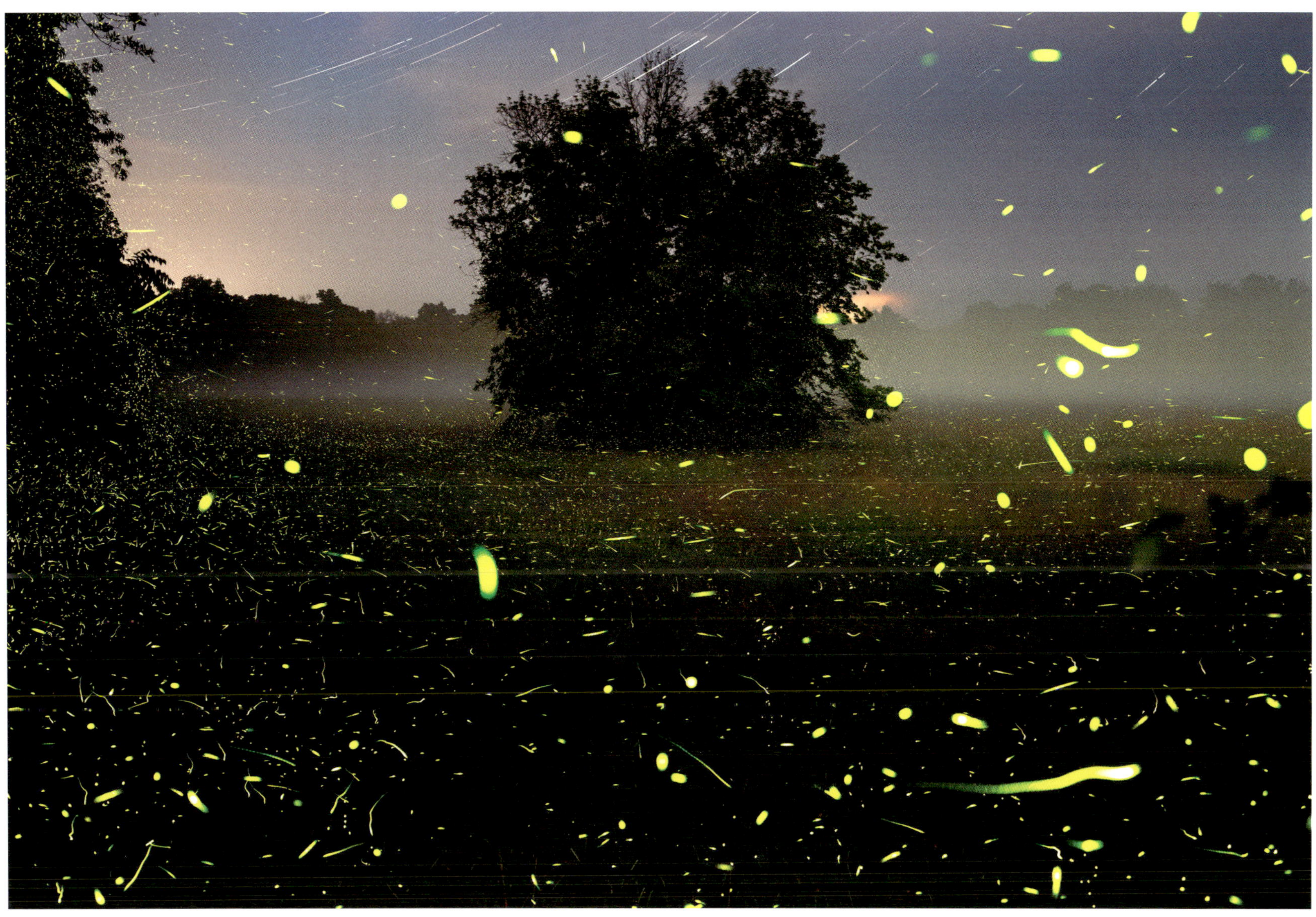

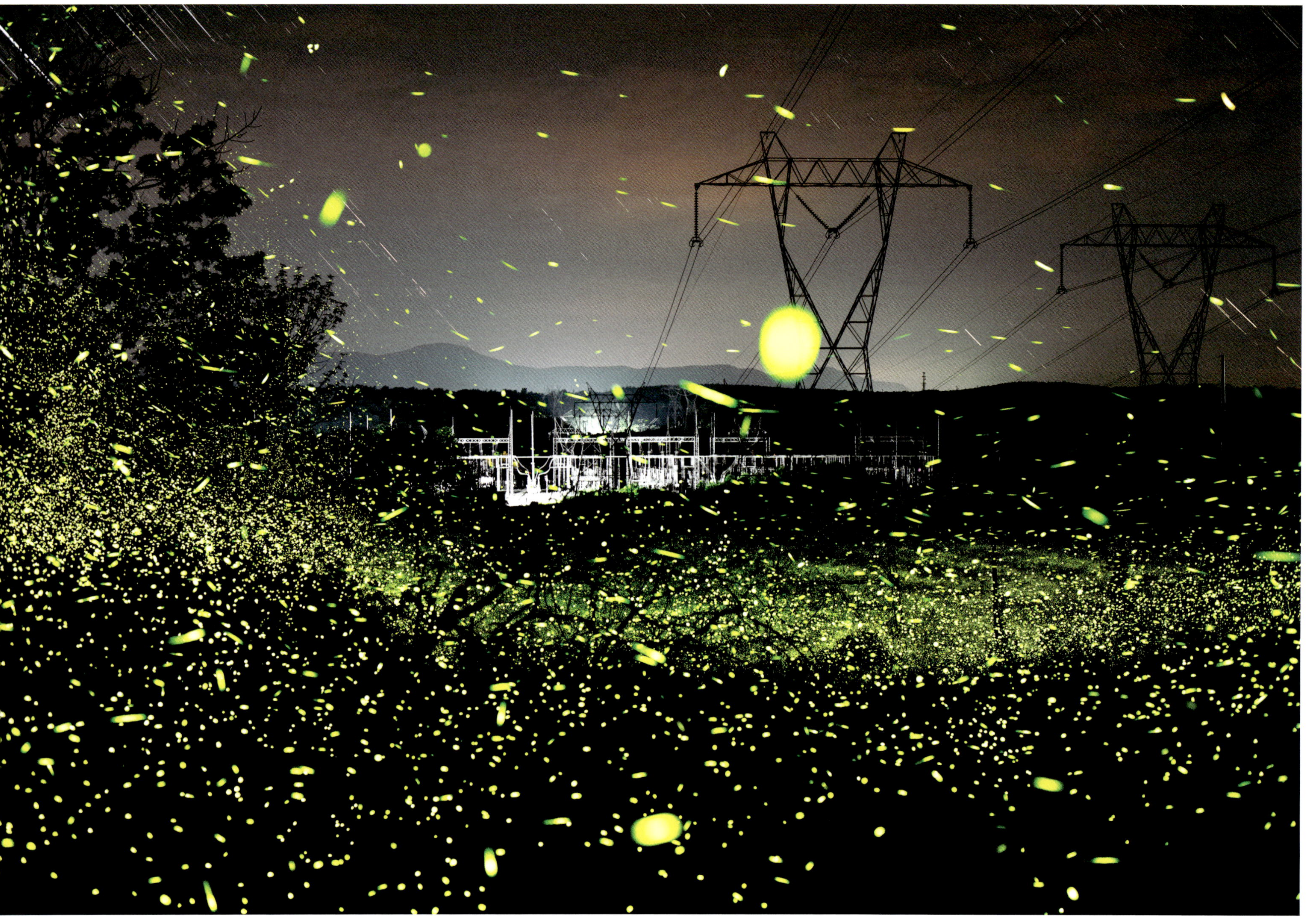

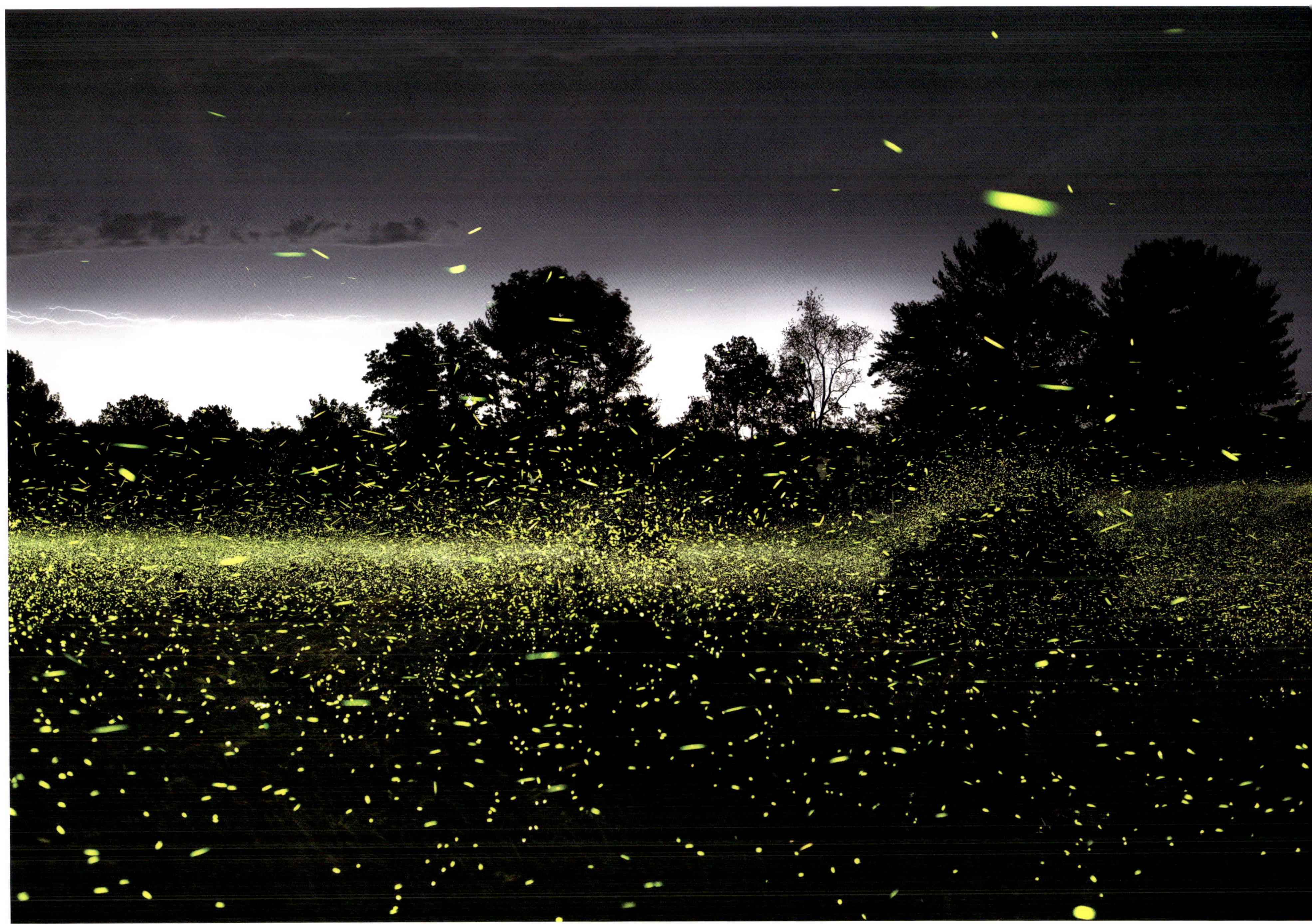

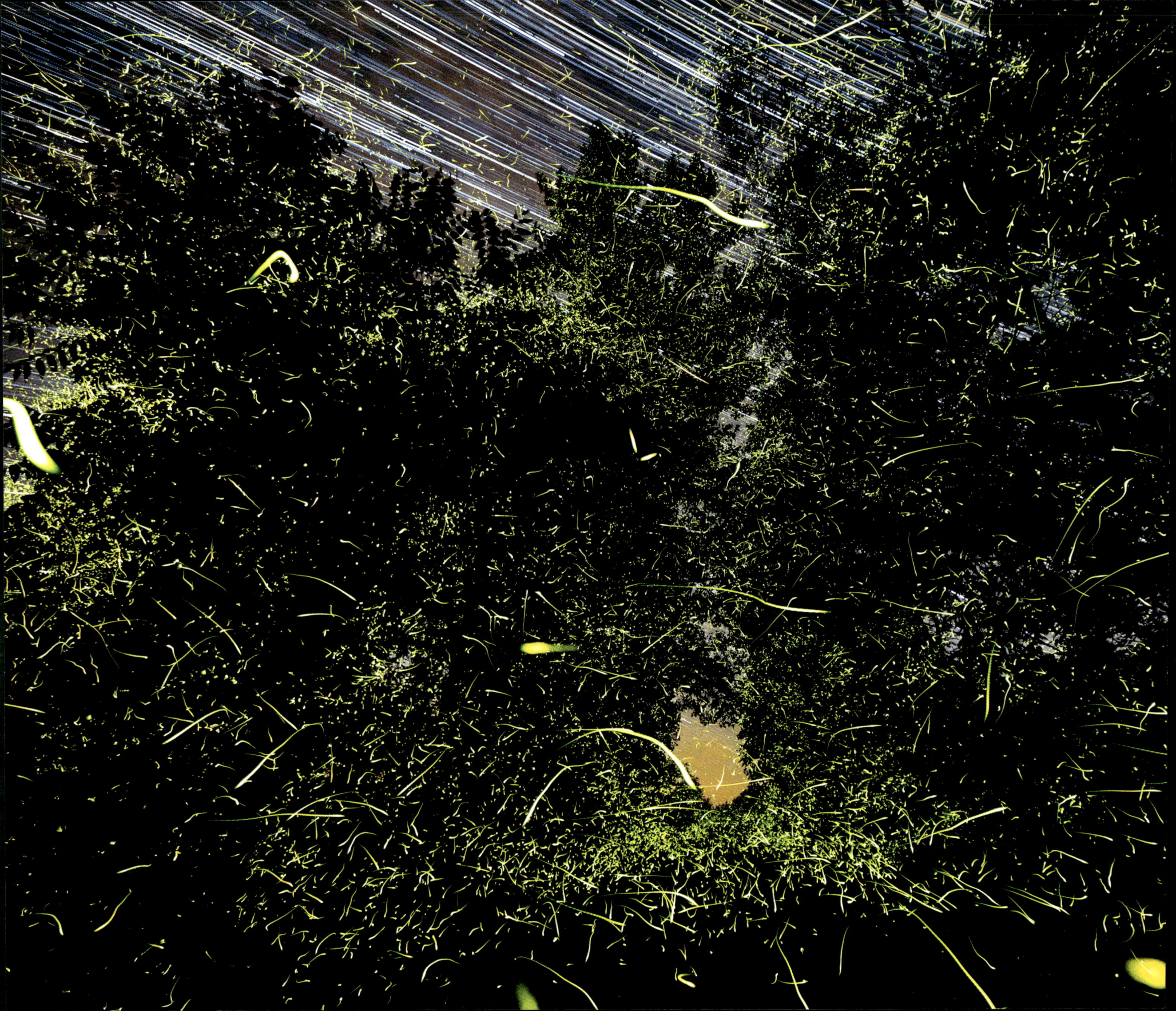

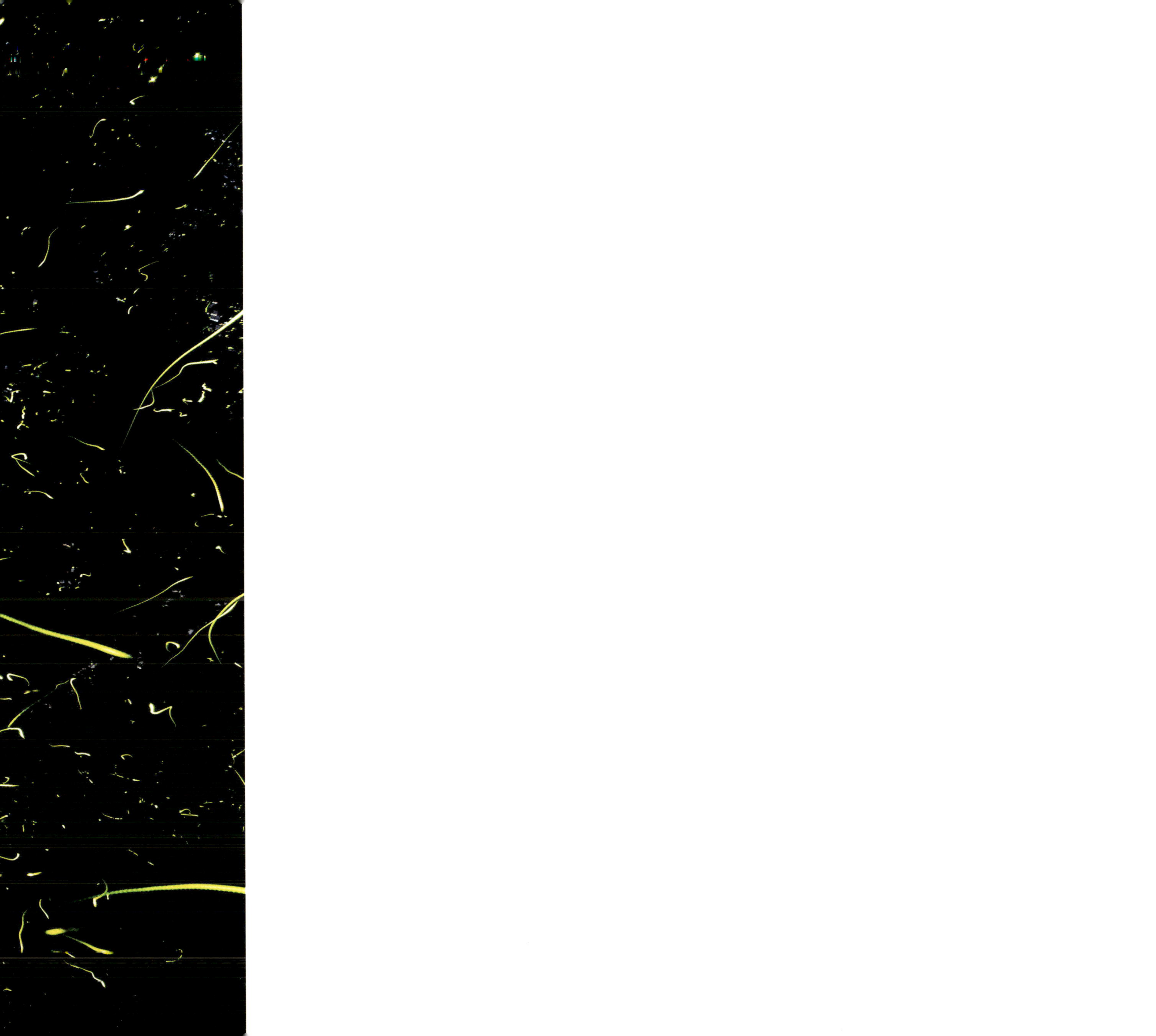

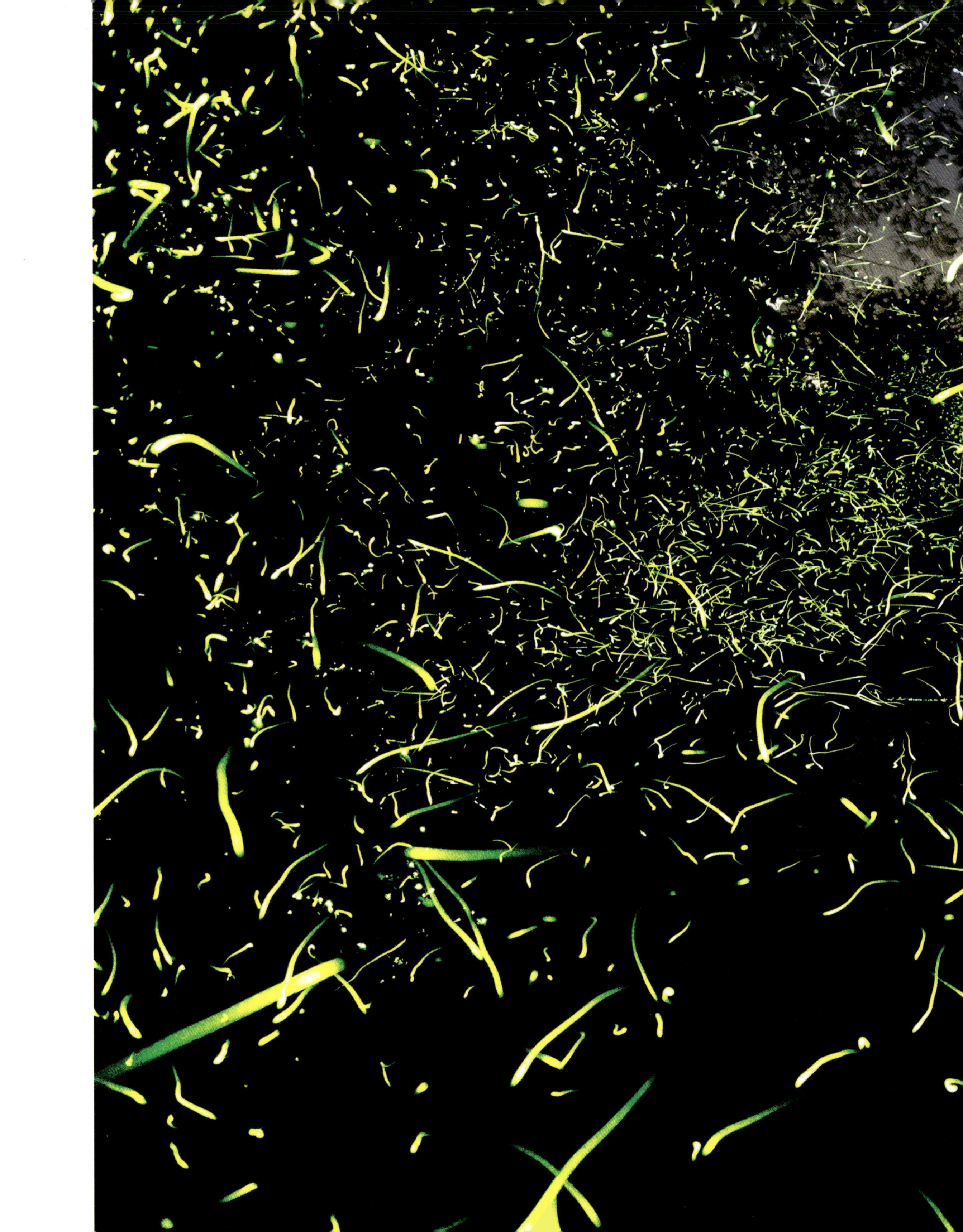

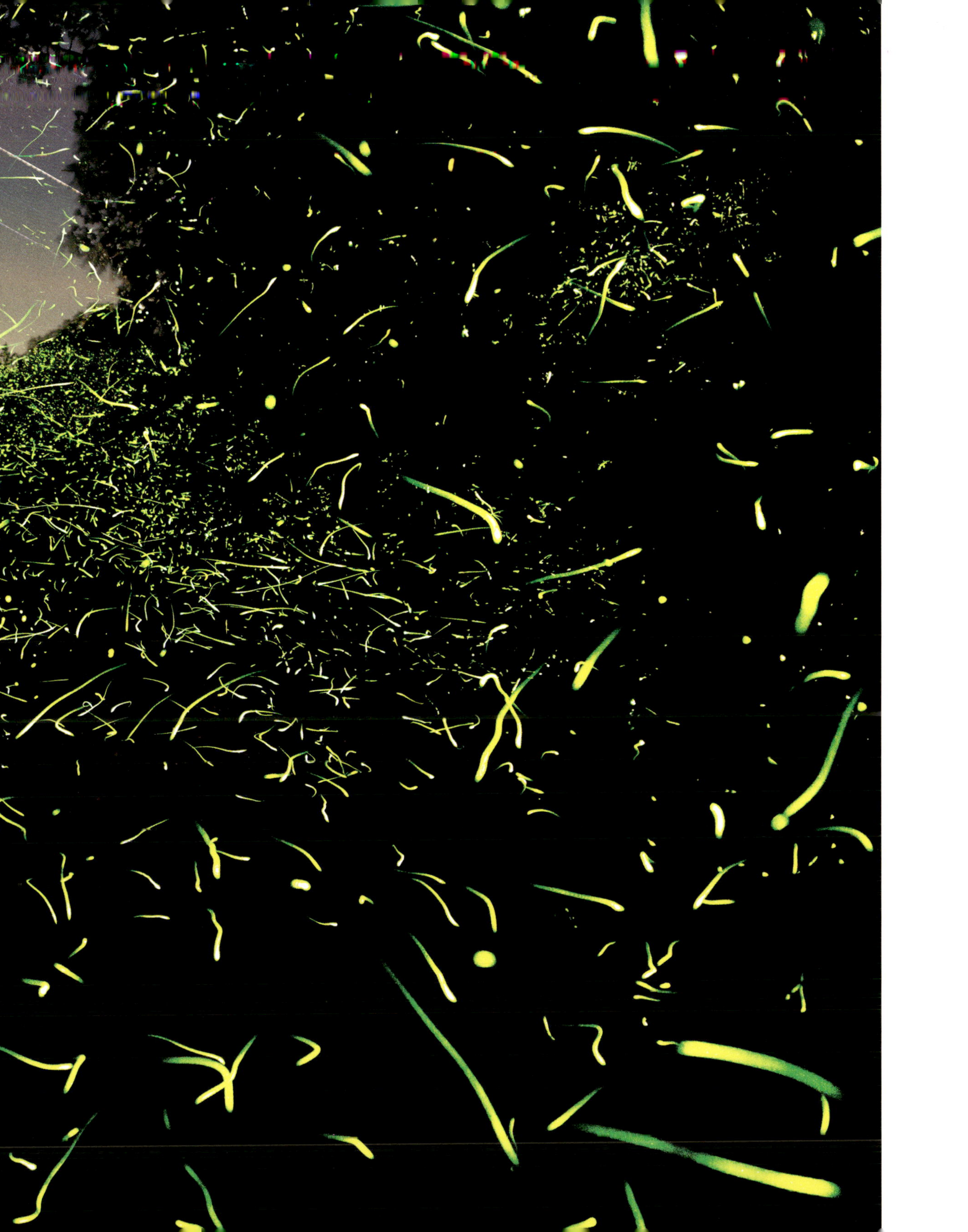

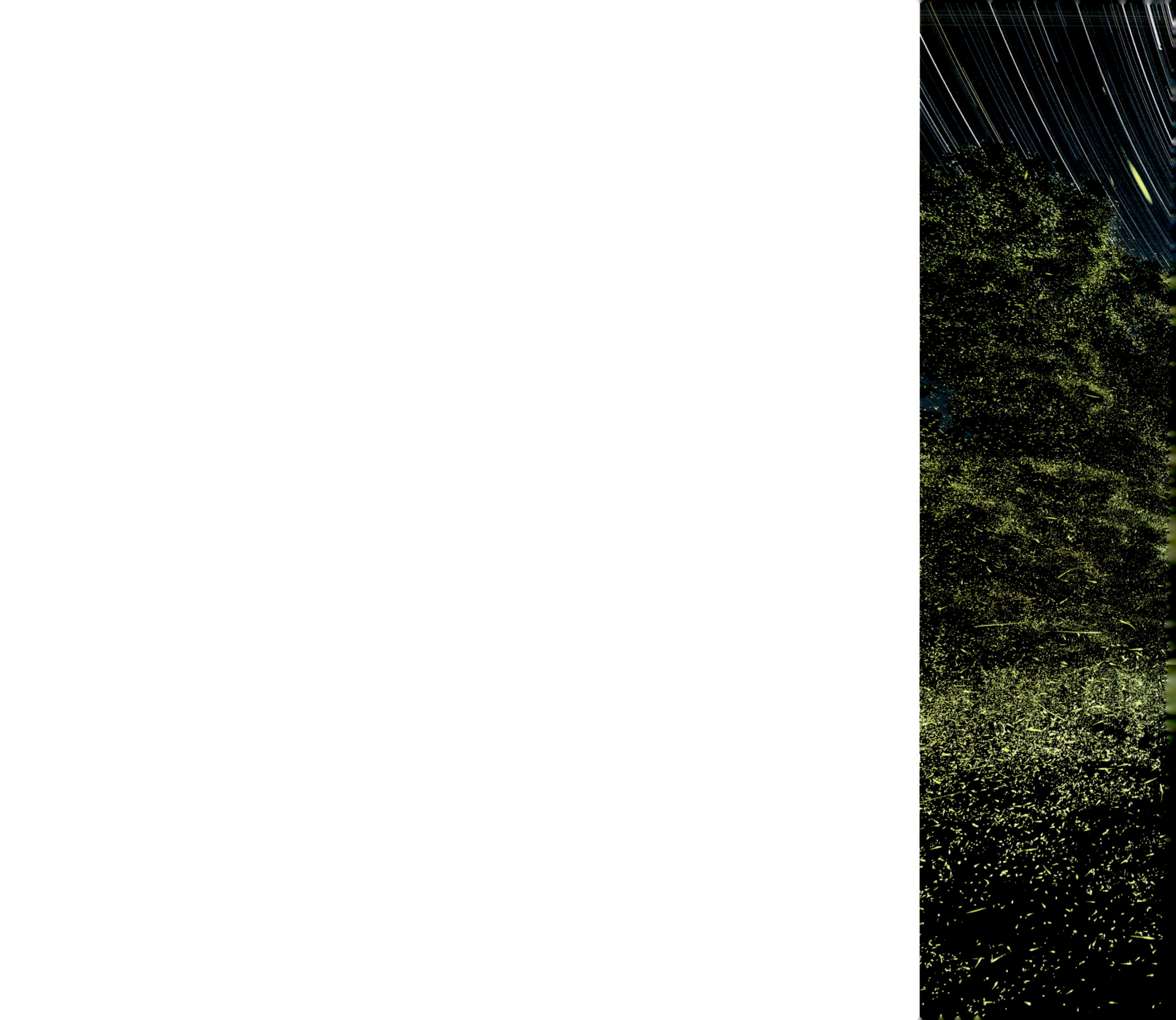

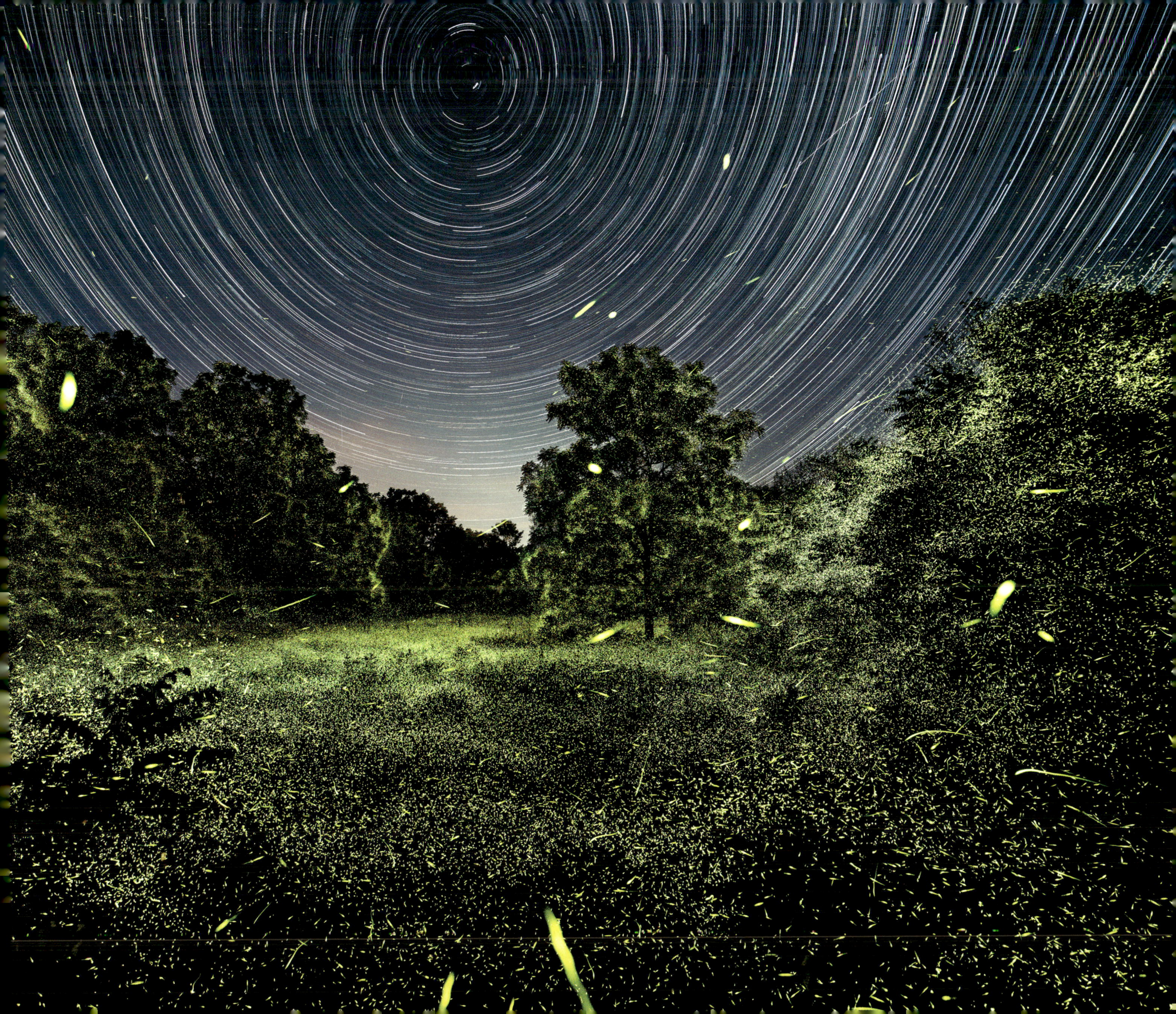

In your process, what does making a mistake look like?

Data. Useful data. I think a lot about the value of failure in art-making. Failure in art-making makes you and your art stronger. It gives you information and structure to build on the next time. When I fuck something up, I always learn something new and often start going down a whole different direction because I'm like, wow, it's actually kind of cool that the cameras shifted because I suck. How can I replicate that?

I'm not gonna say that I intentionally go out to fail. I am way too uptight for that. But I will say that I don't shy away from it, not in the least. I welcome what I learn from it each and every time. It really is all about data and learning. Even if simply to remind myself to tighten that stupid ball head so the background doesn't look smeared. This whole process has helped me learn to not spend so much time trying to predetermine things.

I also like how some of the imperfections or mistakes you've made that could have been controlled to your standards are occasionally images you end up loving. How do you decide what is a good photo?

There's a sound that I get in my head when I see a picture come to life that I know is right. Can I quantify or qualify that? Not really. I just know that it makes a little sound go off in my head. And that is something that I've learned to trust, even though it's not always right. If it's something that I try to conjure, it disappears. It's just that there are certain ones where I feel it, and hear it.

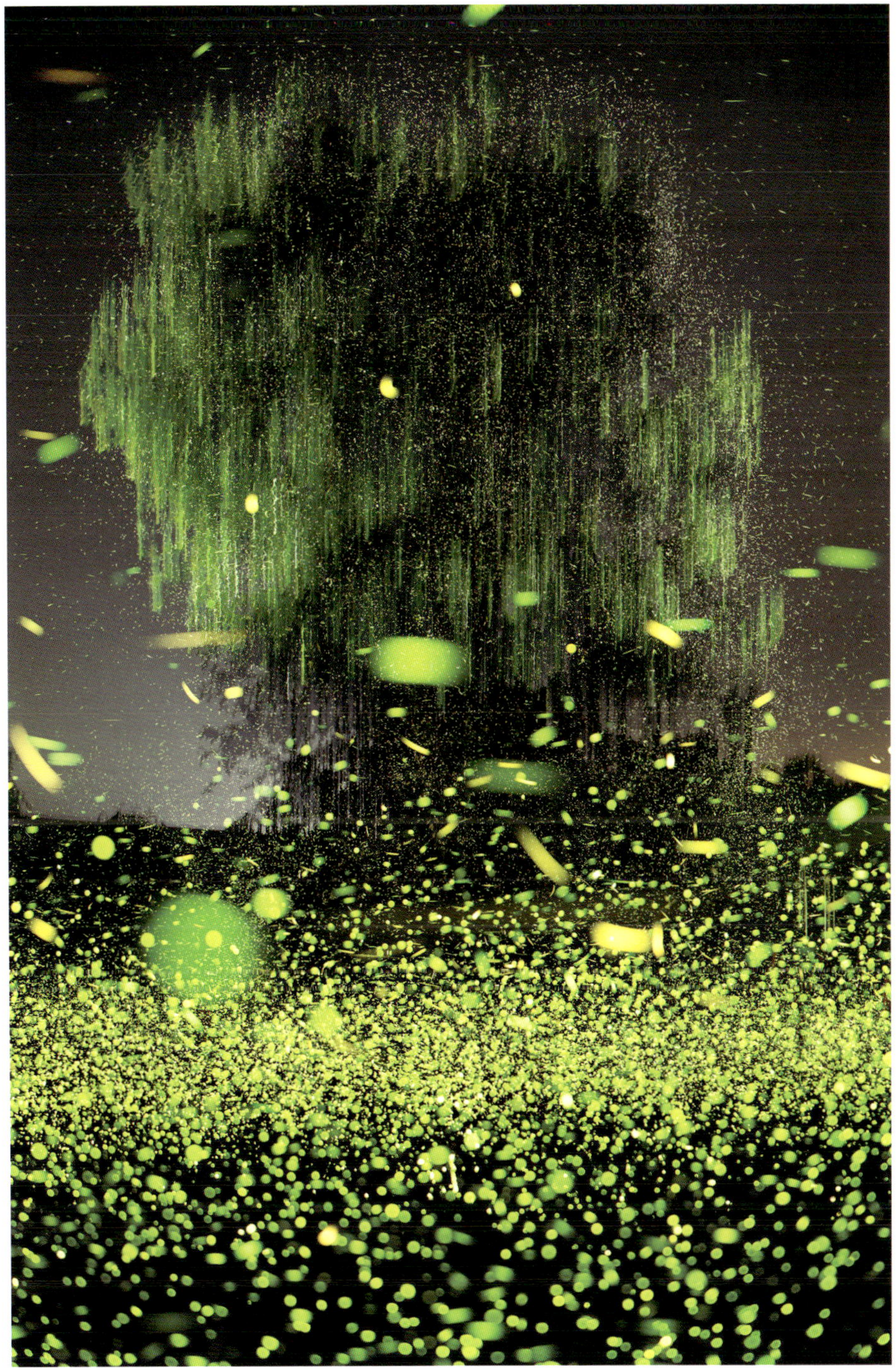

Failed attempt? June 19, 2021.

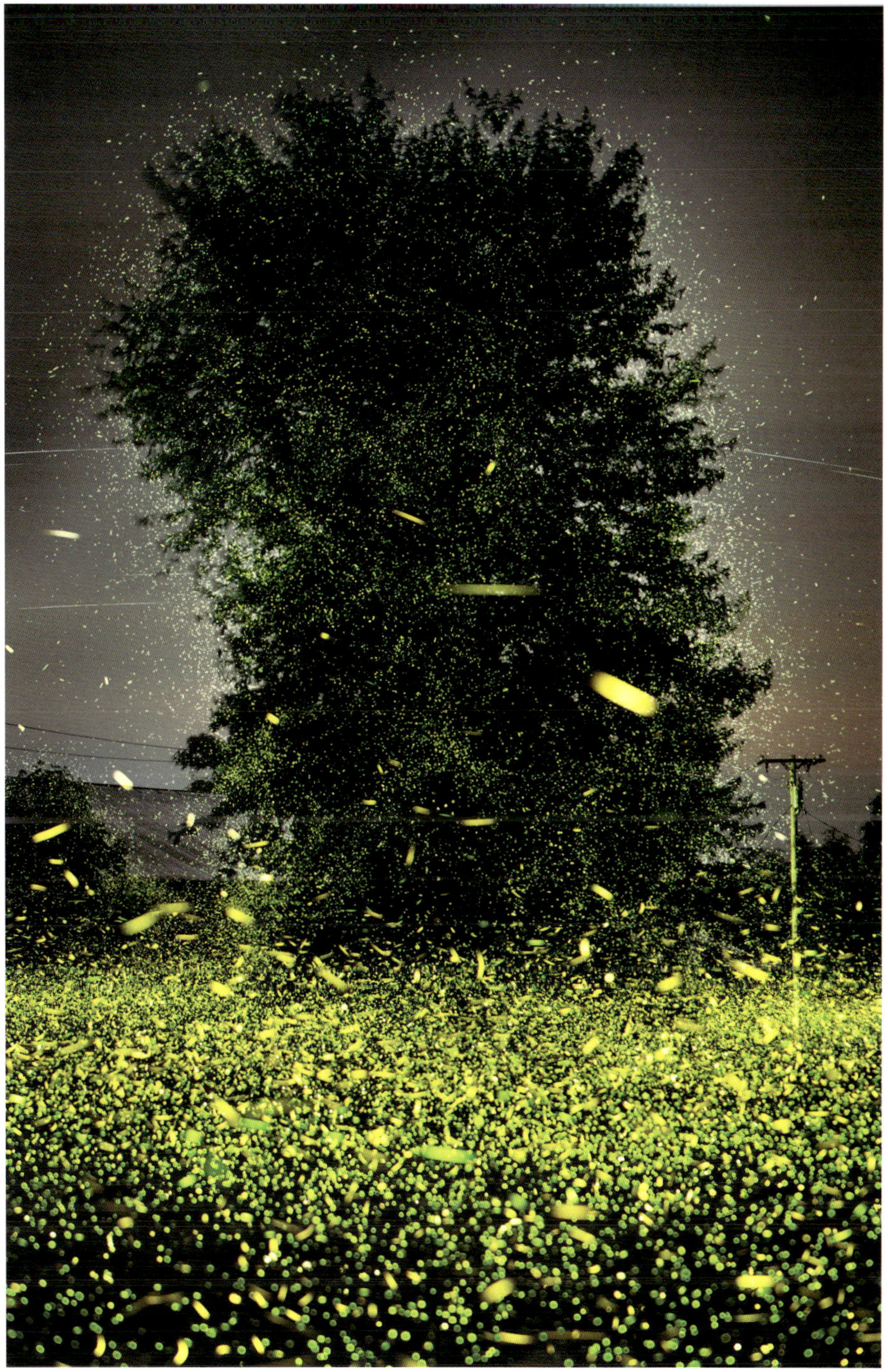

Success? June 20, 2021.

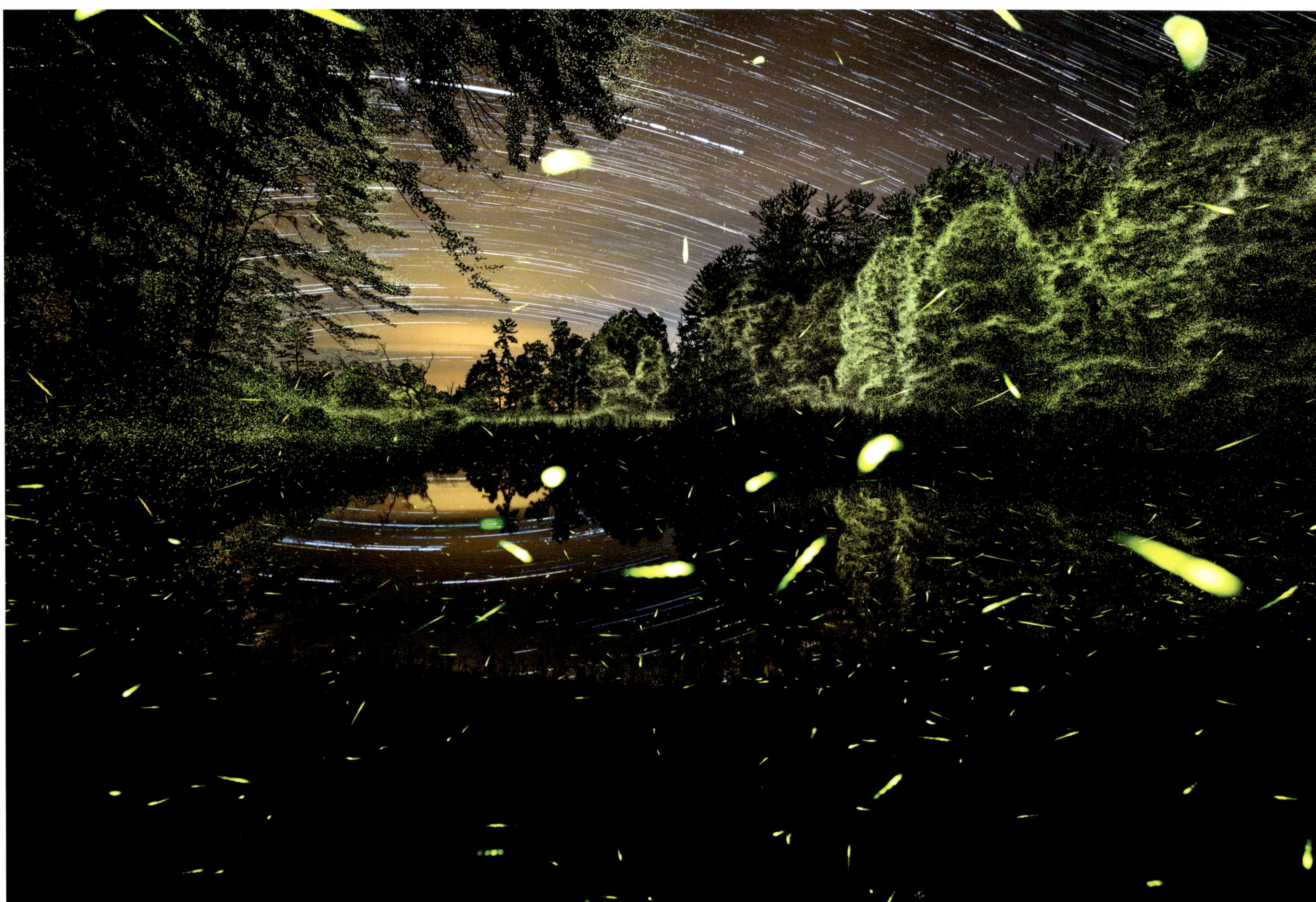

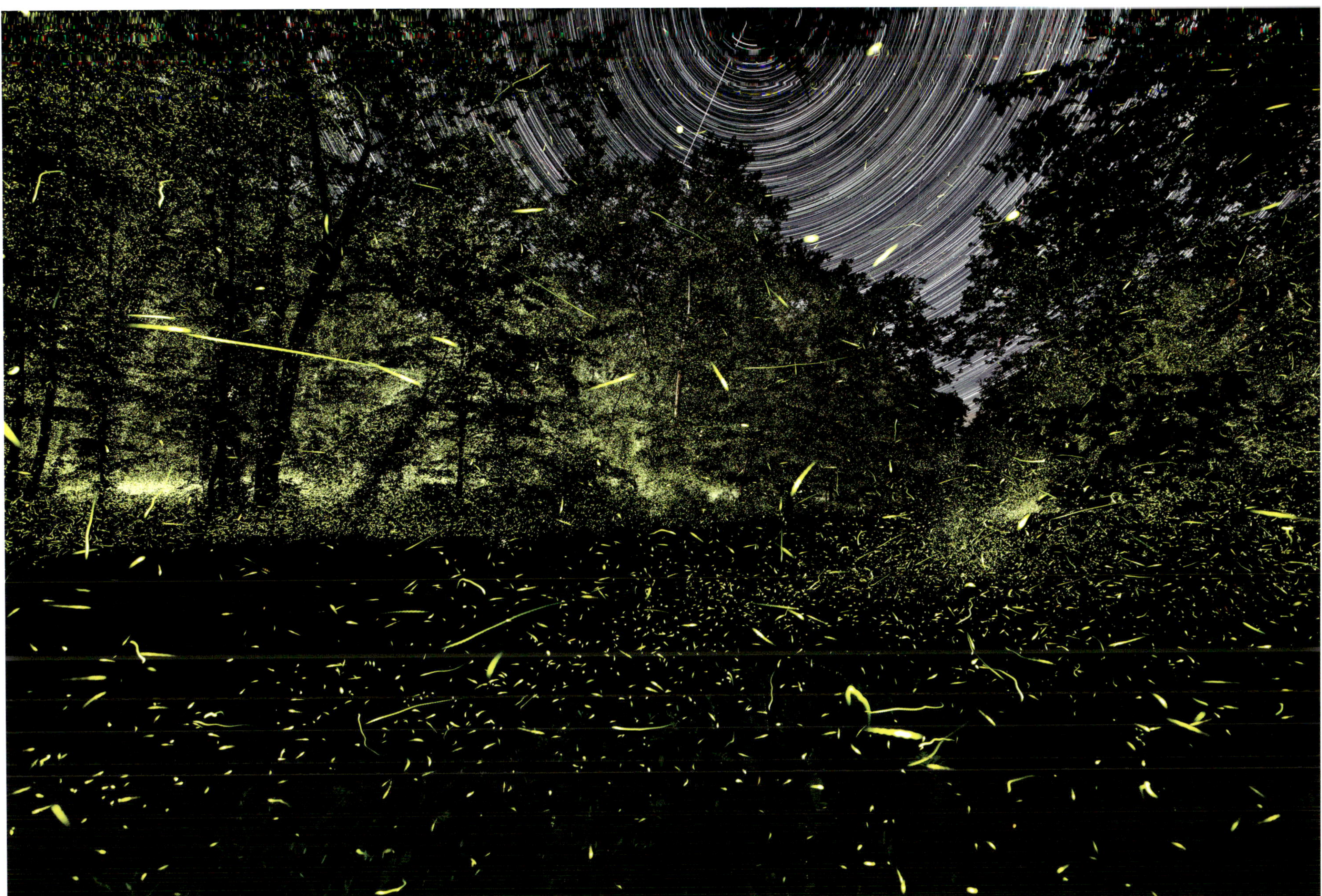

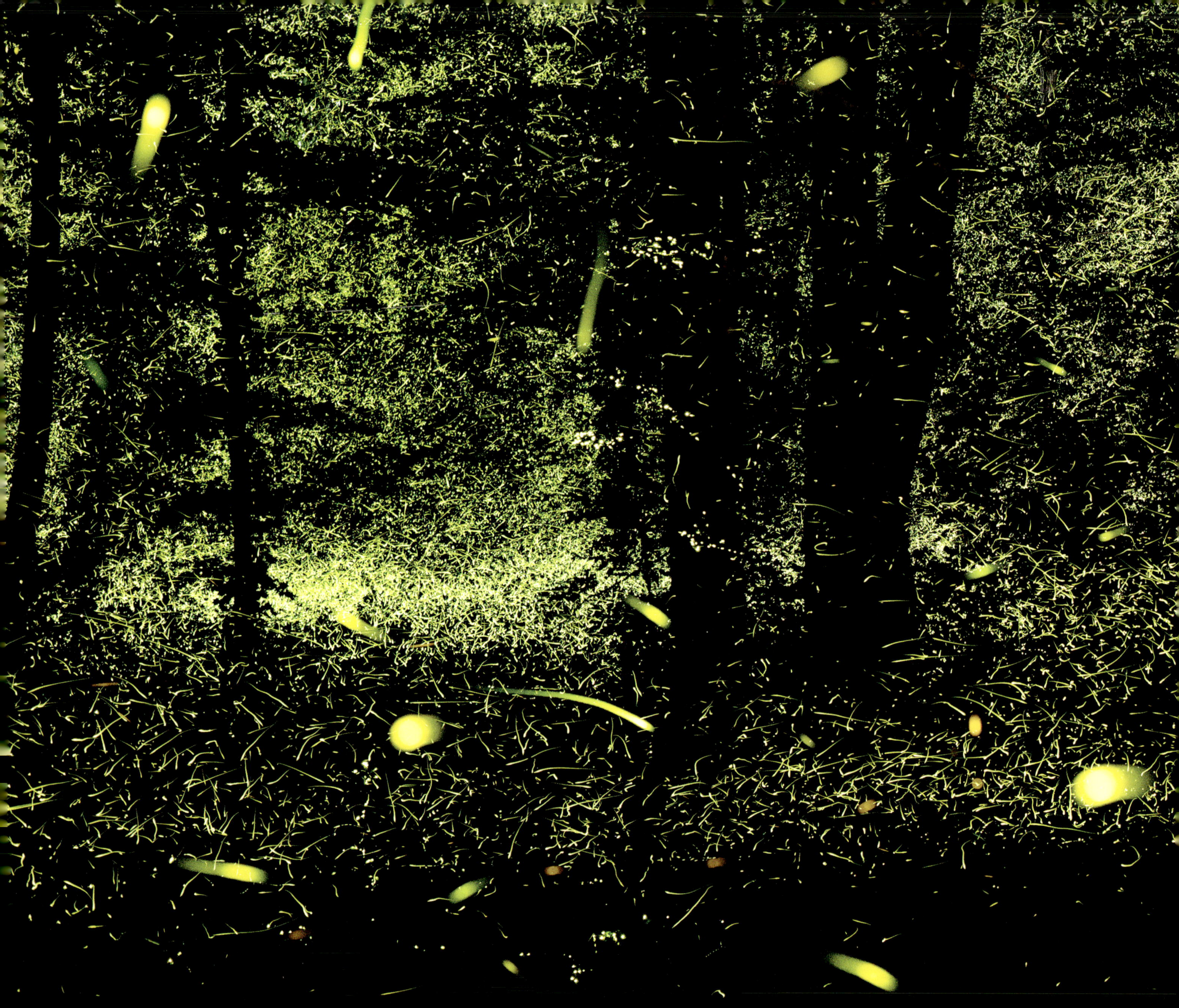

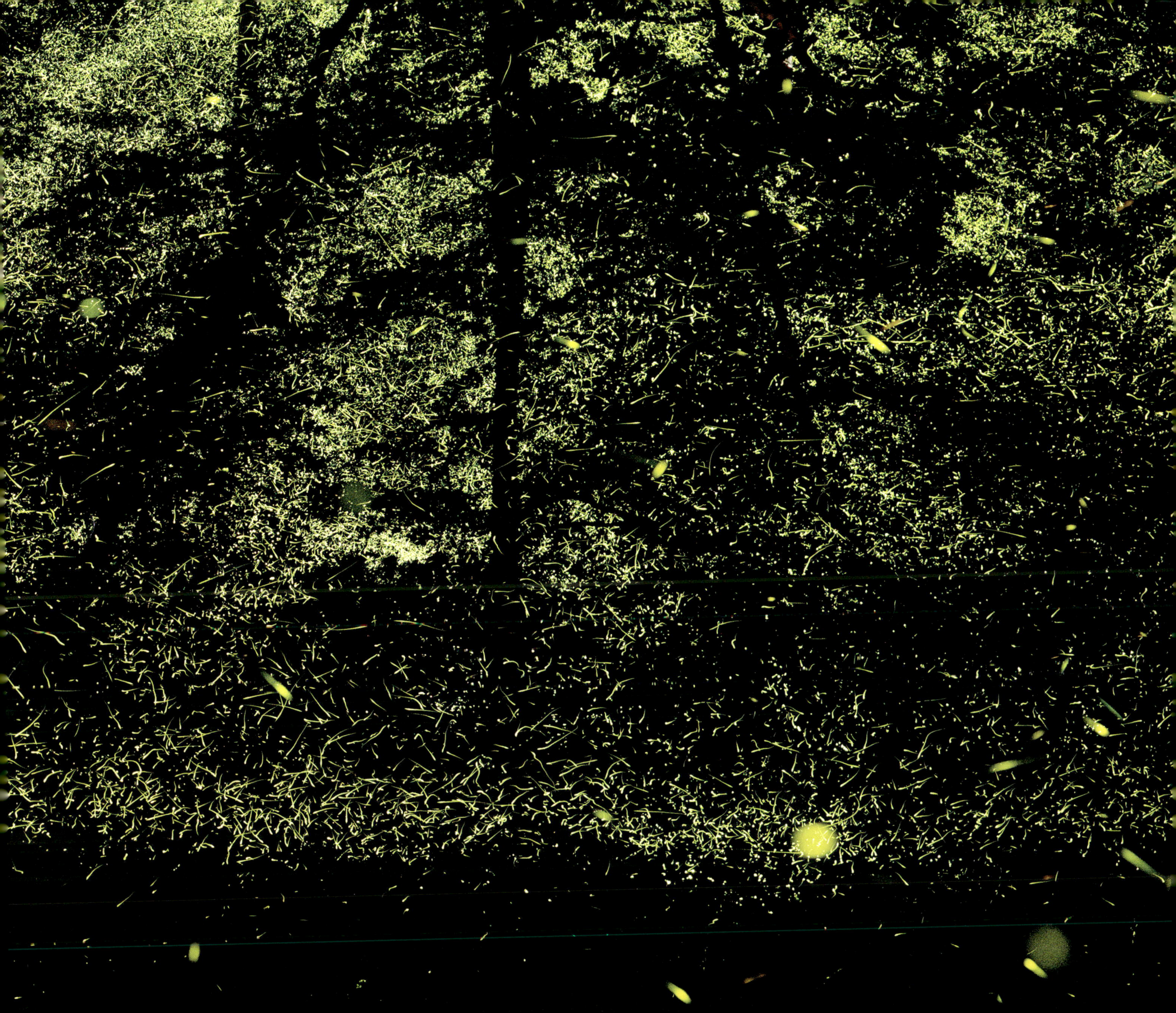

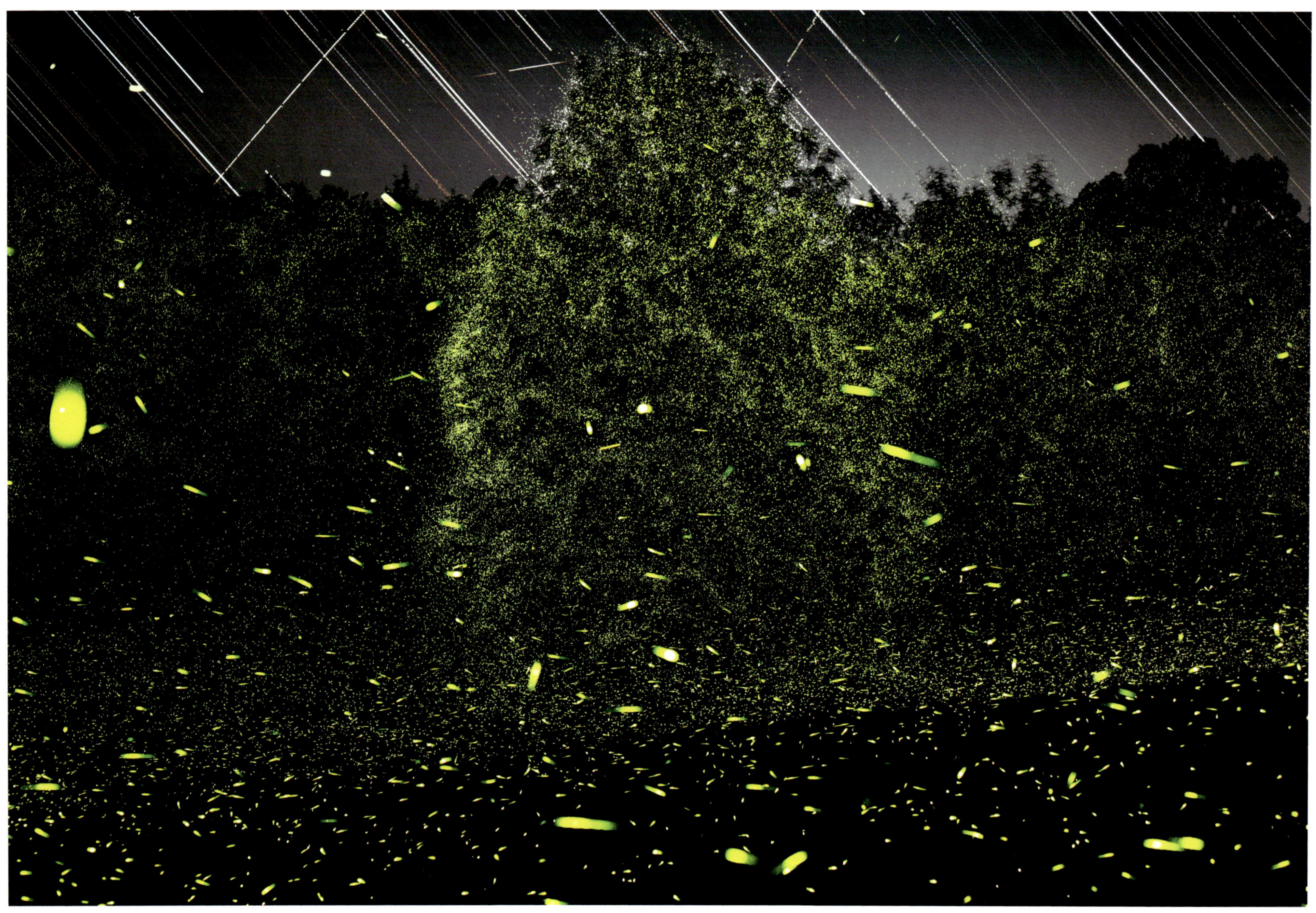

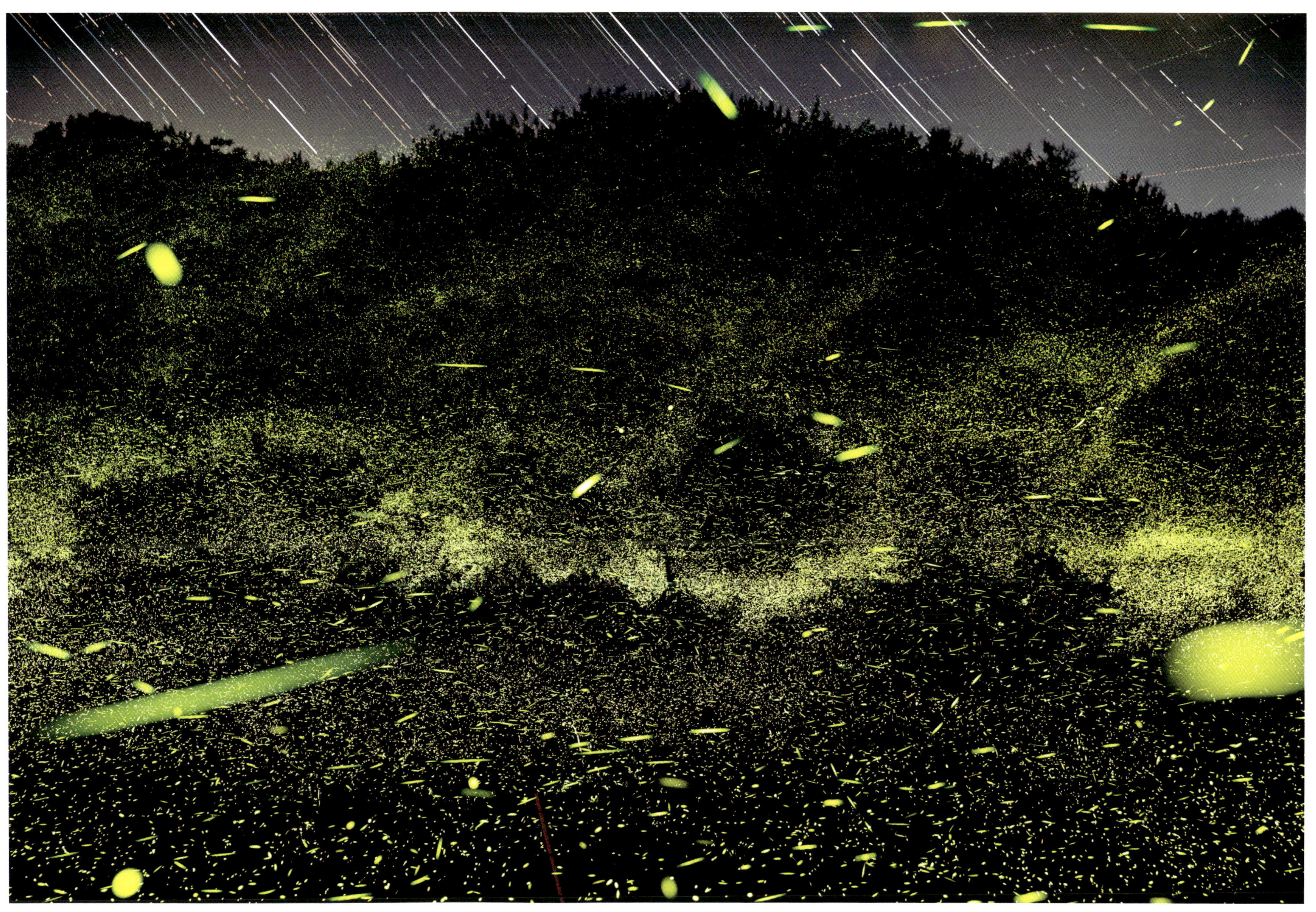

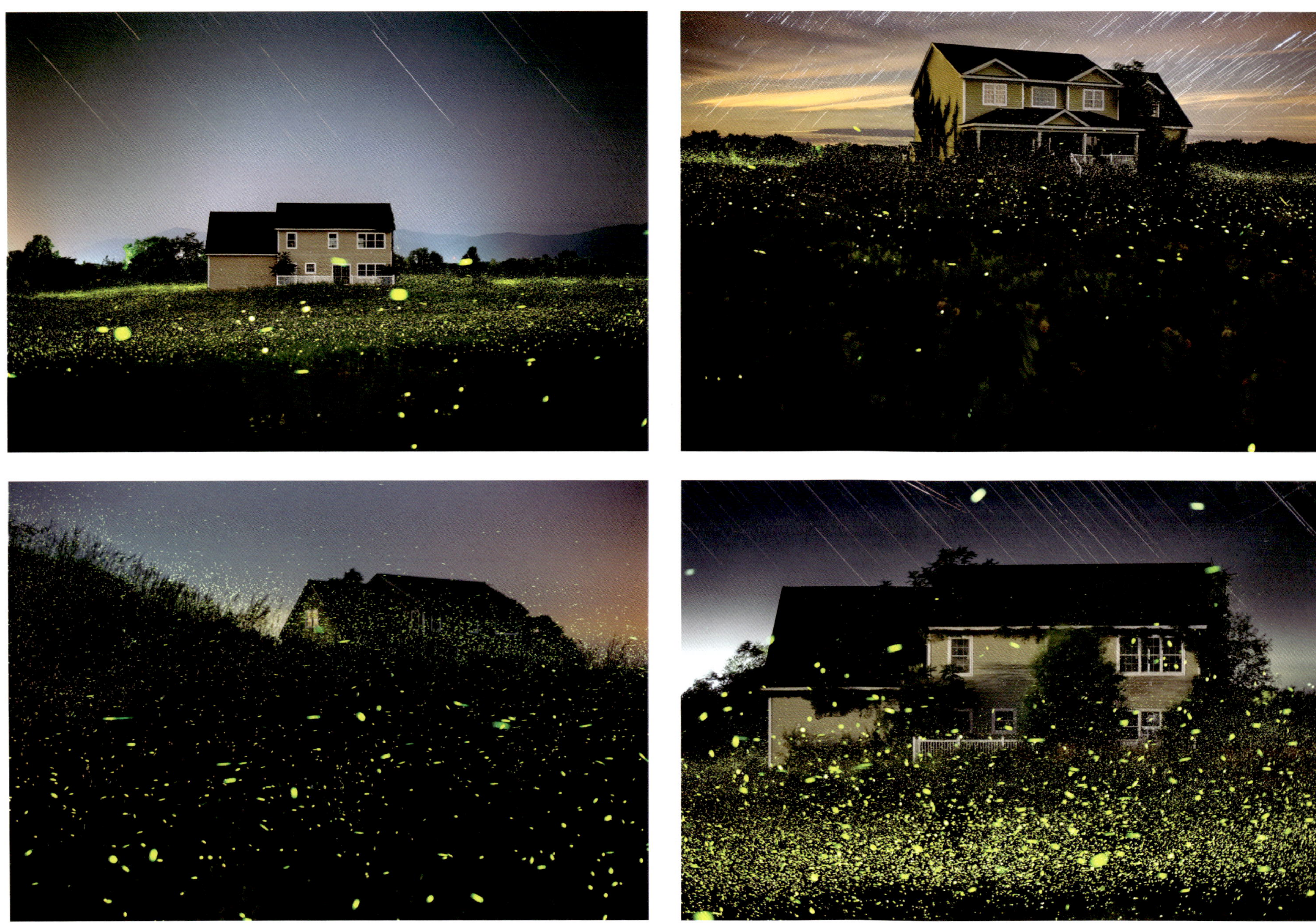

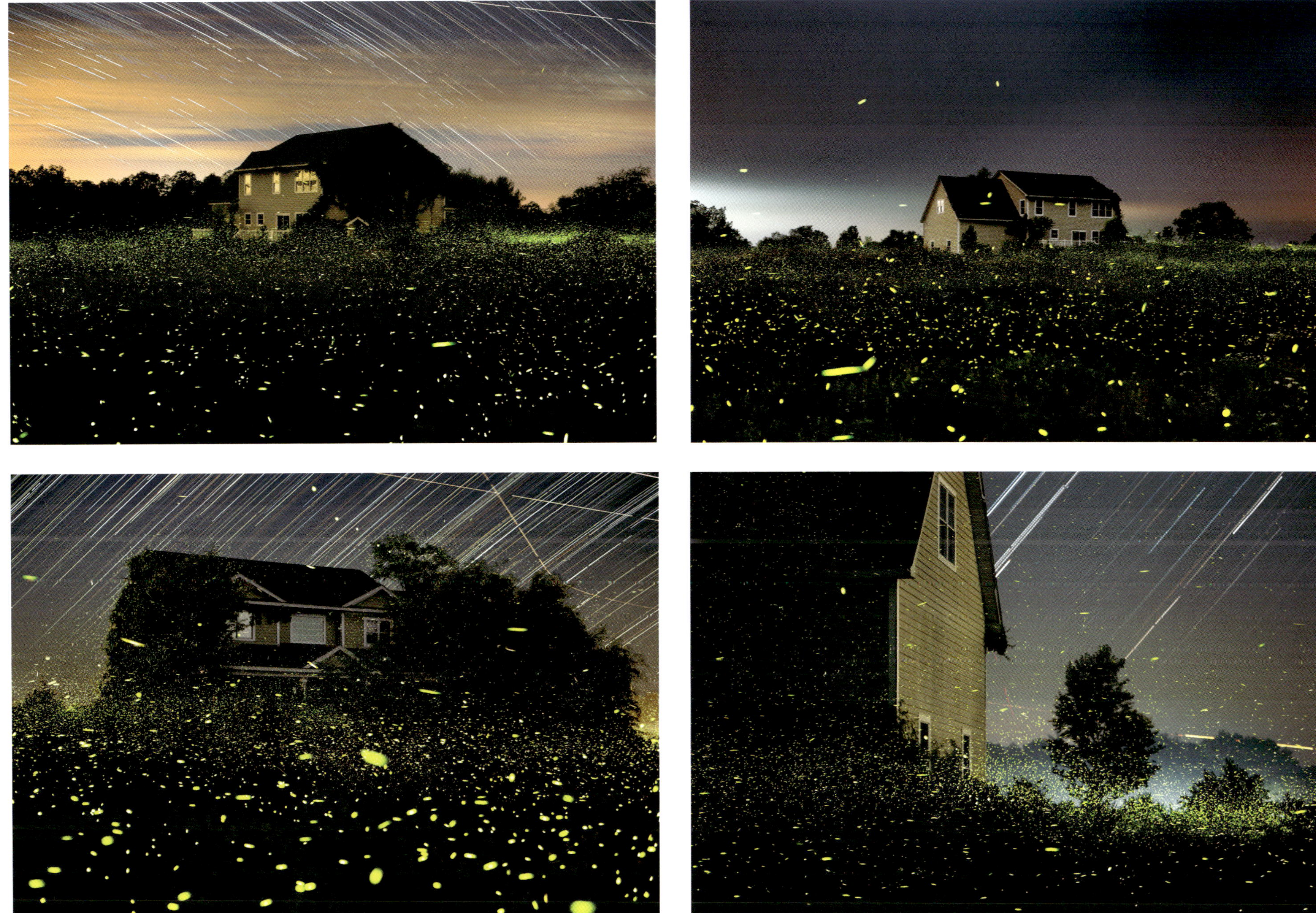

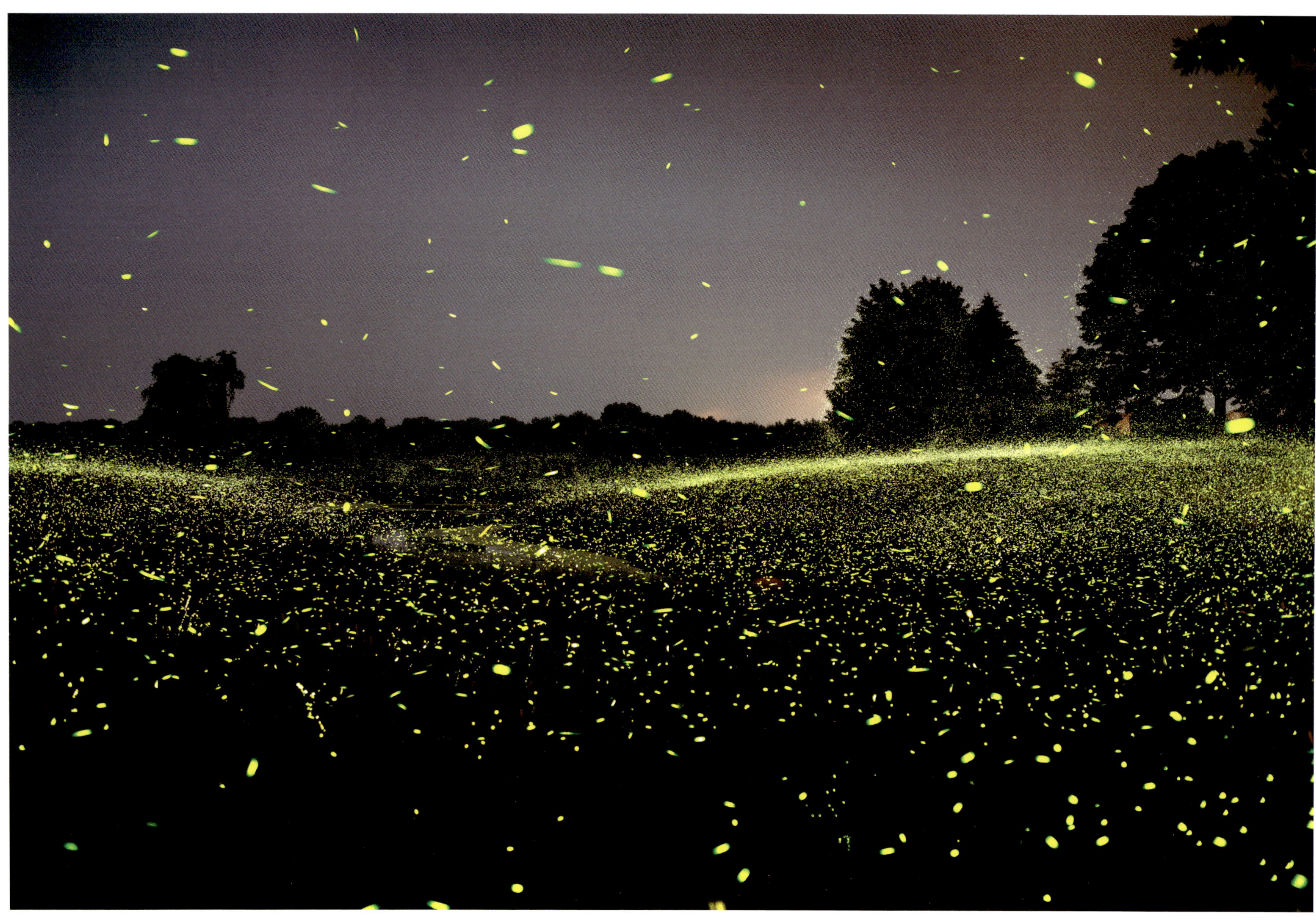

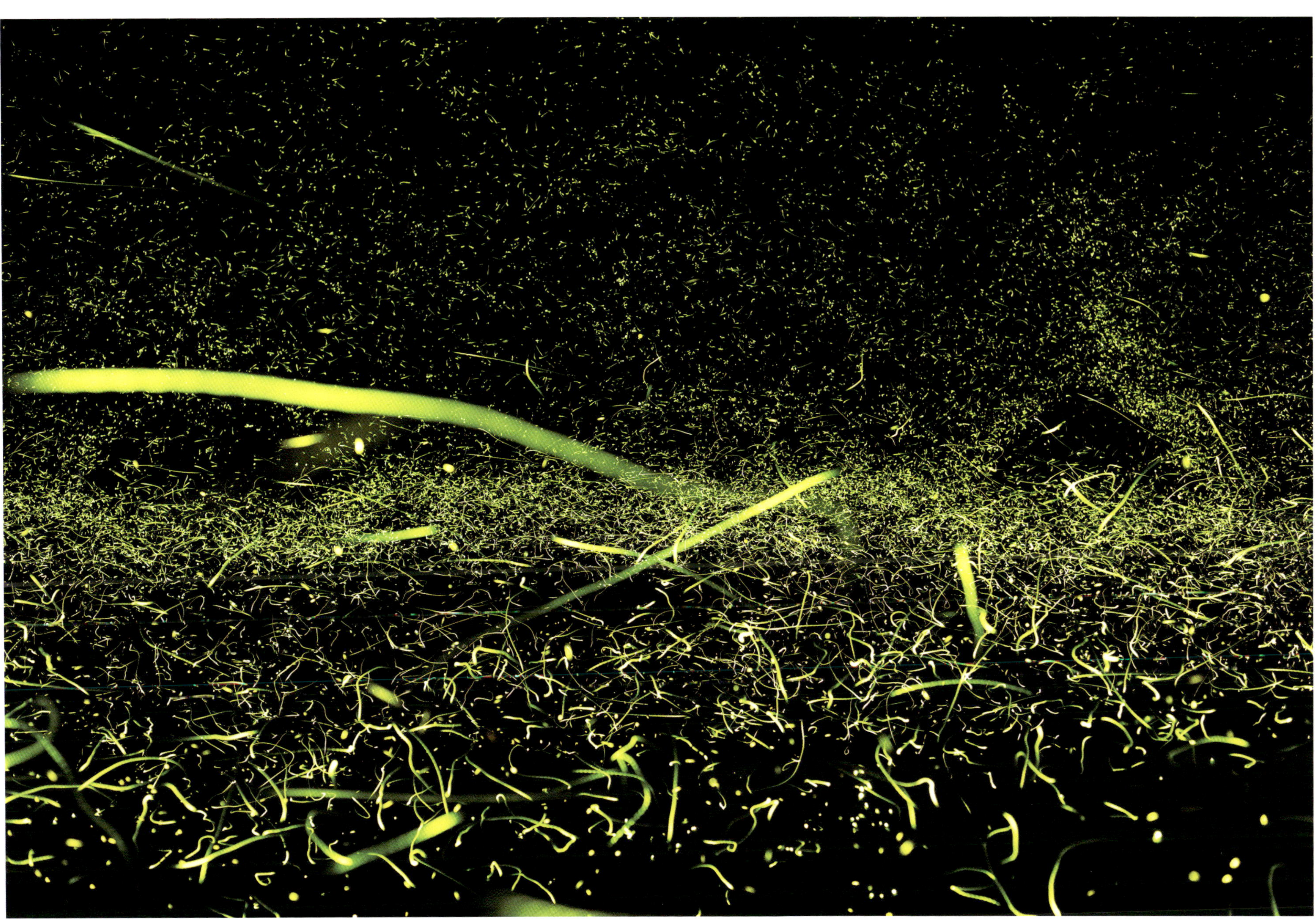

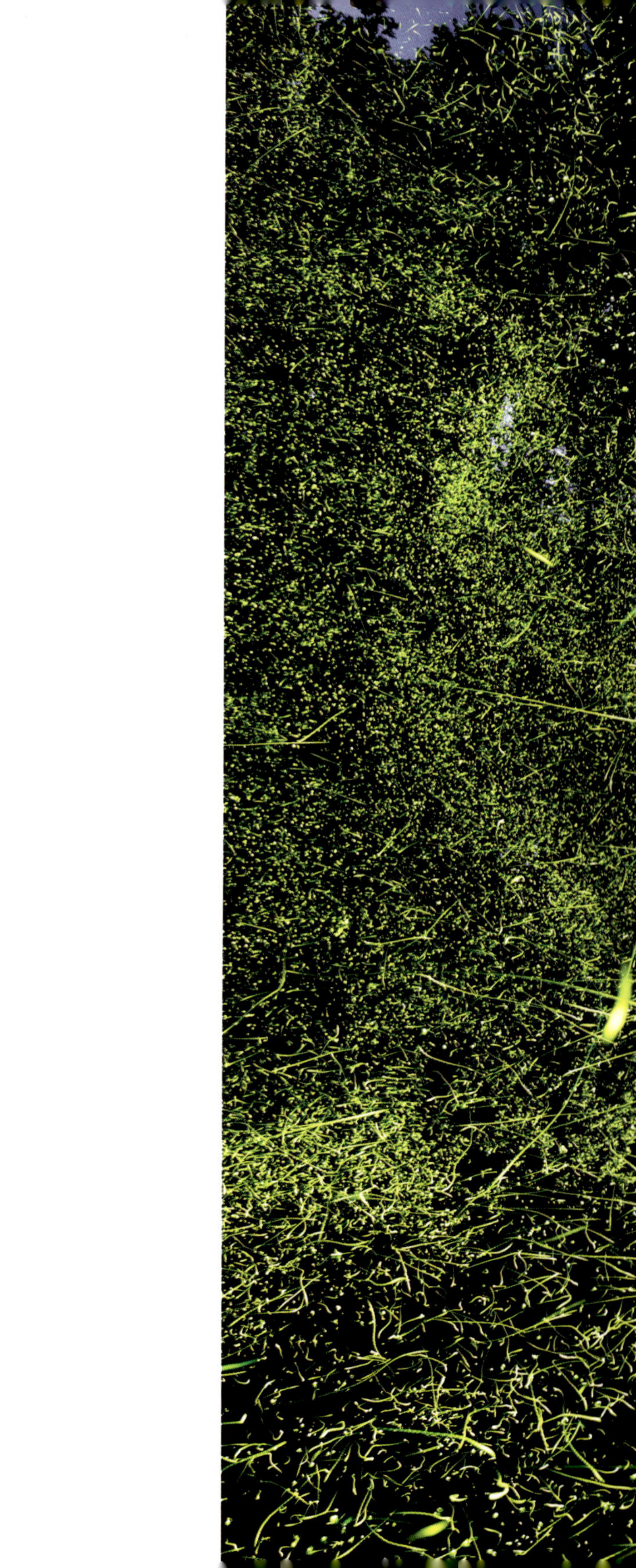

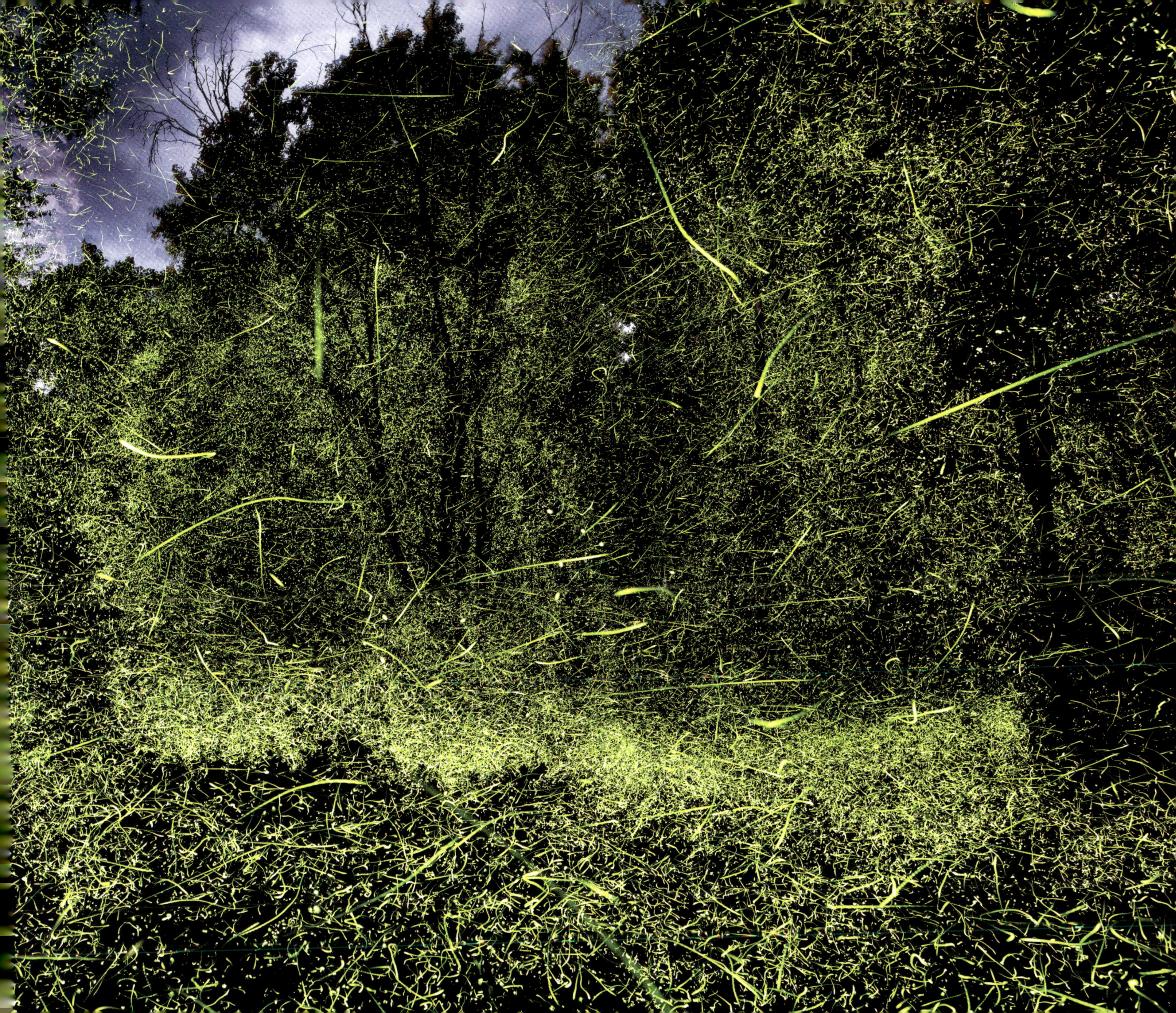

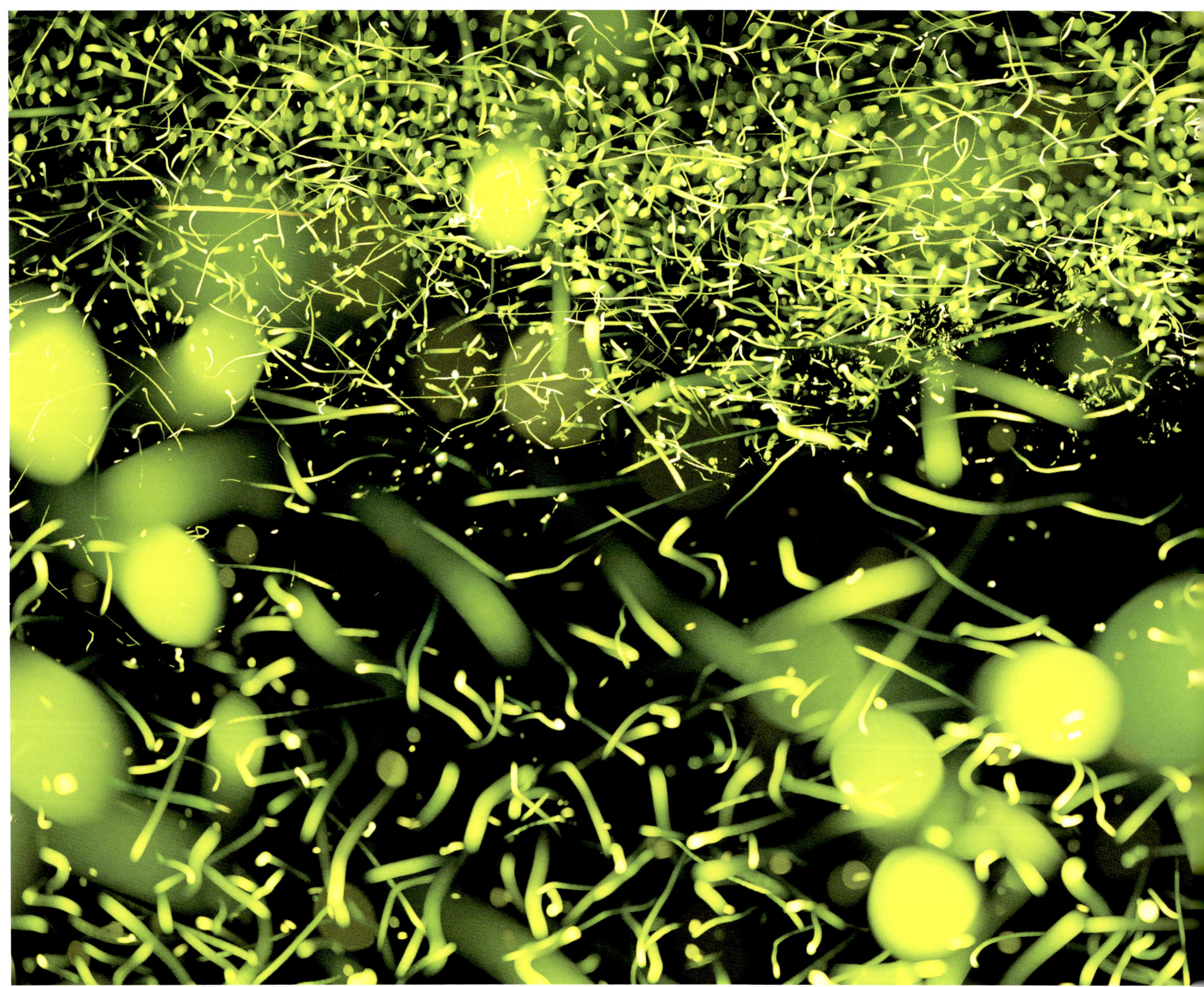

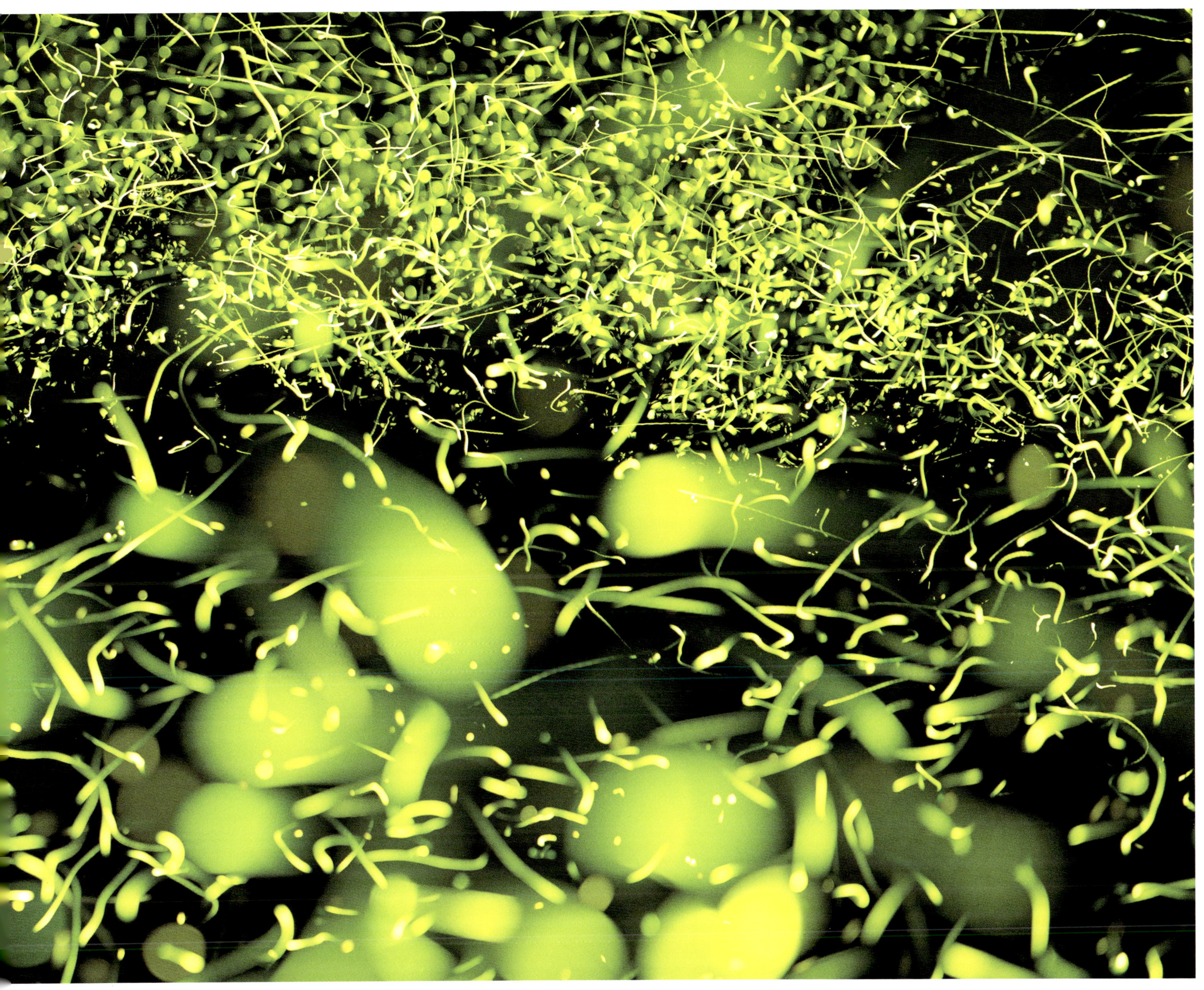

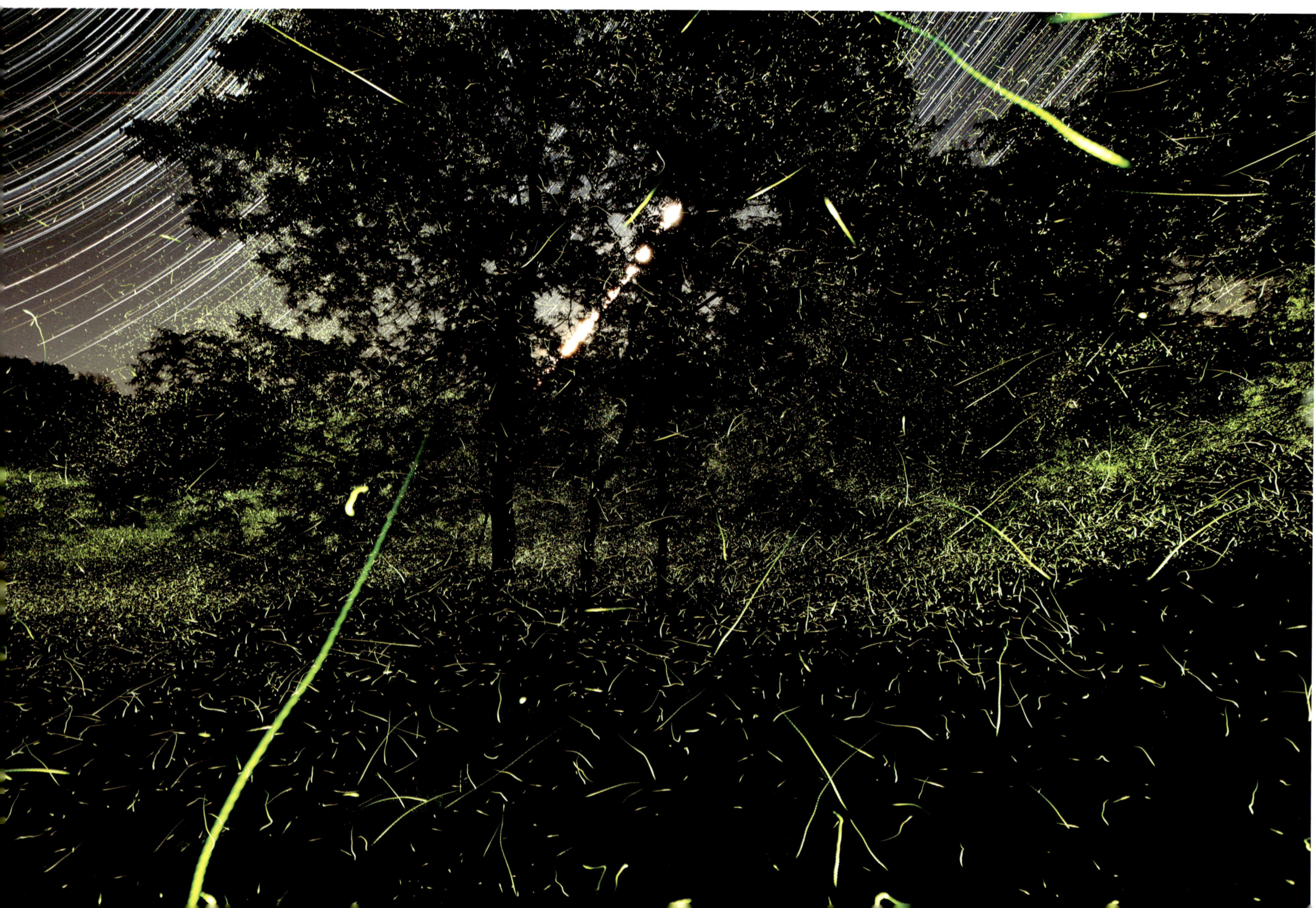

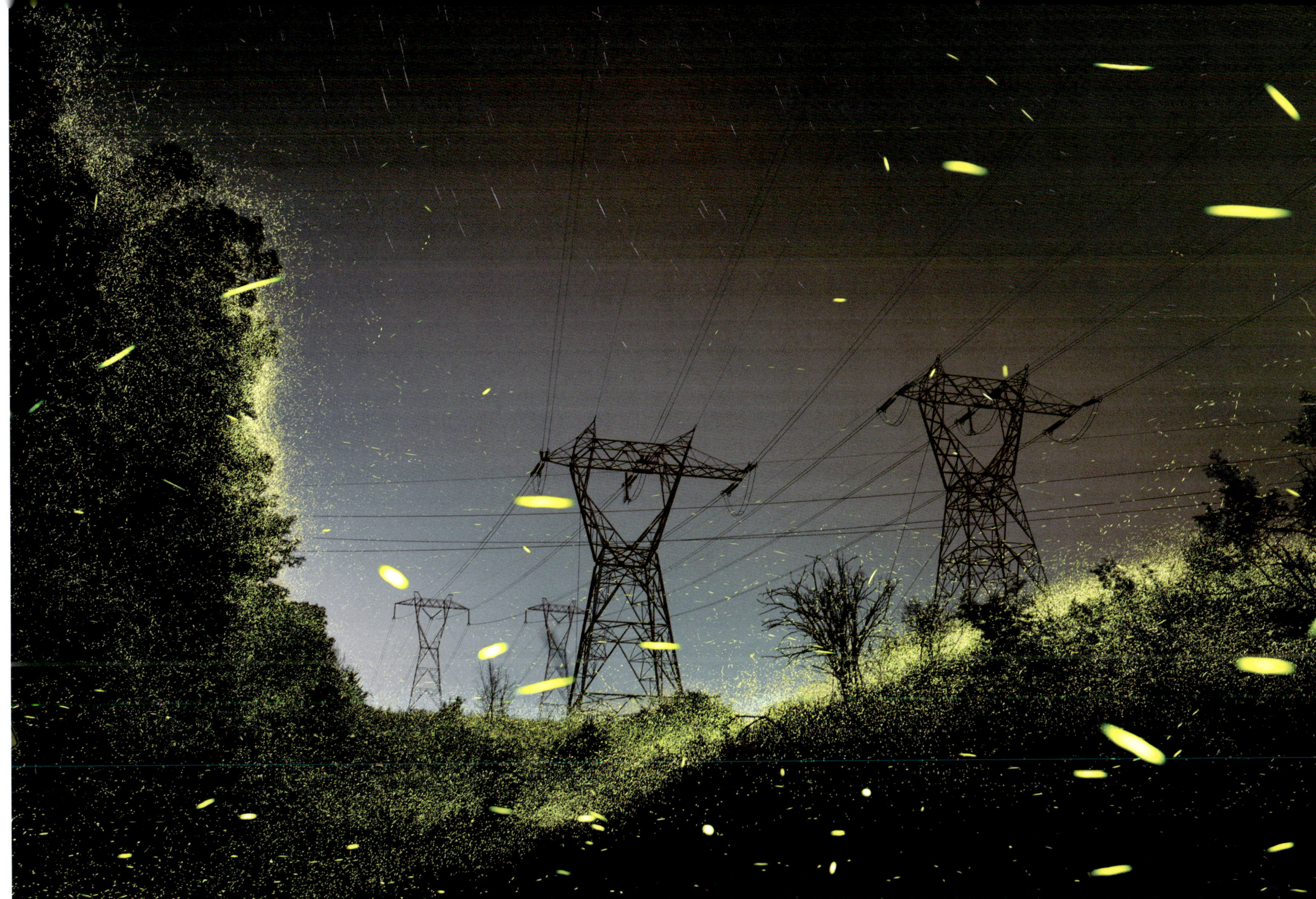

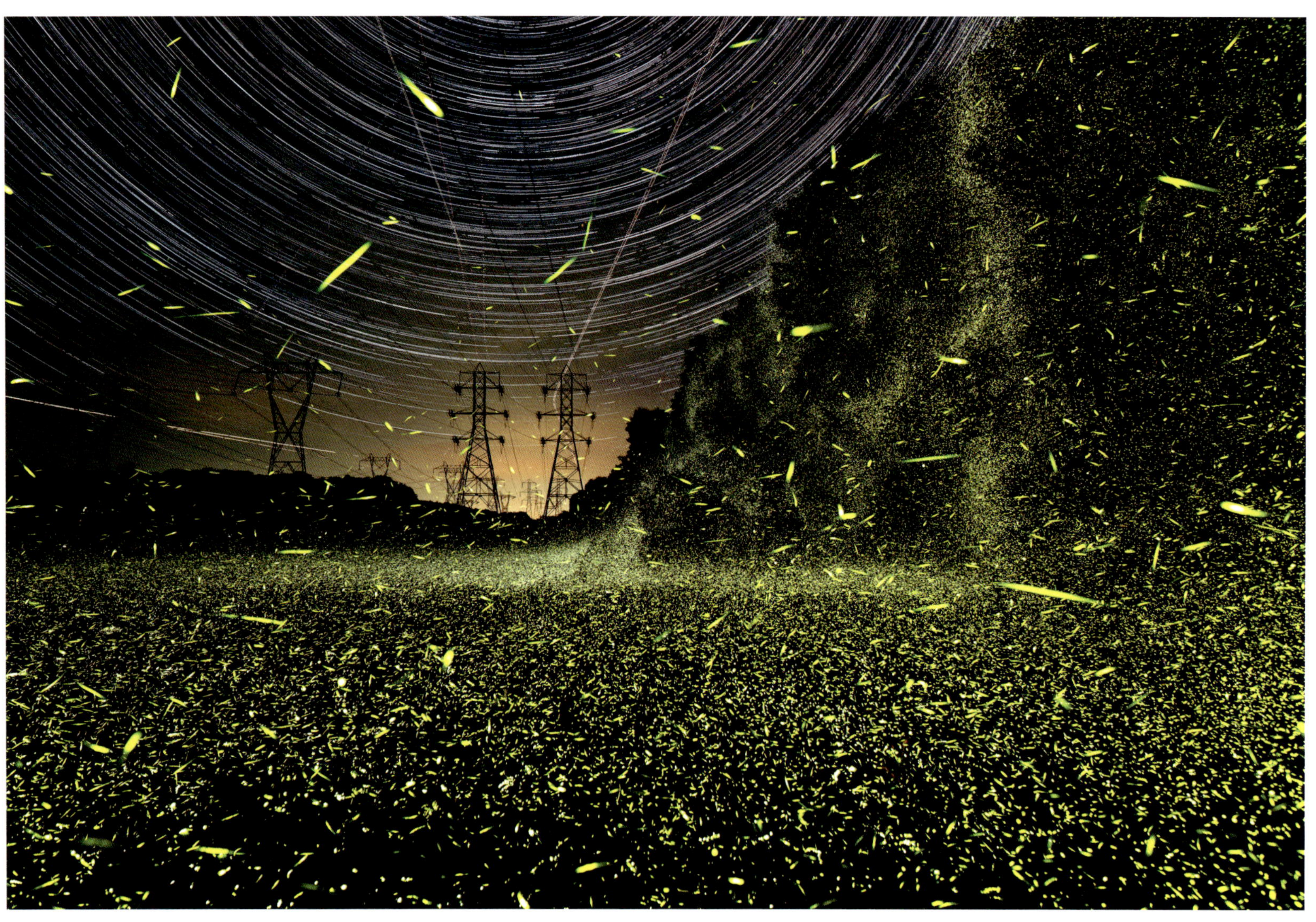

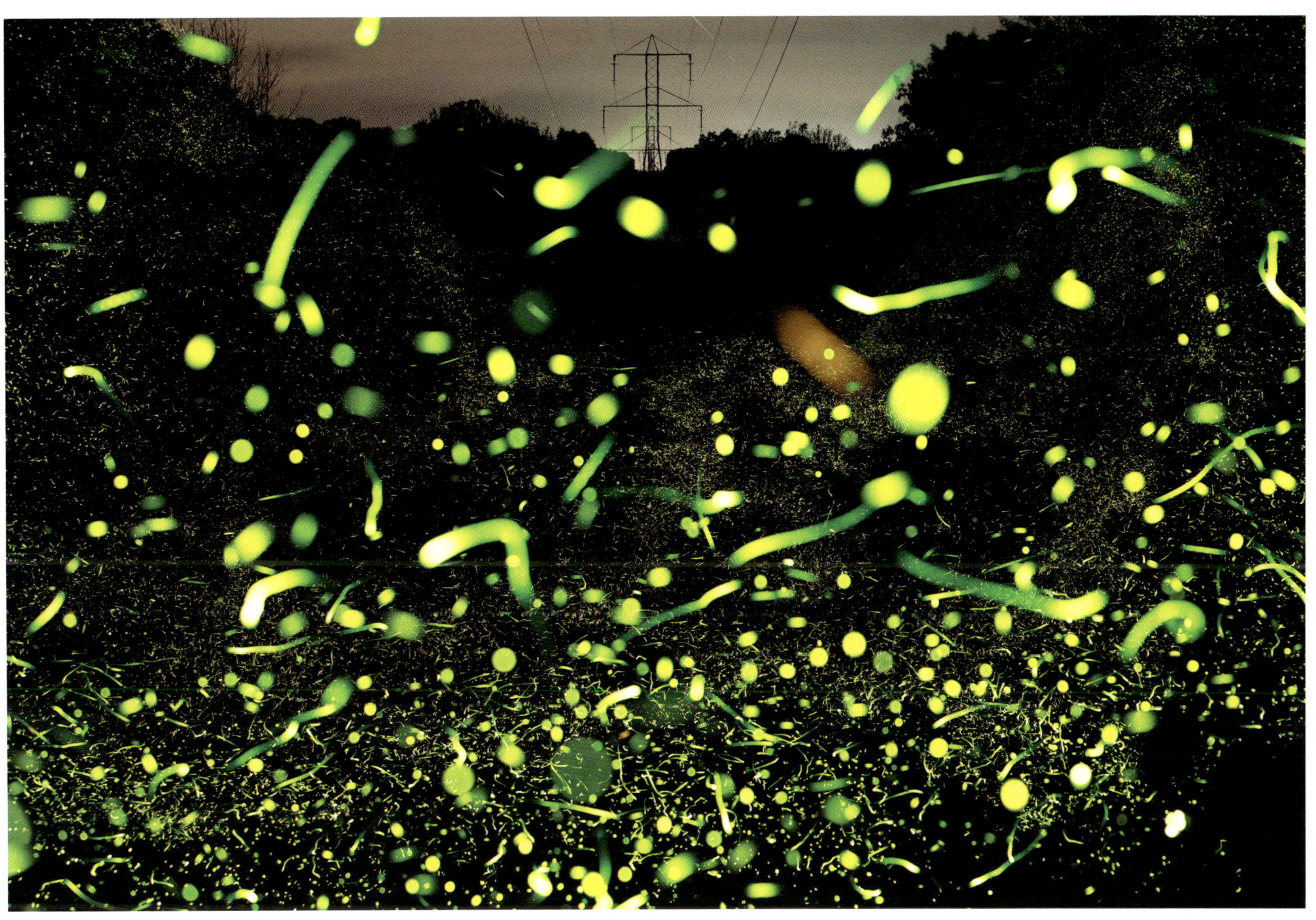

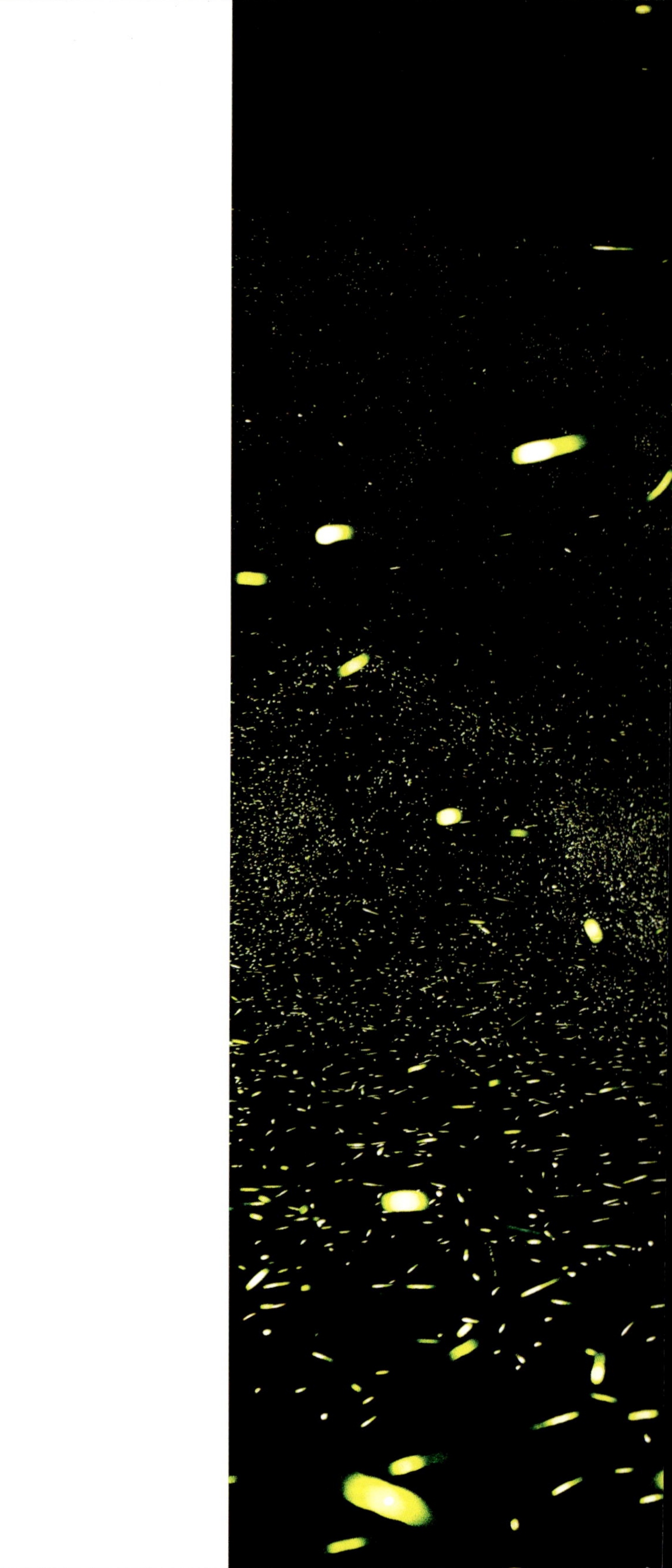

BENEATH THE STARLIGHT:
PHYSICS OF FIREFLIES

In our immense and chaotic world, the graceful interplay of matter and time orchestrates countless facets of our existence. This complexity reflects the somber depth of the human condition, encompassing not just our bodies and minds but also entangling our social interactions in its grasp. It's a continuum of connections where the smallest of interactions between individual elements can spiral into significant, global consequences. Atoms and molecules, in their silent dance, converge to form cells, which in turn build tissues, then organs, culminating in the intricate mosaic that is human life and societies.[1]

Within this bewildering complexity, I, as a physicist, grapple with a deep personal need to make sense of it all. This pursuit, often operating at the fine line between fascination and madness, is a quest for understanding in a world where the mechanisms of human behavior remain an enigma. This stands in stark contrast to our understanding of many non-living systems, from the smallest atoms to the vast astronomical bodies, whose behaviors and interactions we can predict with remarkable precision. Yet, amidst this existential quest, there lies a peculiar solace in the pursuit of deciphering the mysteries of other complex systems, particularly those that mirror the social structures and dynamics found in nature.

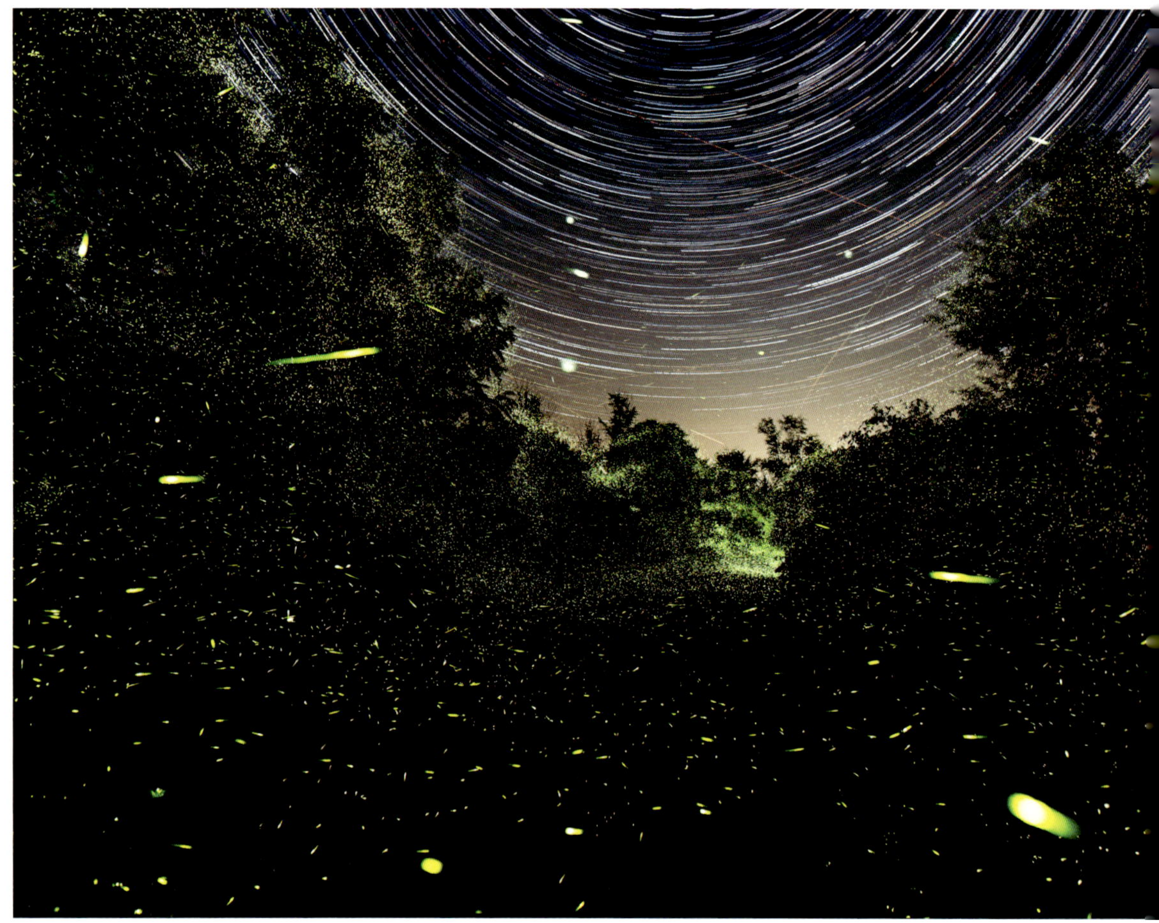

One marvel that seamlessly blends the simplicity of physics with the complexity of biology is the firefly. These tiny luminescent creatures, fluttering through the night, communicate with a species-specific pattern of light signals, much like Morse code.[2,3] This language of light is much more than a pretty display. It plays a crucial role in courtship rituals: male fireflies, adrift in the air, use these bioluminescent signals to broadcast their suitability as mates to the observant females below. In turn, these females, with their selective roles, favor the males that display a species-specific "ideal" sequence of flashes.[4]

A myriad of fireflies flashing within a group can overwhelm the senses, making it challenging to spot suitable partners. This sensory overload is further amplified when different species, each with its unique flash sequences, join the fray. To cut through this visual noise, some male fireflies resort to synchronized flashing, allowing them to enhance the visibility of their signals.[5,6] My lab members and I established advanced techniques to capture these displays in detail, yielding critical data that uncover how singular exchanges between individual fireflies amplify into a unified, global display.[7,8,9]

Yet the true scope of our challenge only becomes clear when one considers the sheer biodiversity of fireflies. With thousands of species each broadcasting its own unique light pattern, our documented patterns represent only a tiny fraction of this rich system.[10,11] Our goal is to create a comprehensive catalog of these patterns; yet the elusive nature of firefly swarms, shining brightly for just a few weeks in specific sites, complicates data collection.

To overcome these obstacles we are utilizing crowdsourcing, leveraging a network of volunteers who assist in recording data, thus extending our reach despite the brief existence of each firefly swarm display.[12,13] Pete Mauney is a dedicated member of our volunteer network. As an exceptionally talented photographer passionate about capturing fireflies in their natural settings, Pete understands the allure of these creatures. His photographs, teeming with activity, have been instrumental in our research. Through his lens, we have expanded our catalog and assembled a few more pieces of the puzzle that defines the various species of fireflies. But our quest is far from completion. As we dive deeper into the quiet dialogues of fireflies, the wide and nuanced workings of our universe become increasingly evident. We continue to study how the social lives of fireflies elevate into a harmonious exhibition.

Observing the ephemeral light of these small beings, we uncover hints of the grand patterns of nature, inching ever closer to understanding the complex web that weaves together the fabric of our existence.

ORIT PELEG
JANUARY 4, 2024

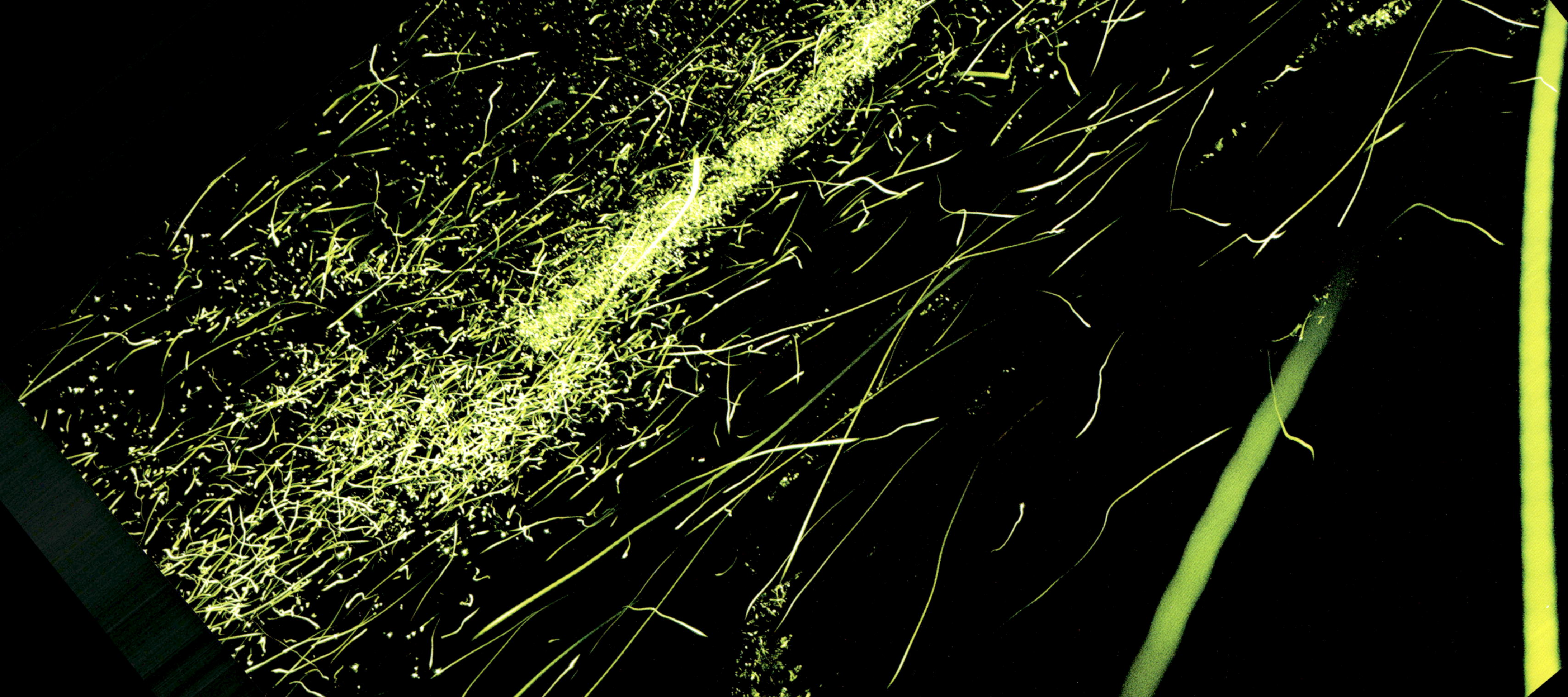

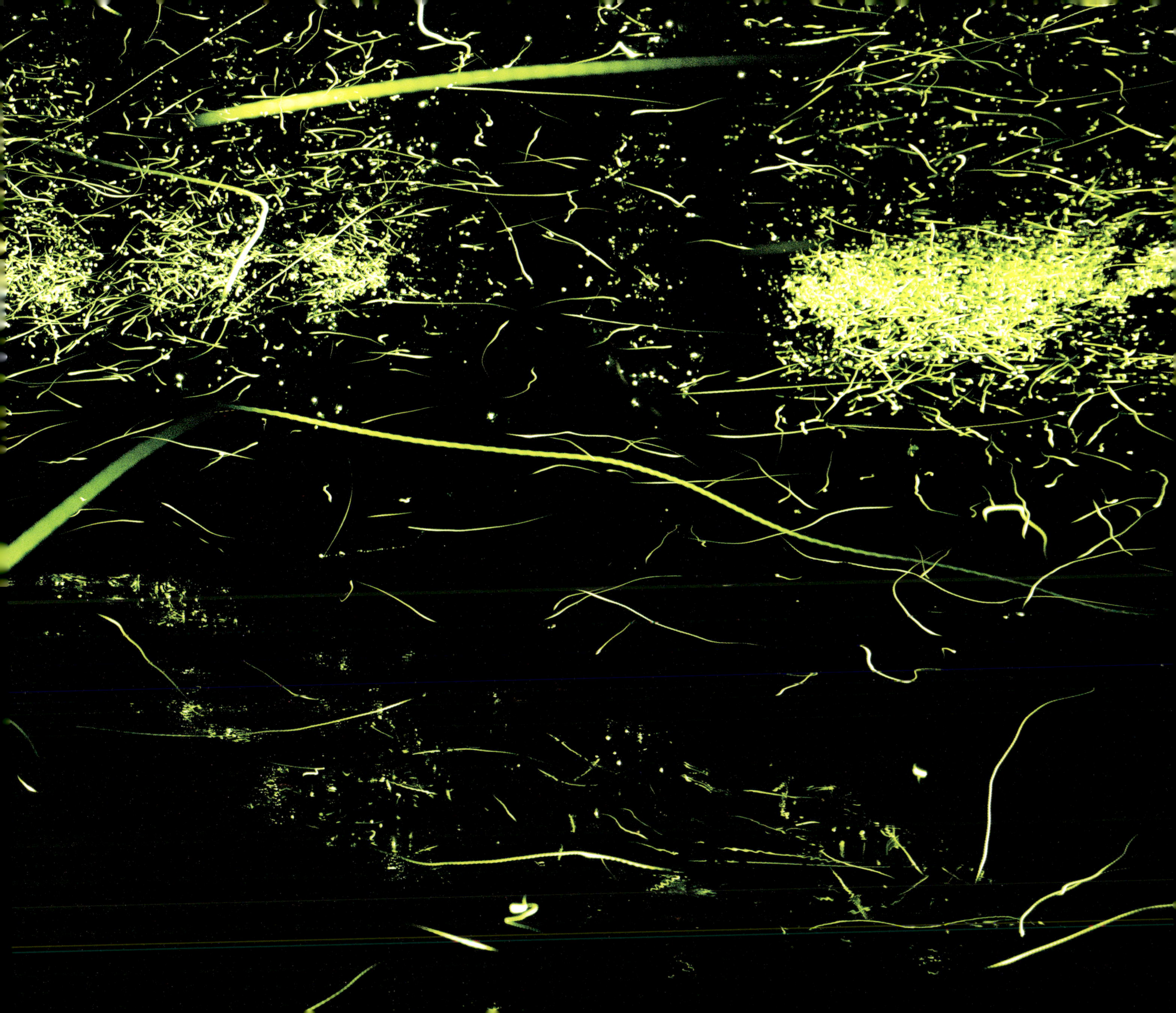

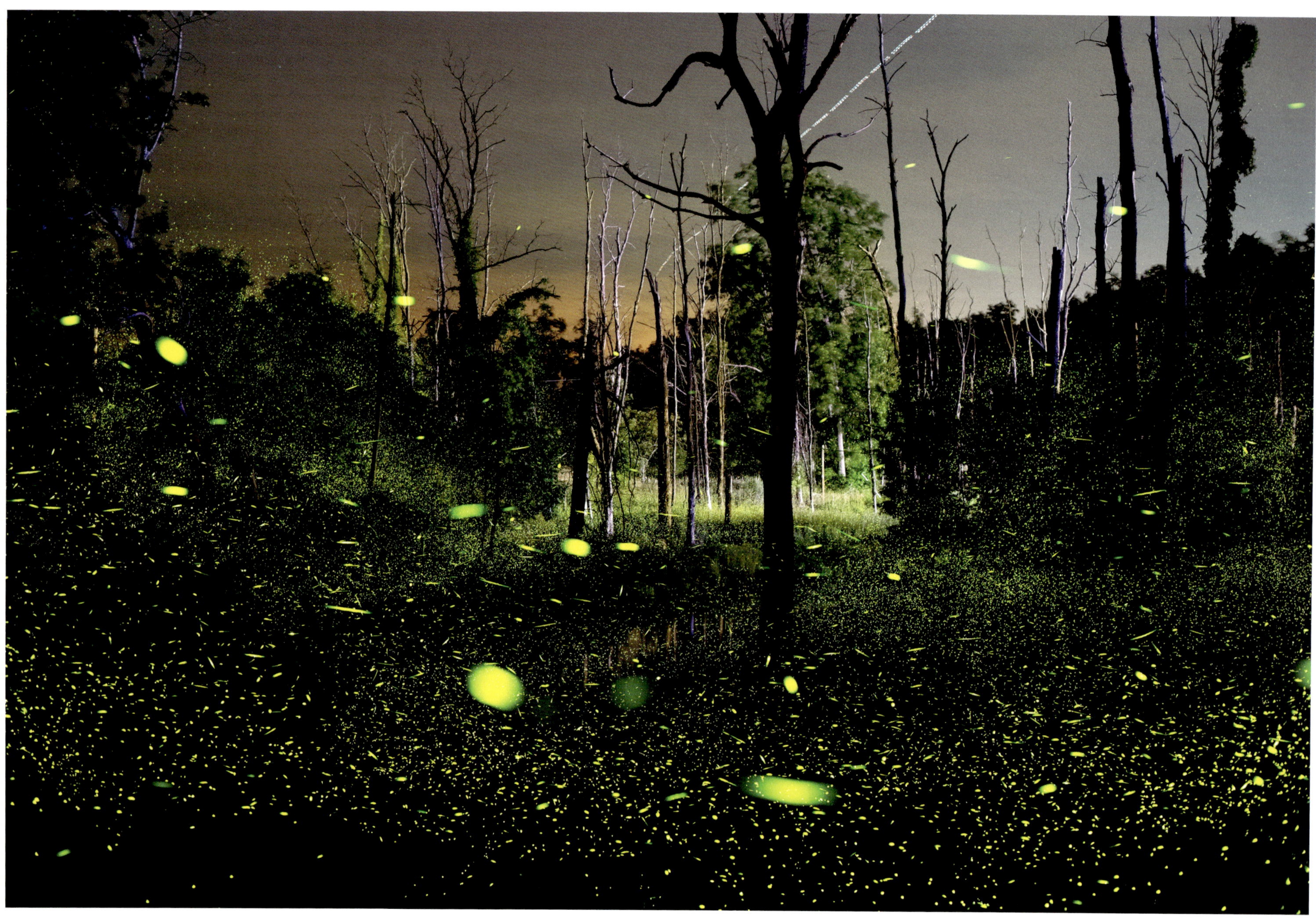

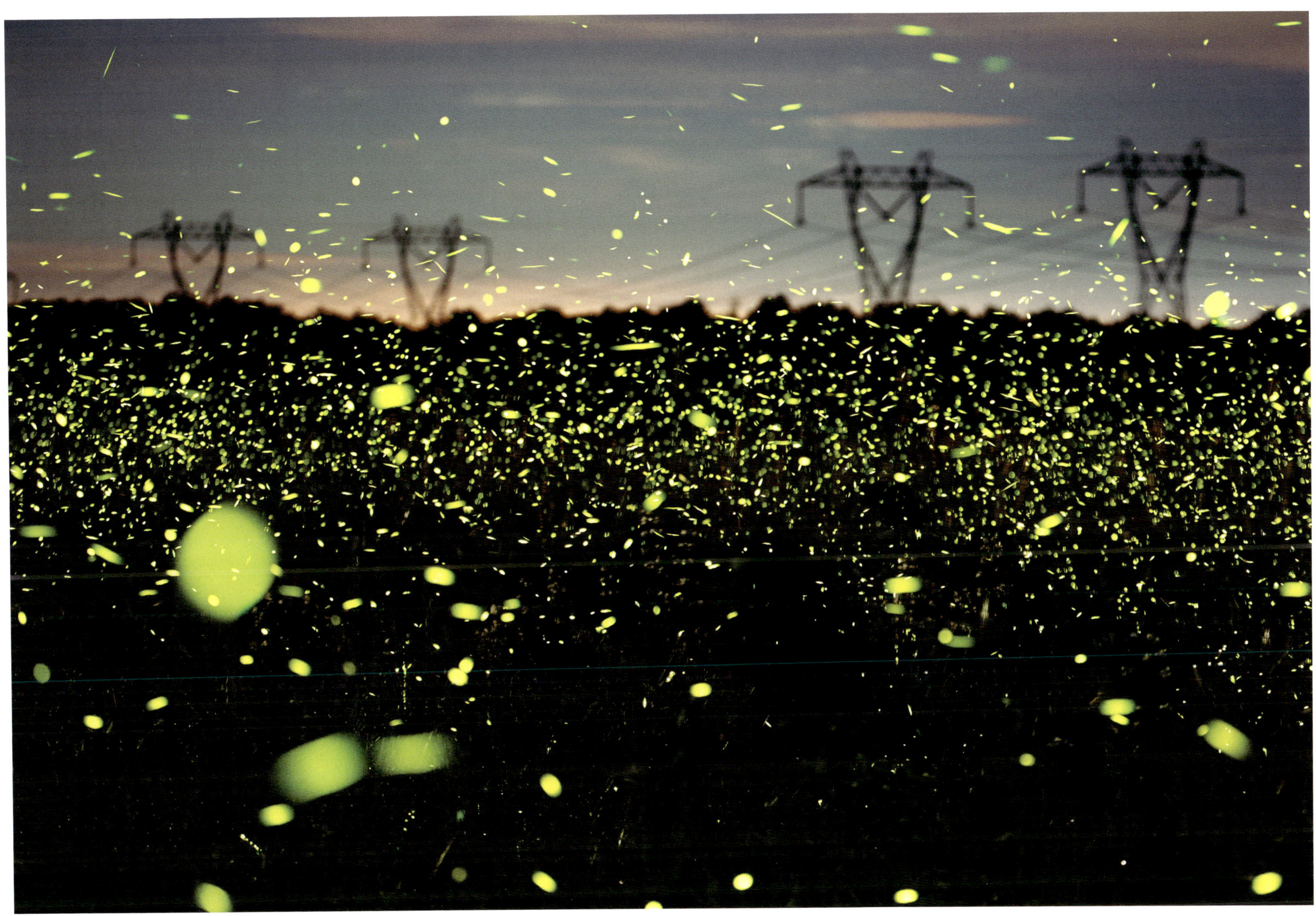

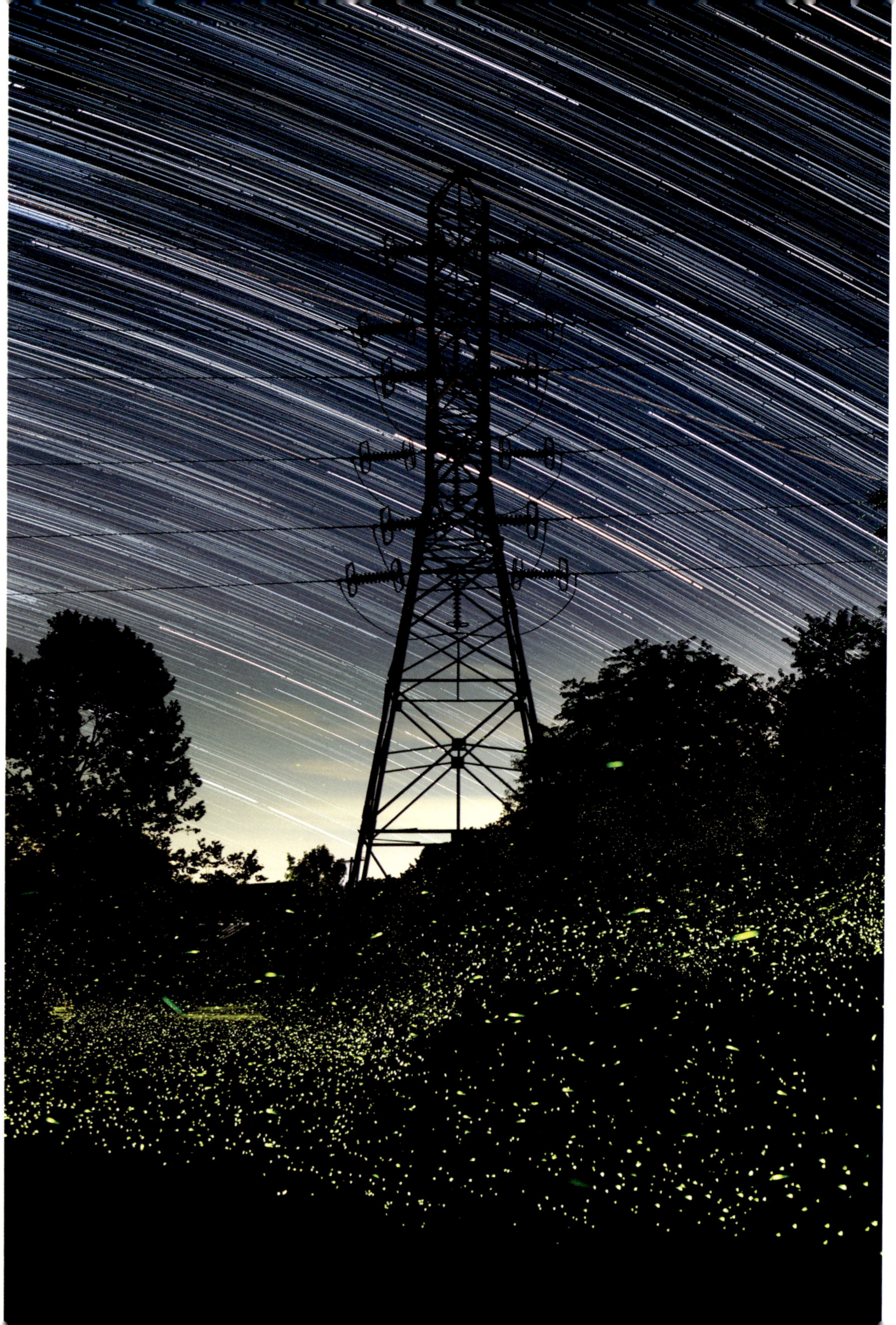

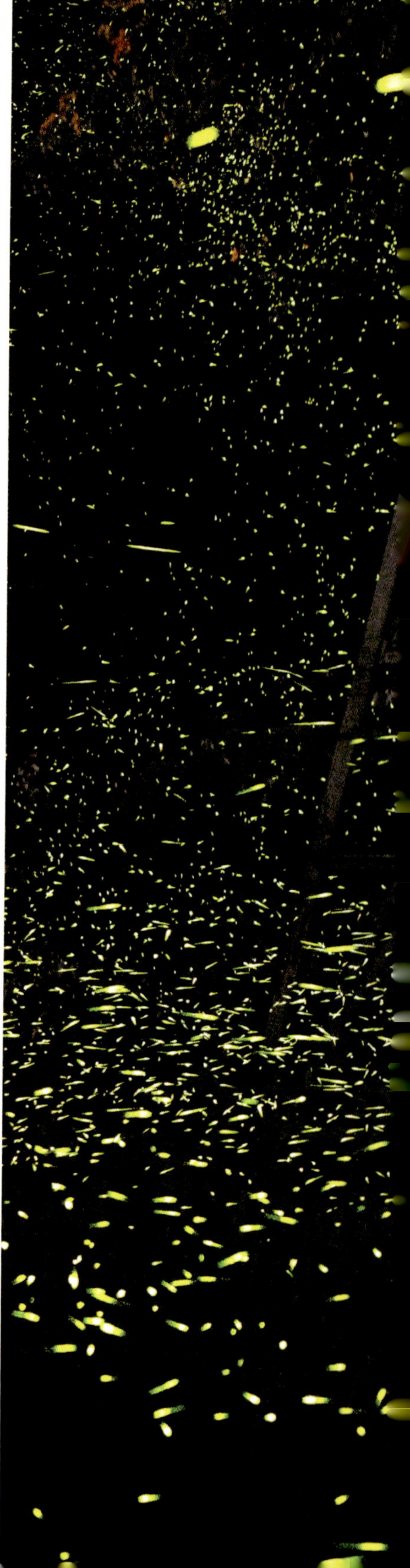

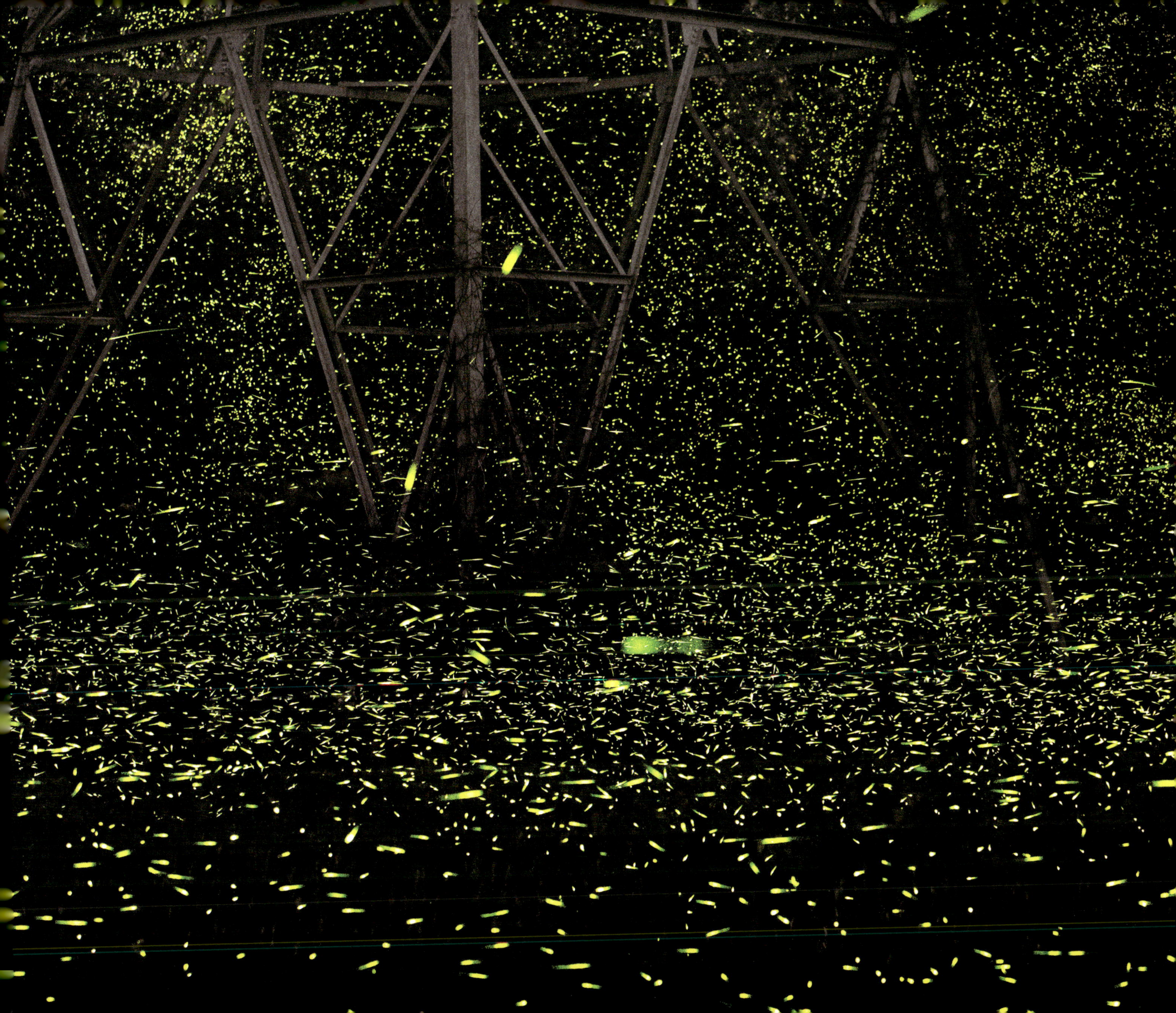

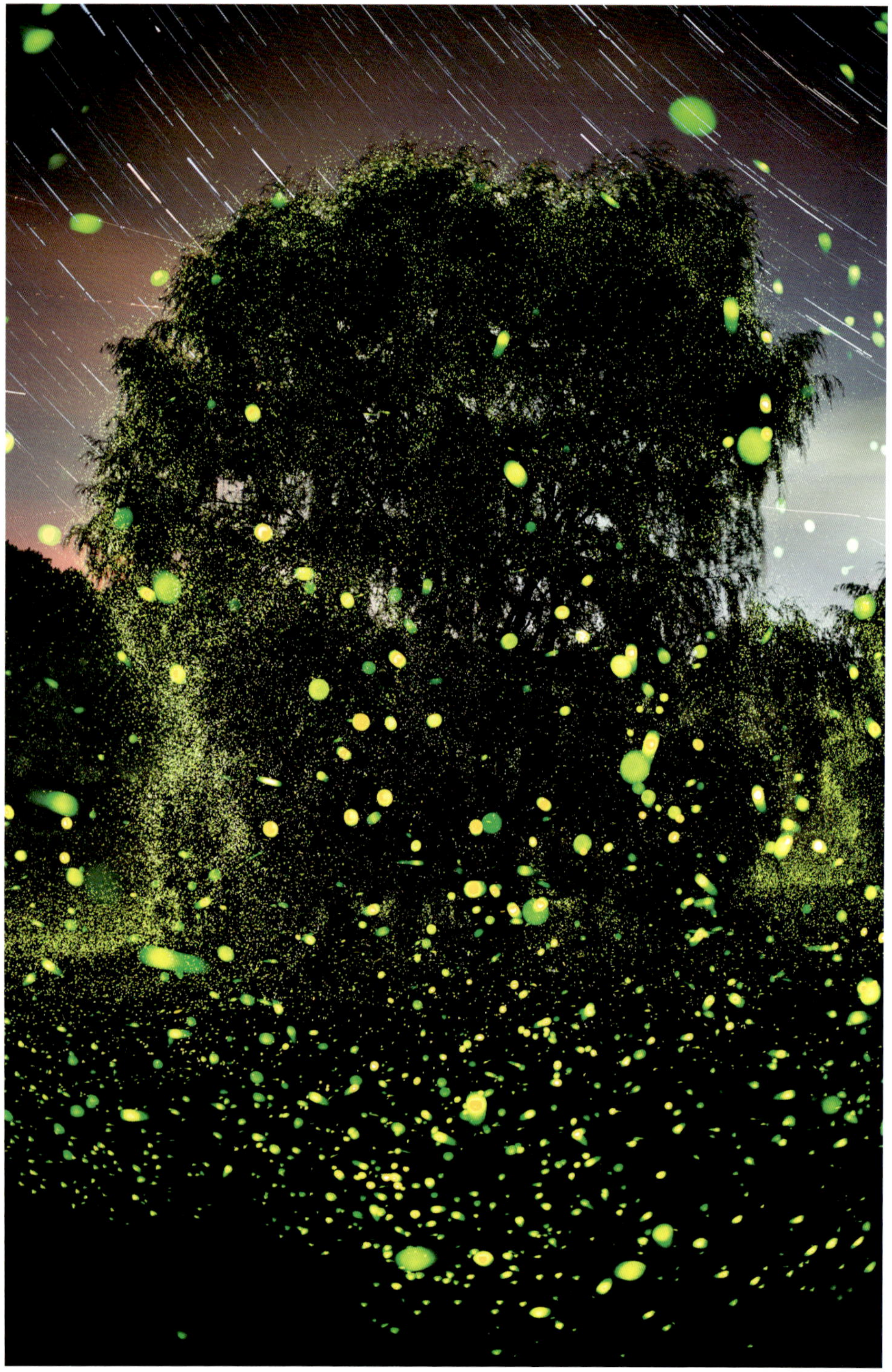

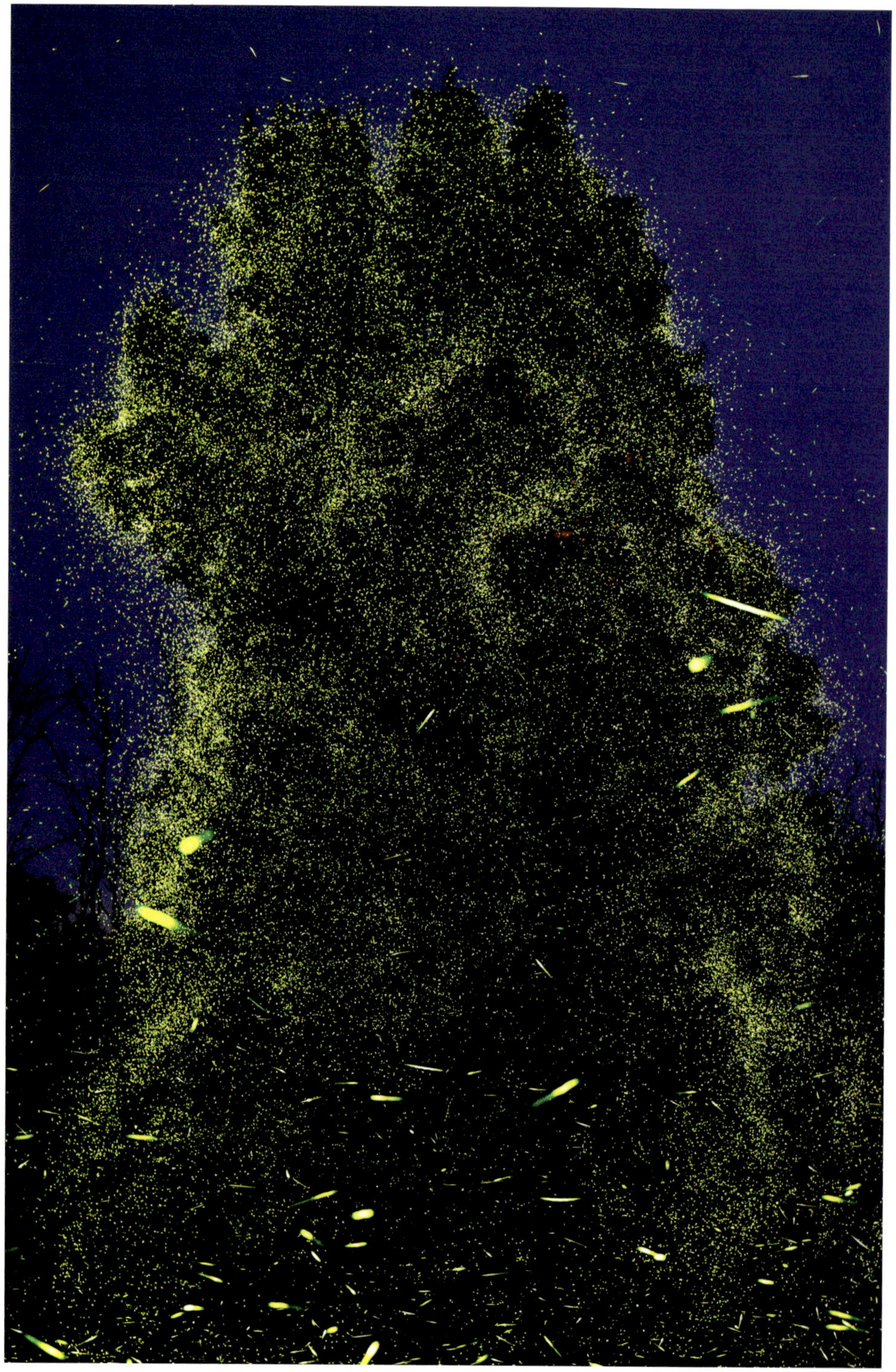

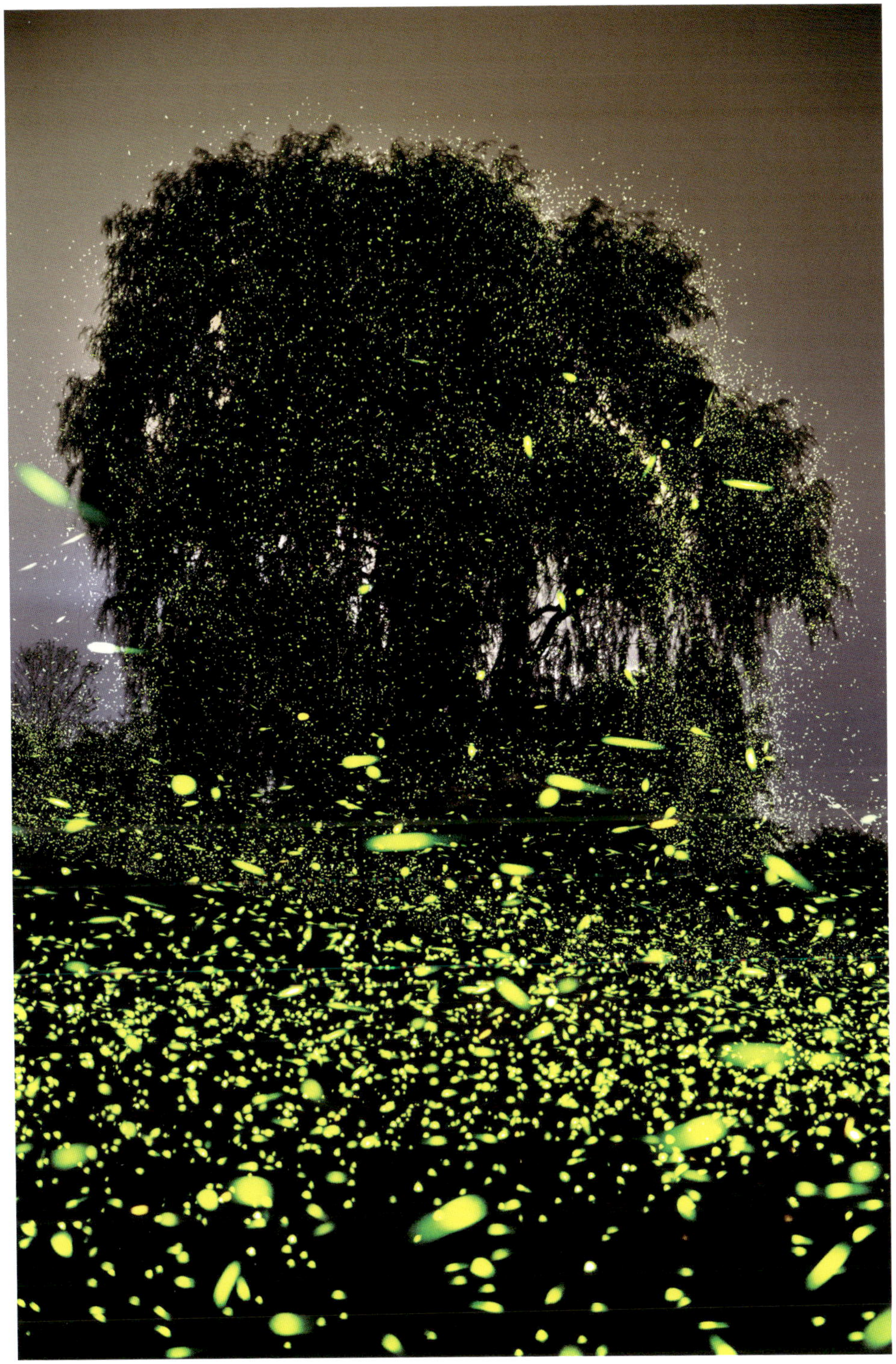

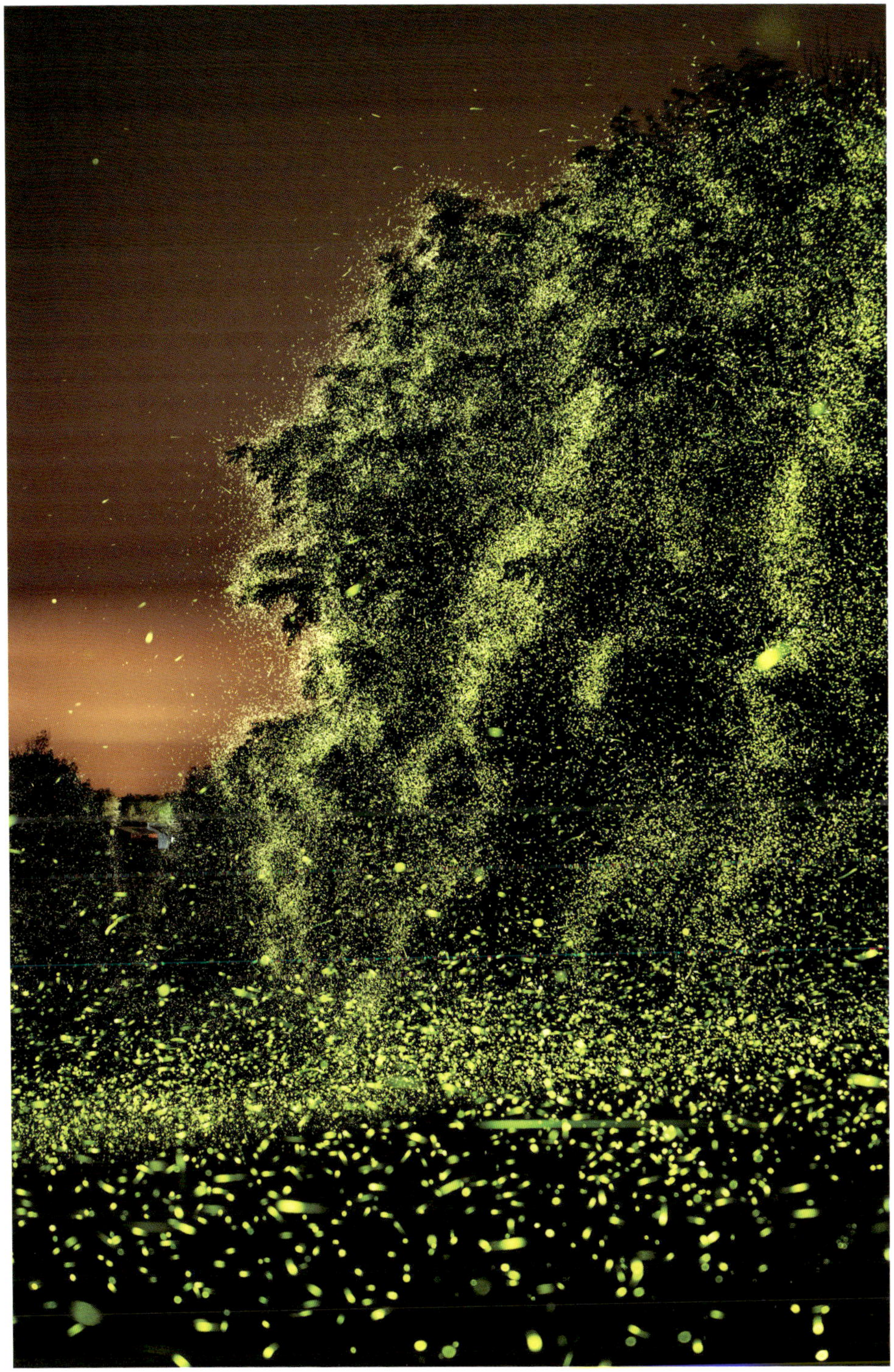

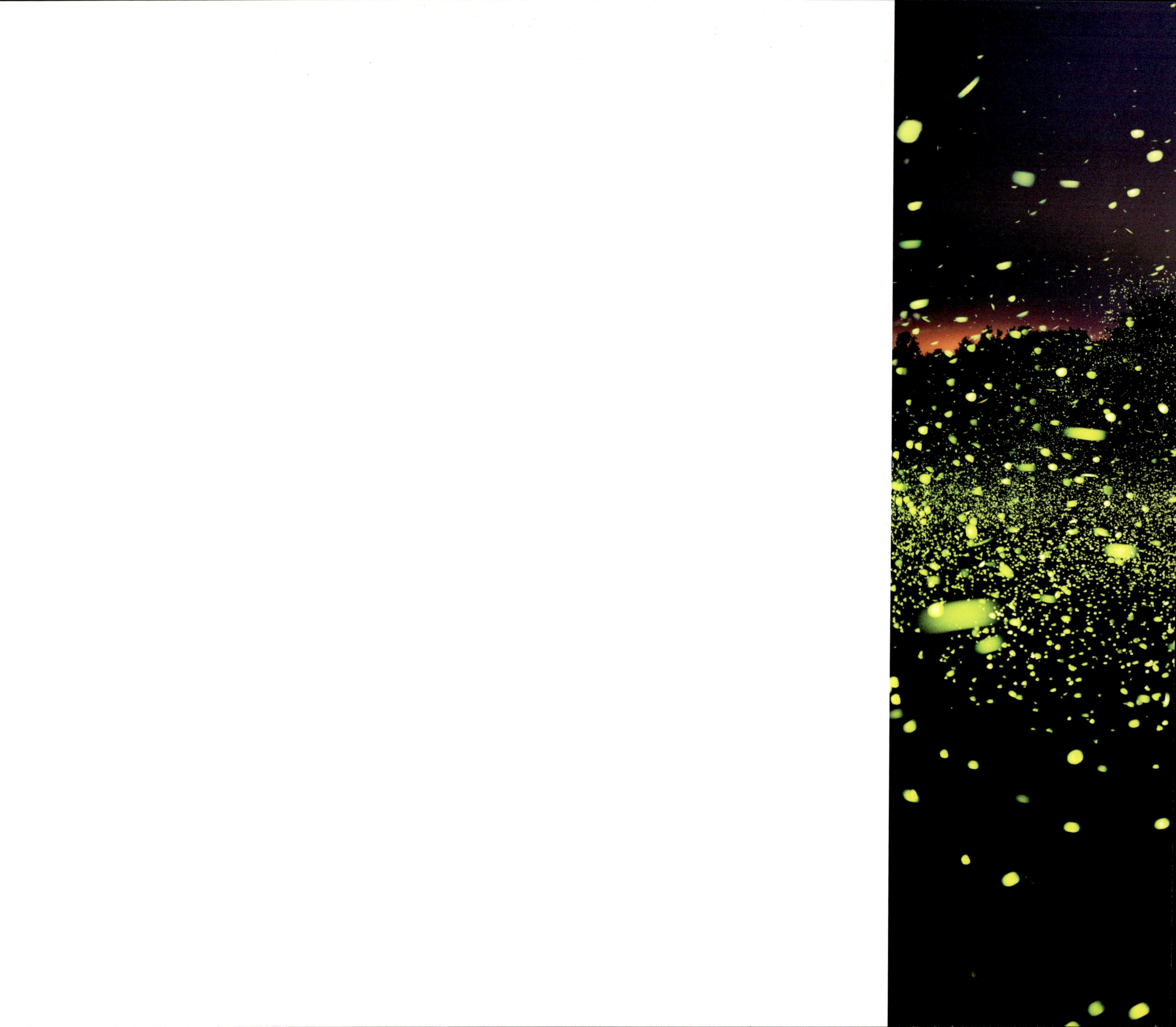

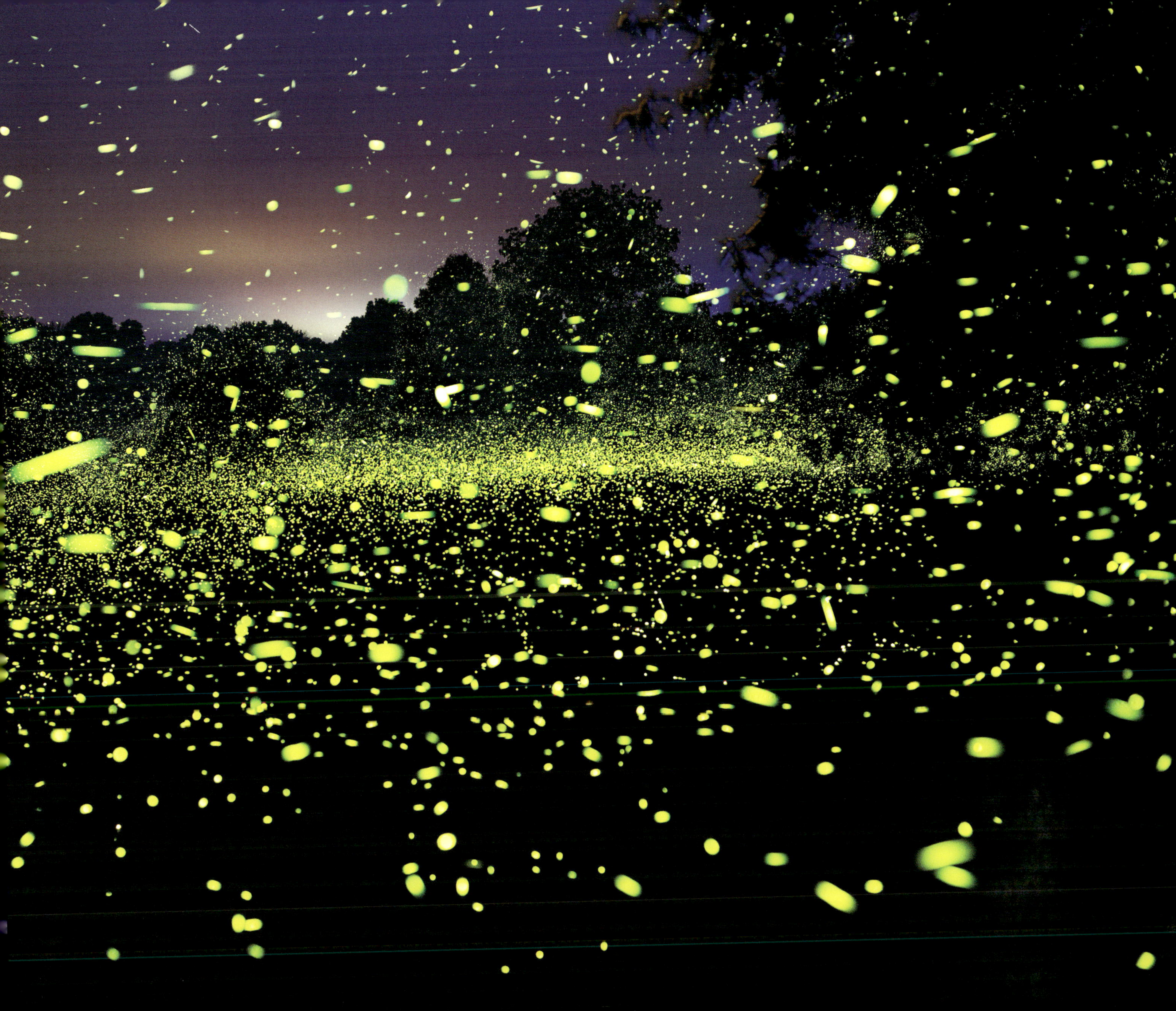

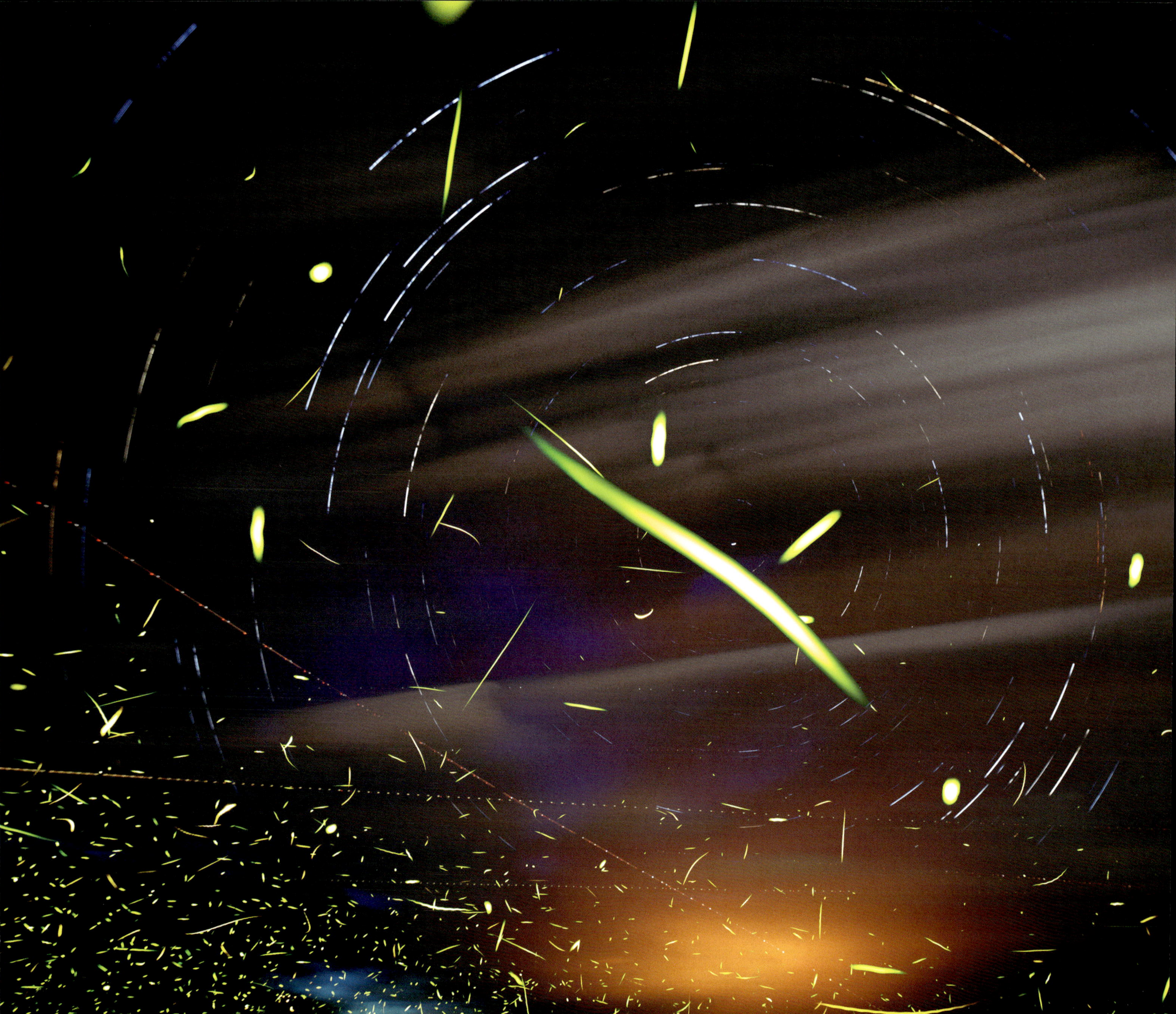

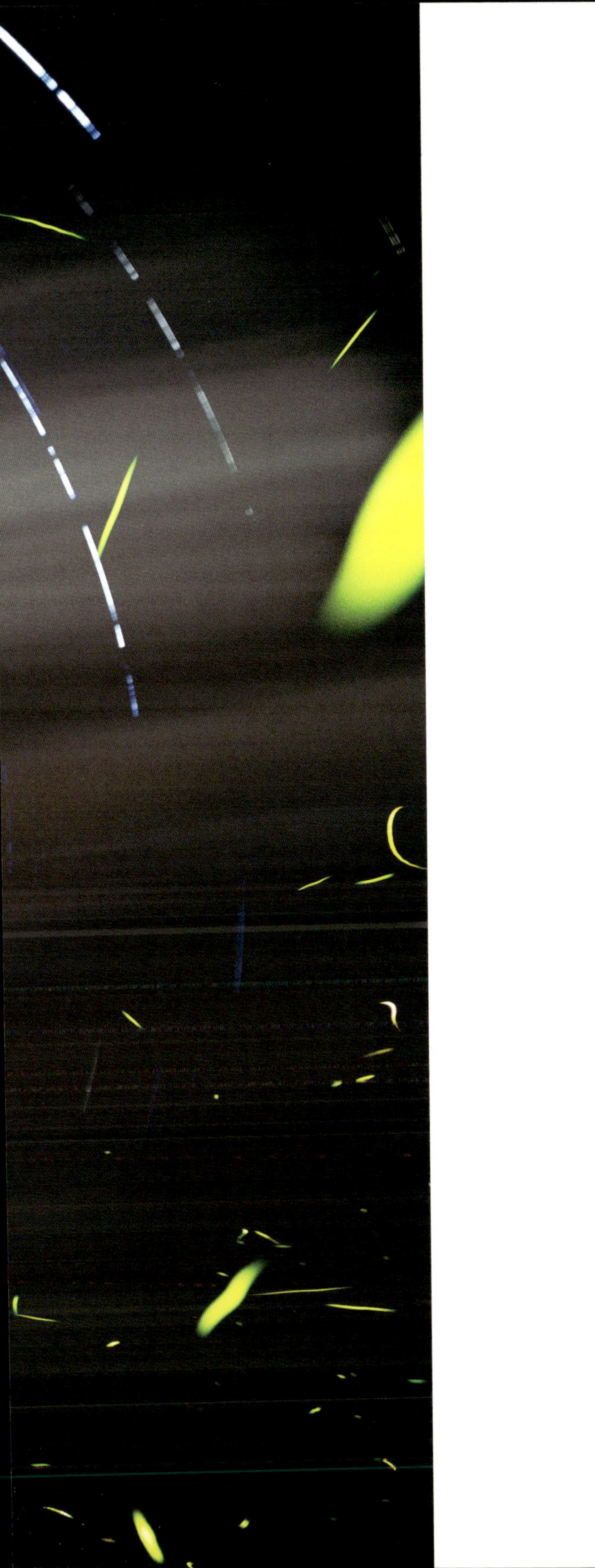

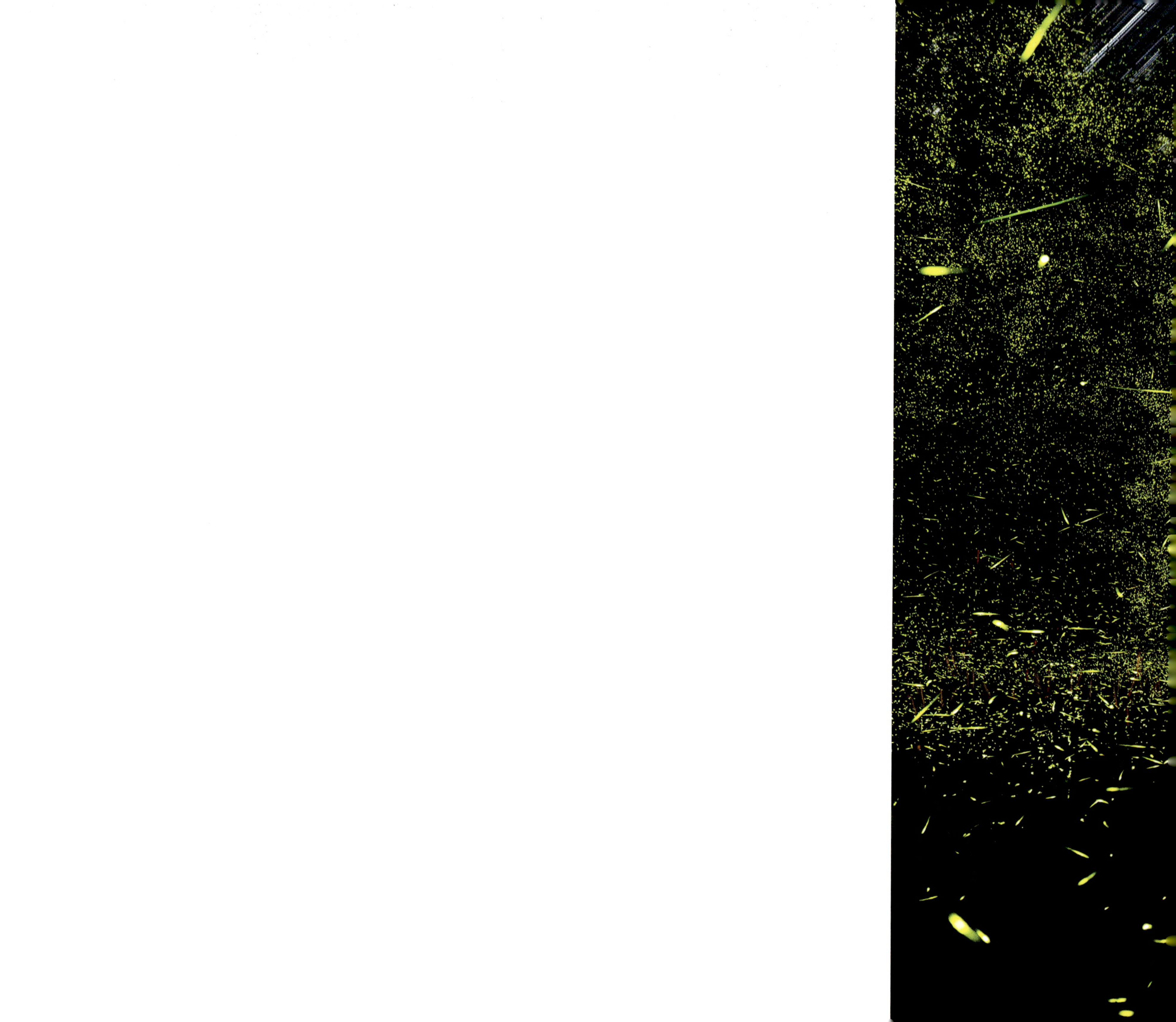

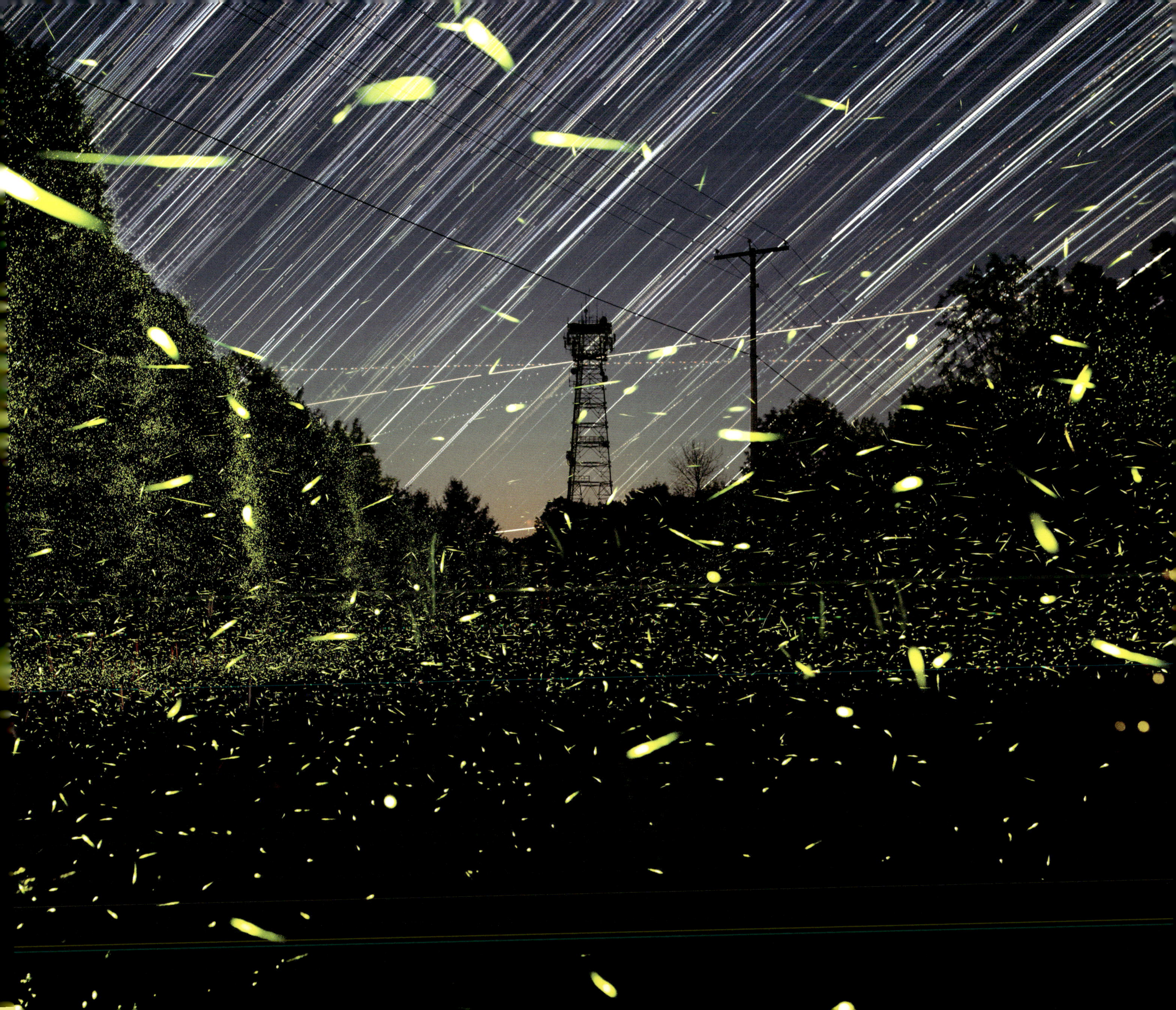

**HOW LUCKY ARE YOU, MY COMPANION DEAR,
TO NAVIGATE THROUGH THE NIGHT,
ILLUMINATING A WORLD FROM YOUR REAR...**

—A SNIPPET FROM "ODE TO A FIREFLY," A POEM BY
JULIANNA MARIE CLAIRE

And how lucky are we that Pete Mauney has divined a way to illuminate the enchanting world of fireflies. We humans can now fully appreciate the extent of their luminescent and shimmering spectacle. His work has produced a supernova of lightning-bug brilliance. This is a master class in artistic and scientific photography, bringing you images not visible to the human eye. It is a splendid, or dare I say, an enlightening achievement.

Pete spends long summer nights in fields near his home in upstate New York, surrounded by blinking-butted beauties. He puts his camera on a tripod and leaves it in the same spot for hours, taking hundreds of long exposures. Later, Pete assembles those bursts of light into one stunning image. What we mortal observers see in that field are just intermittent blinking pinpoints of light against a dark backdrop. Pete has turned that placid and pleasant scene into a visual cacophony of swirling blobs, streaks, and spheres of greenish yellow, a veritable insect-driven Fourth of July. The stars caught in his long exposures, form bright circular shapes. The trail of light caused by the occasional passing aircraft provides a brilliant slash in the sky. What emerges is a kaleidoscope of kinetic energy that dazzles the mind.

My first impression of Pete's photographs linked them to other artist's work—specifically painters, rather than photographers. To me, his pictures conjure up Pete as Vincent van Gogh reincarnated. Instead of a brush, this "Dutchman" carries a camera and has materialized to shoot lightning-bug variations of one of the greatest paintings of all time, *The Starry Night*. In 1889, when van Gogh created that nocturnal masterpiece he was in an asylum in southern France fighting deep depression. The view from his window inspired the iconic painting. Like van Gogh, Pete finds respite under his own starry skies.

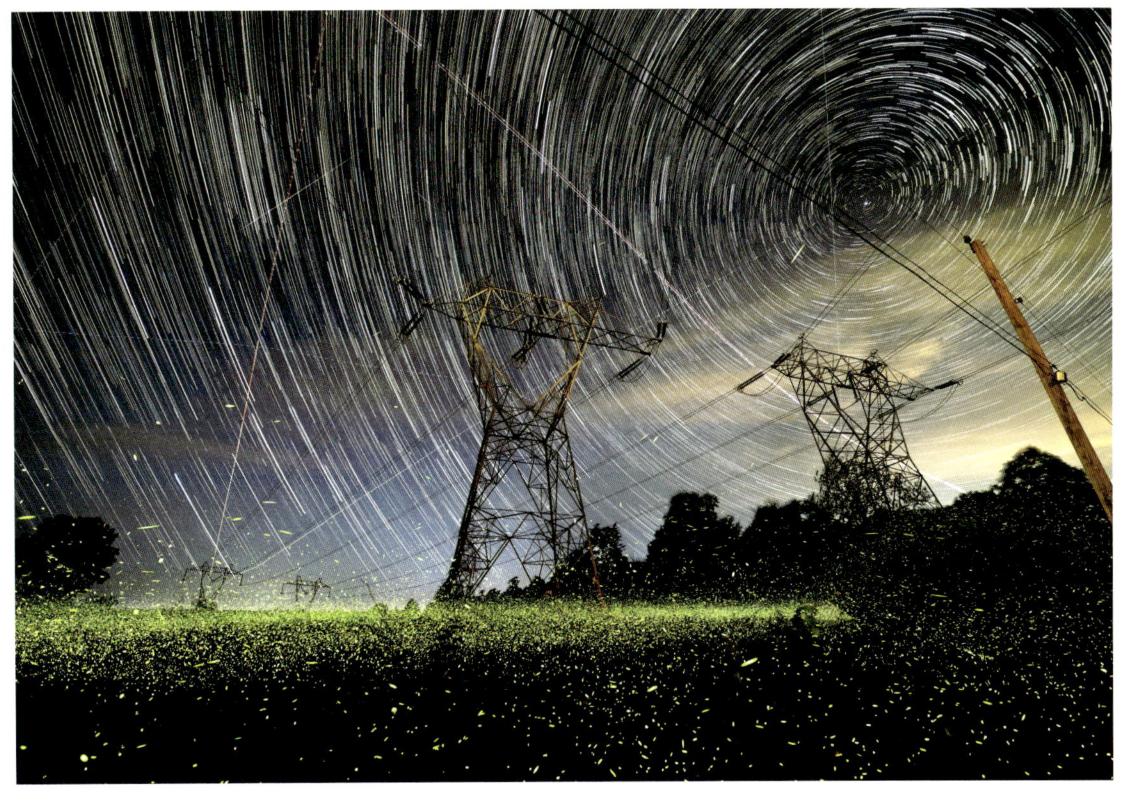

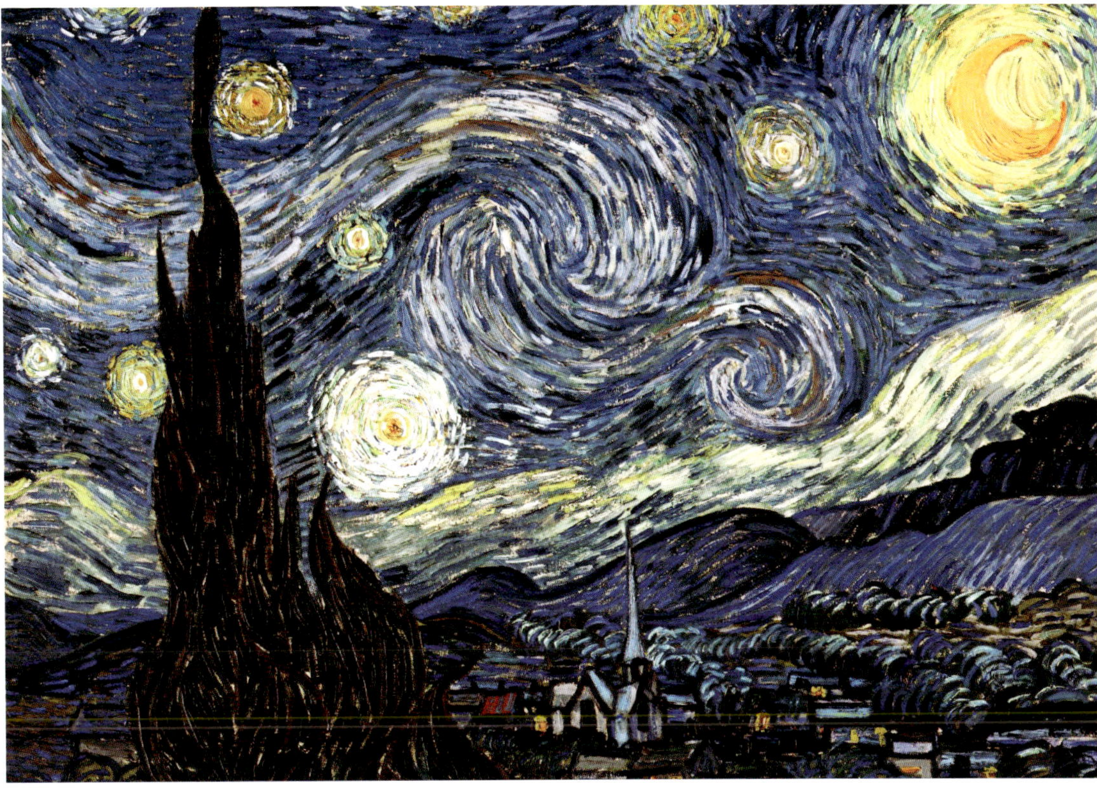

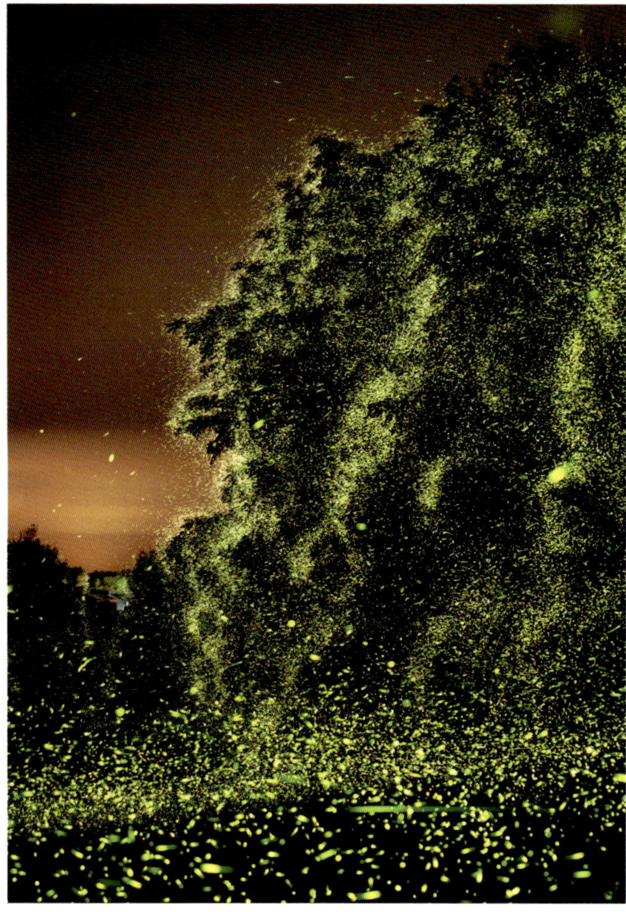

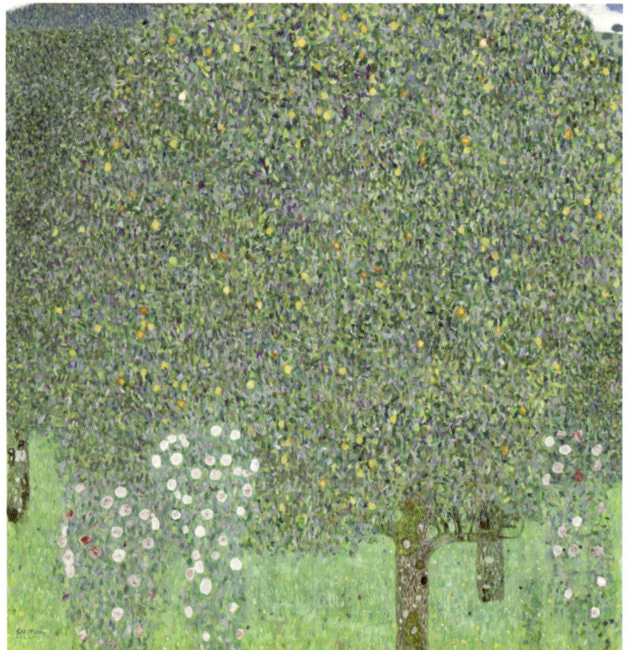

Another evocative work is by the Austrian painter Gustav Klimt, who was also inspired by van Gogh. One image that could have been snatched right out of Pete's playbook is *Roses Among the Trees*, painted in 1905, and features iridescent dabs of yellow fruit against dense green foliage. The green and blue colors are similar to Pete's mélange of fireflies, interrupted only by white climbing flowers.

And then there are the fairies. Anyone looking at Pete's pictures and not seeing a fairy or two or three isn't paying attention. I count hundreds. To me every little orb of light represents one of those wispy, elusive entities.

A painterly reference from fairyland is *Midsummer Eve* by the English artist Edward Robert Hughes. His radiant and ethereal 1908 painting is an enchanting view that embodies Victorian fairy tales when they were wildly popular. Shakespeare's play *A Midsummer's Night Dream* was the inspiration for Hughes. His midsummer fantasy features Shakespeare's character Hermia, who gets lost in the forest and is soon surrounded by fairies. The painting illustrates the widely held belief during Shakespeare's time that the fairytale world is narrower during midsummer, allowing mythical spirits entry into ours. Edward's is a romantic vision of magical light containing imps, cherubs, and, of course, fireflies. Pete's electrically illuminated tree and foreground filled with bright flies captures the same spirit.

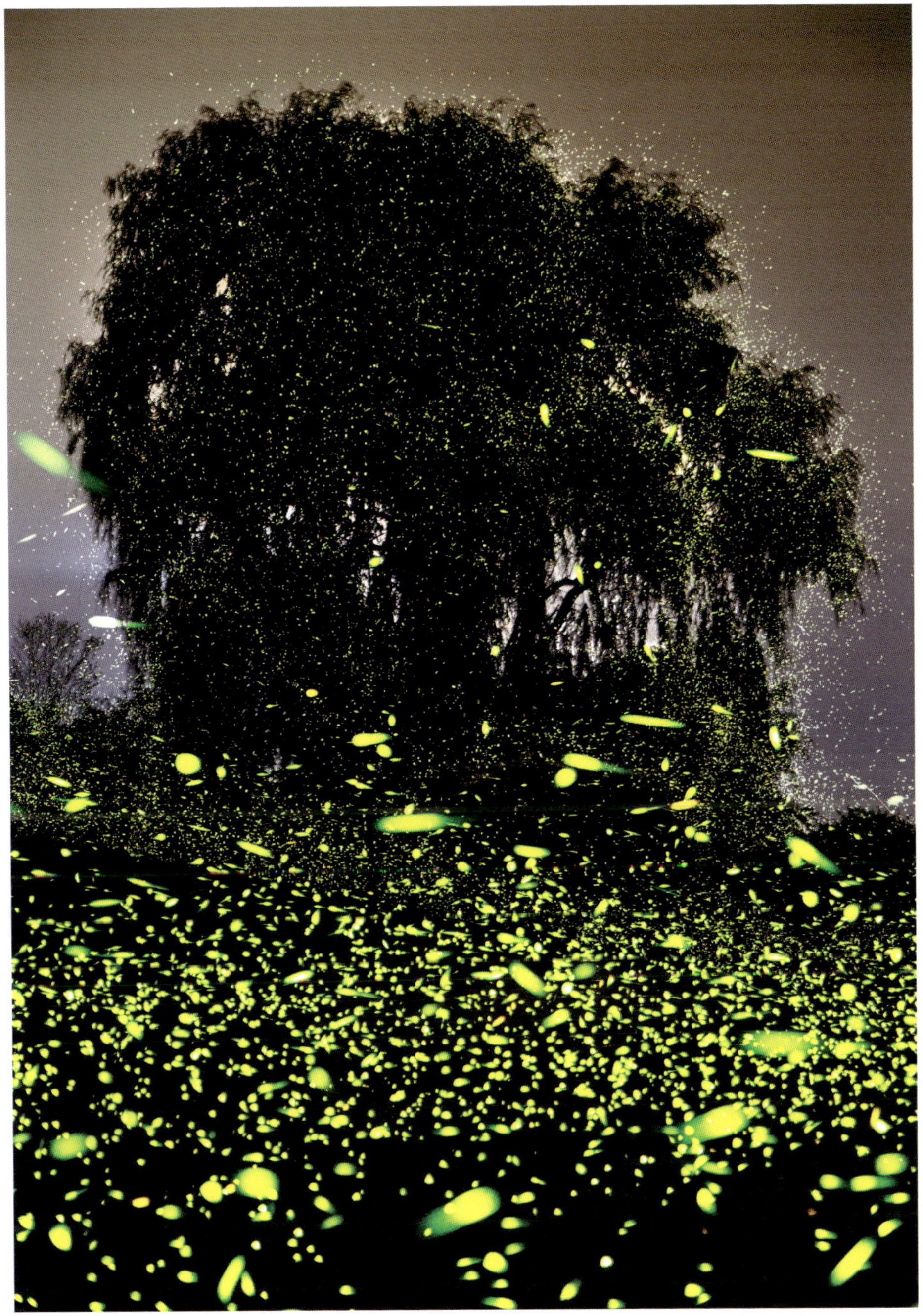

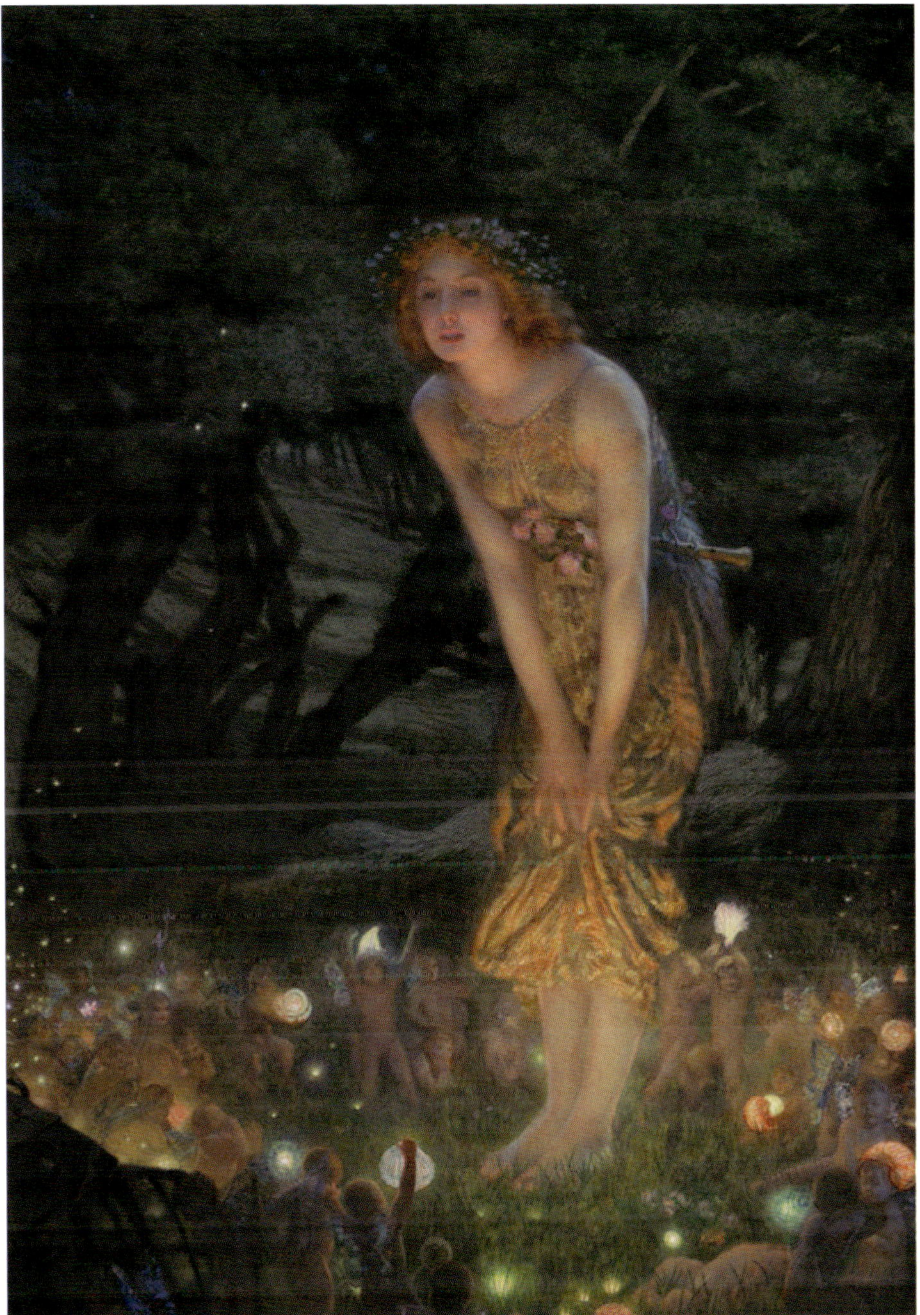

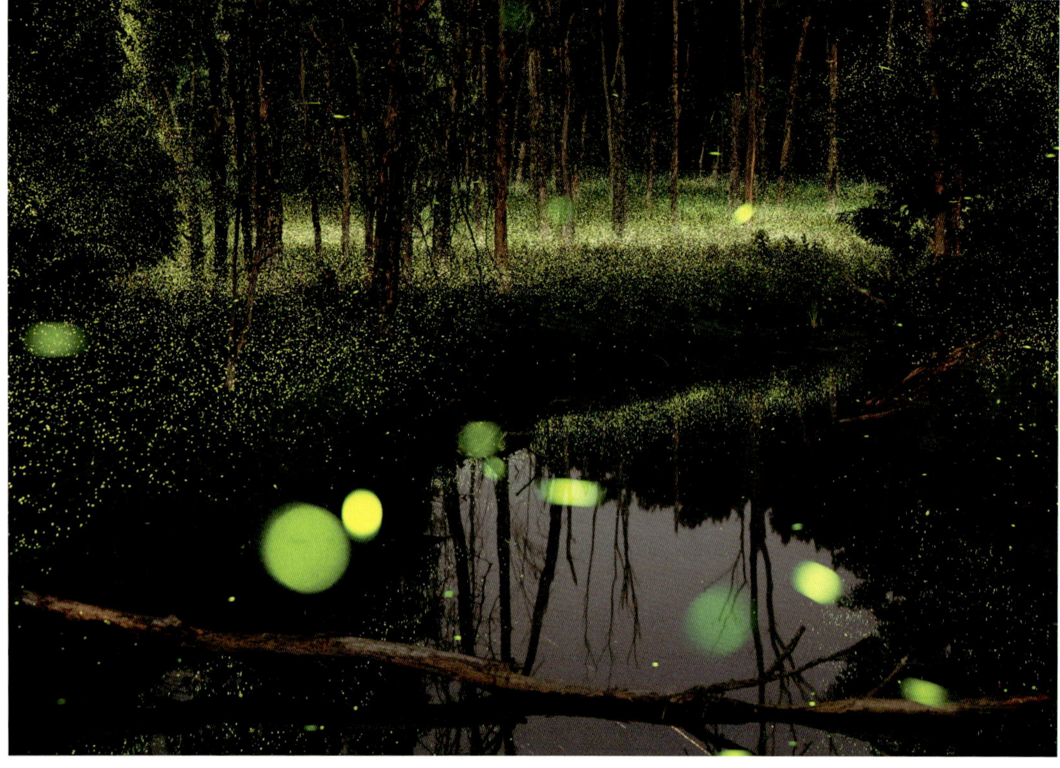

And we must celebrate Claude Monet's *Water Lilies* series, created at his home in Giverny. Monet generated many paintings of his garden and lily pond over the last thirty years of his life, but this one, showing green and yellow with dabs of red and white, much of it reflected in the water, is Mauneyesque, and Pete has the picture to prove it.

Topping my list of brash comparisons of Pete to other great artists' work is *Christina's World*, painted by Andrew Wyeth in 1948. One of the best-known American paintings from the last century, it depicts a woman crouching on the ground in an empty field gazing at a gray house on the horizon. The only thing missing now is a flurry of fireflies, and that's where Pete comes into the picture. His photo of a little house on a hill sits in a field of fireflies. The only thing missing is a semi-reclining woman in the foreground.

As a fellow photographer I have unabashed reverence for Pete Mauney's work. I'm in awe of his patience and perseverance in making these fantastic images. As all artists do, he sees the world in a unique and compelling way, and my comparison of him to other legendary artists is not hyperbole but fact.

Pete never knows what he will end up with after a long night of shooting, and not every evening produces a hit, but he keeps at it, and like those artists of old, he never gives up.

To paraphrase Obi-Wan Kenobi: "Pete, may the firefly be with you."

DAVID HUME KENNERLY

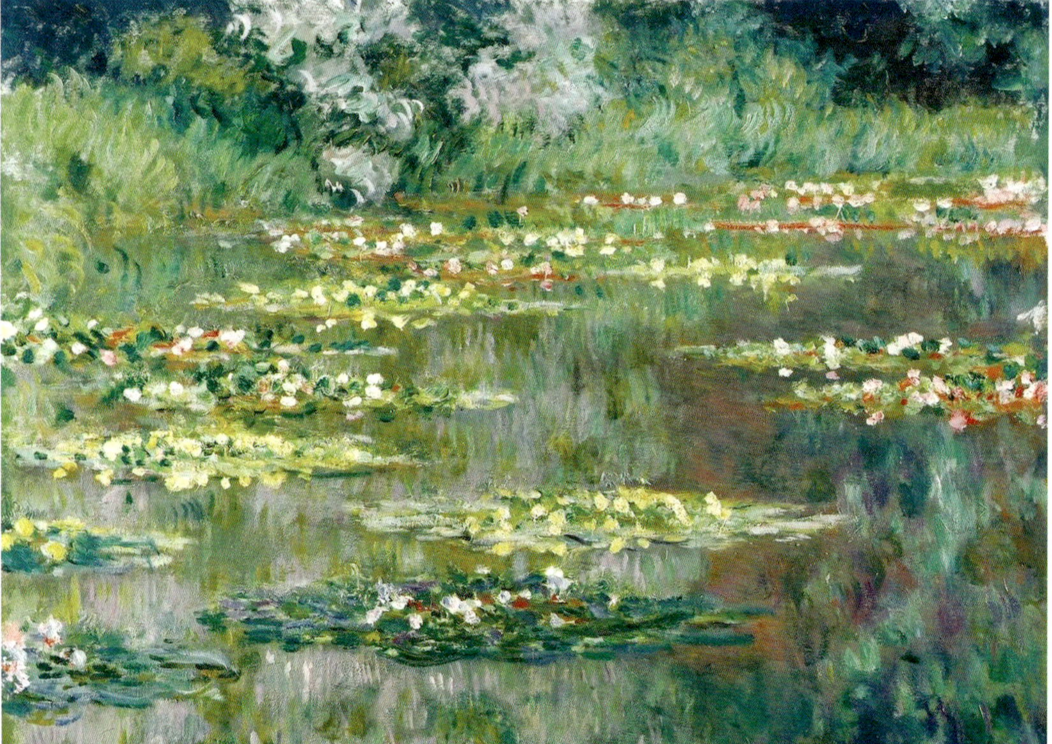

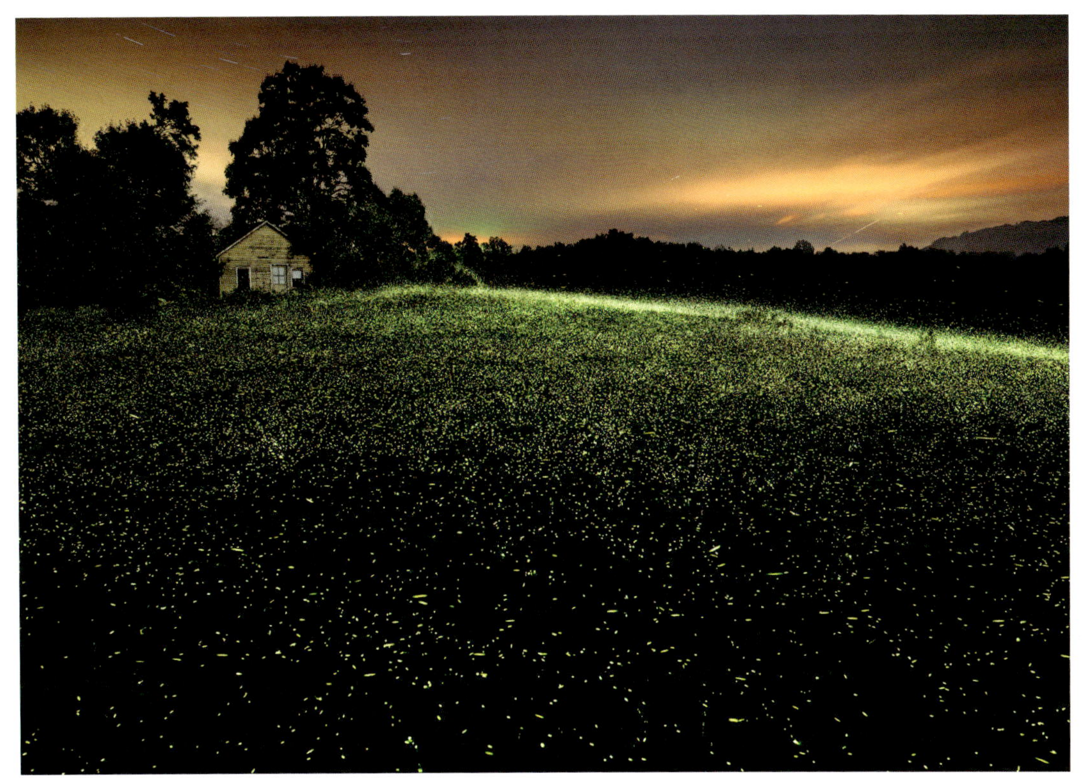

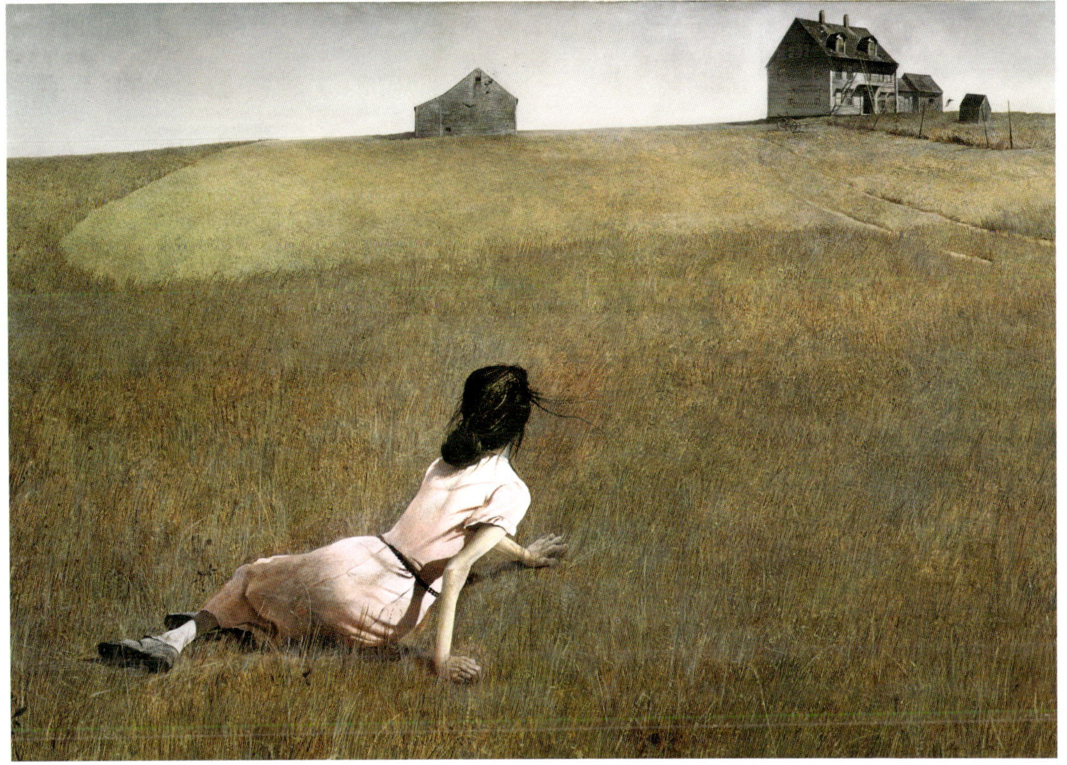

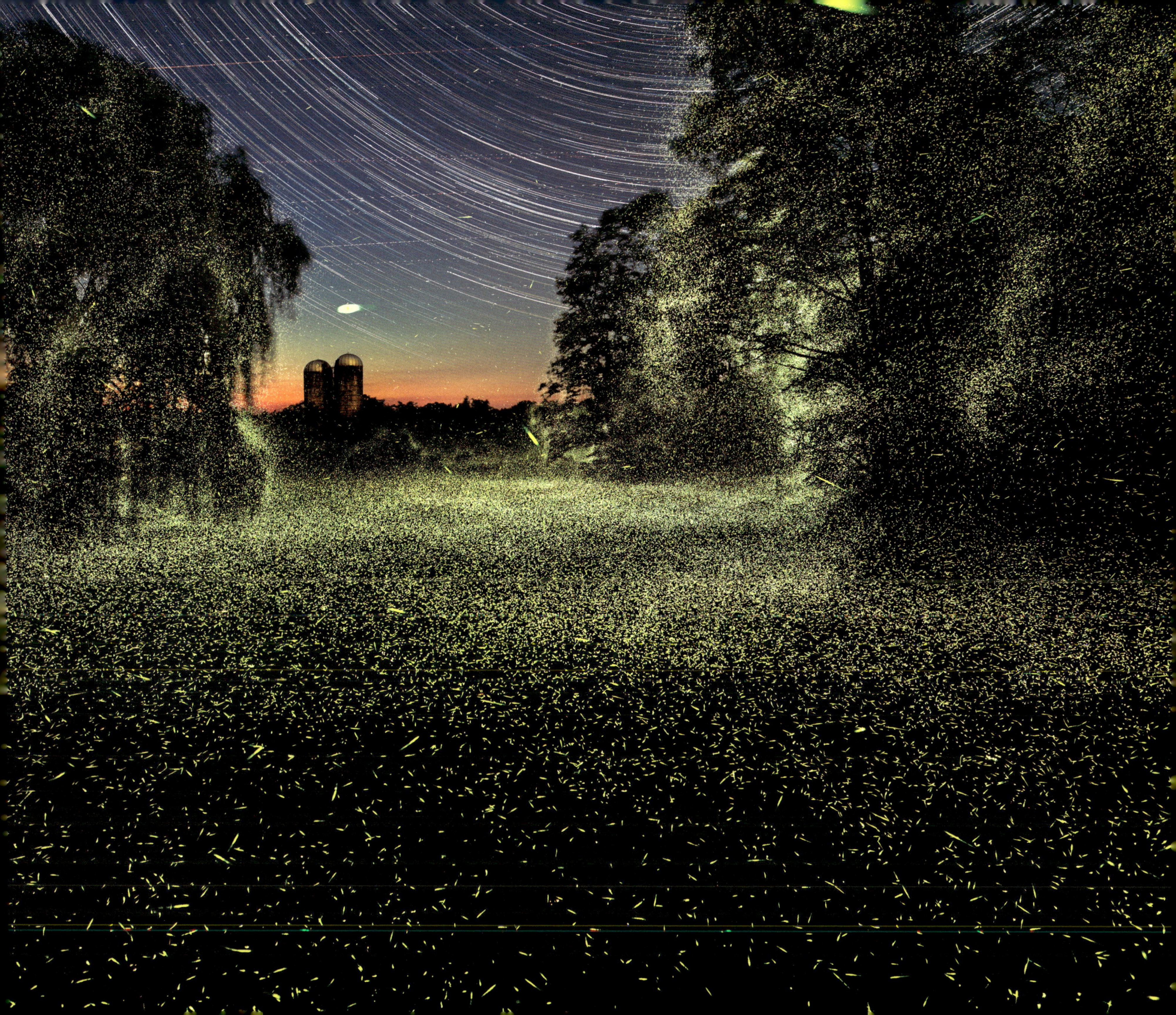

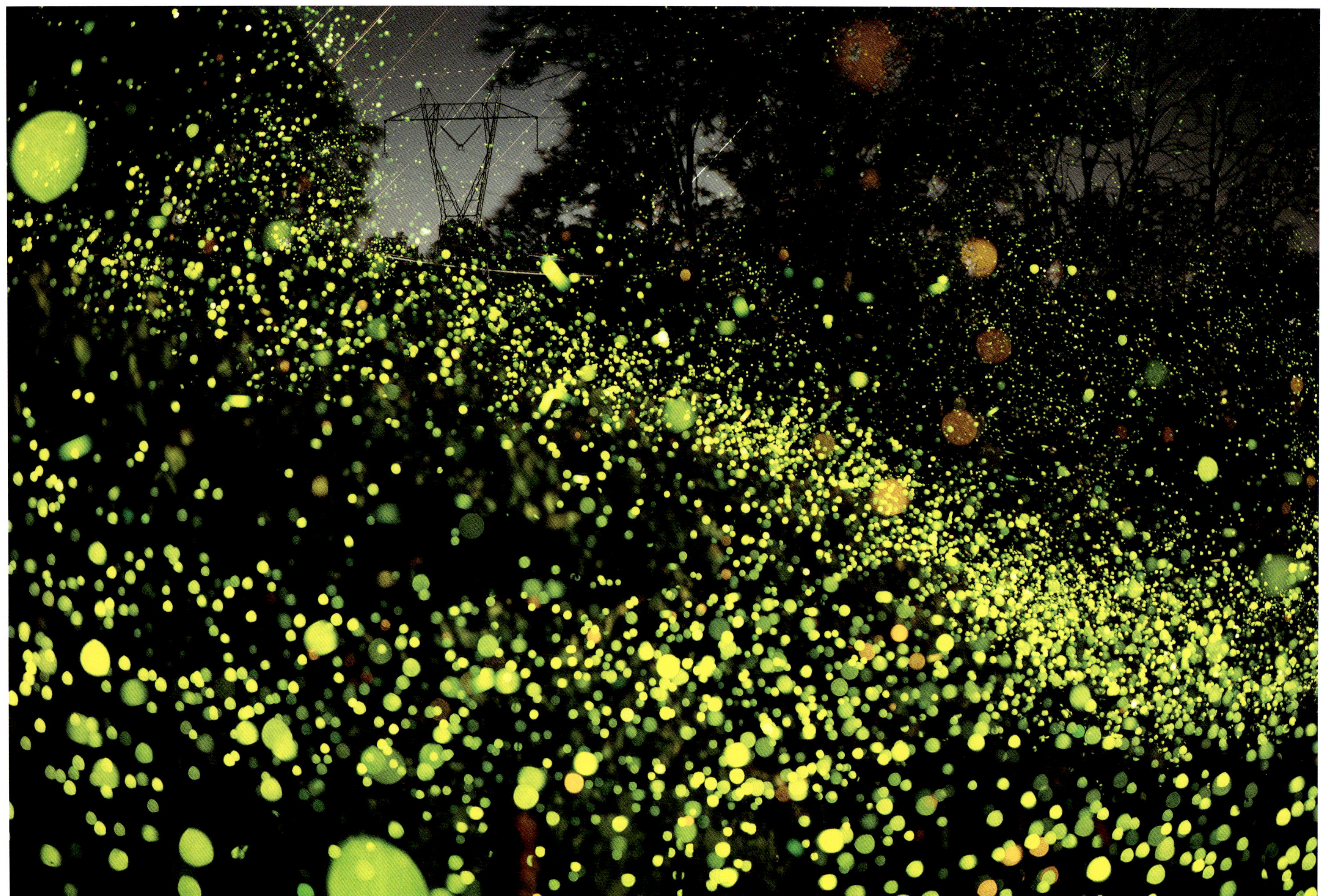

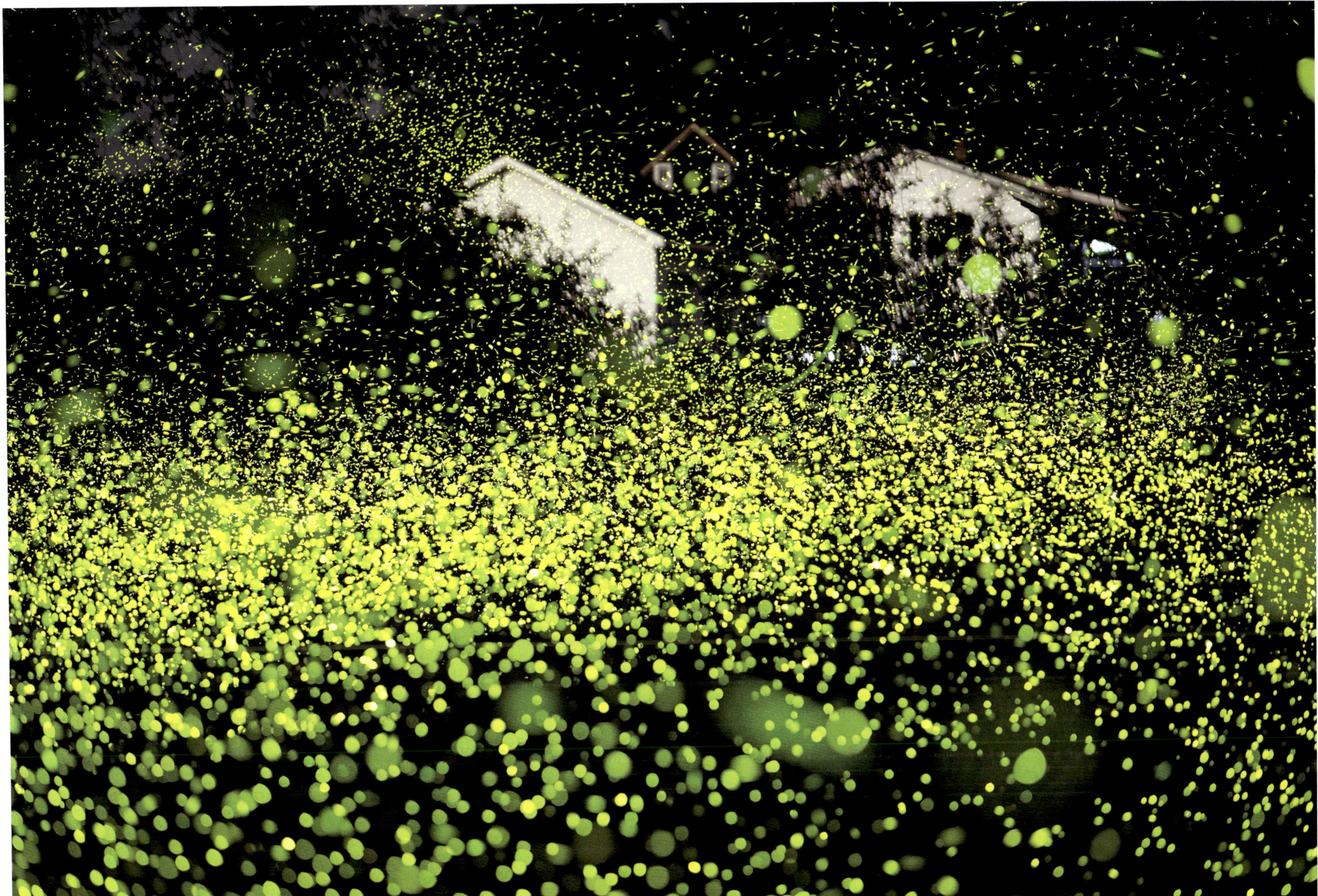

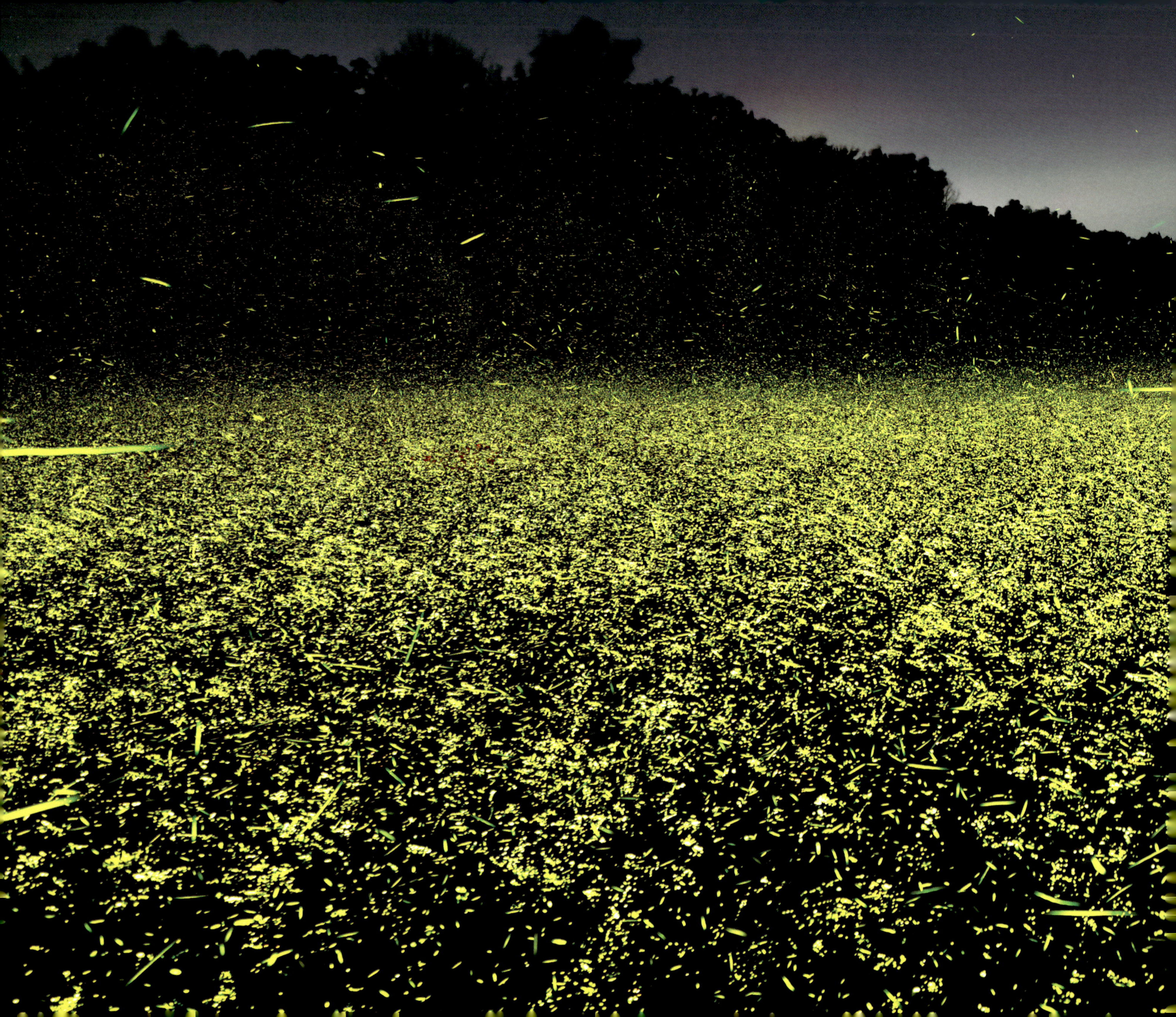

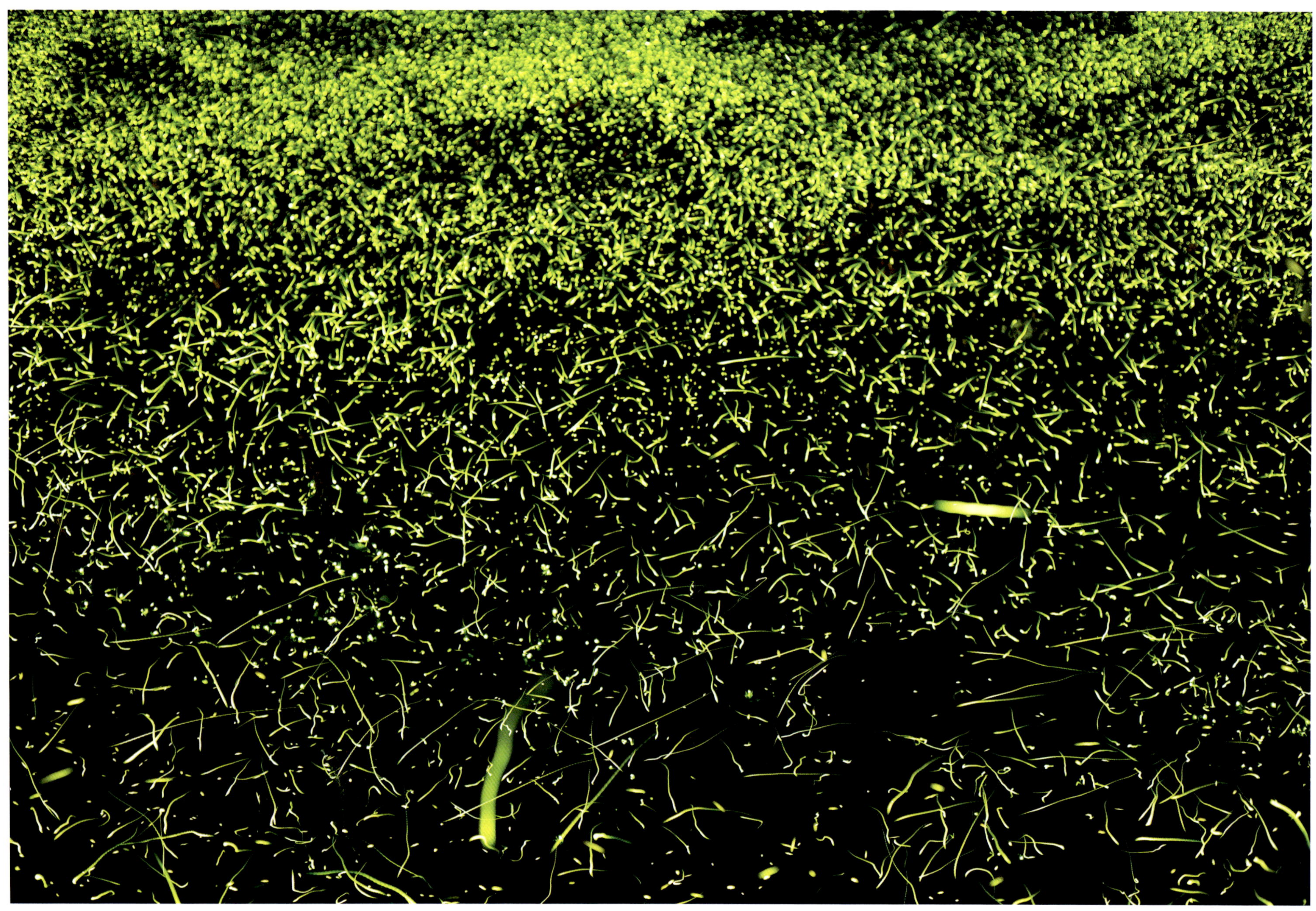

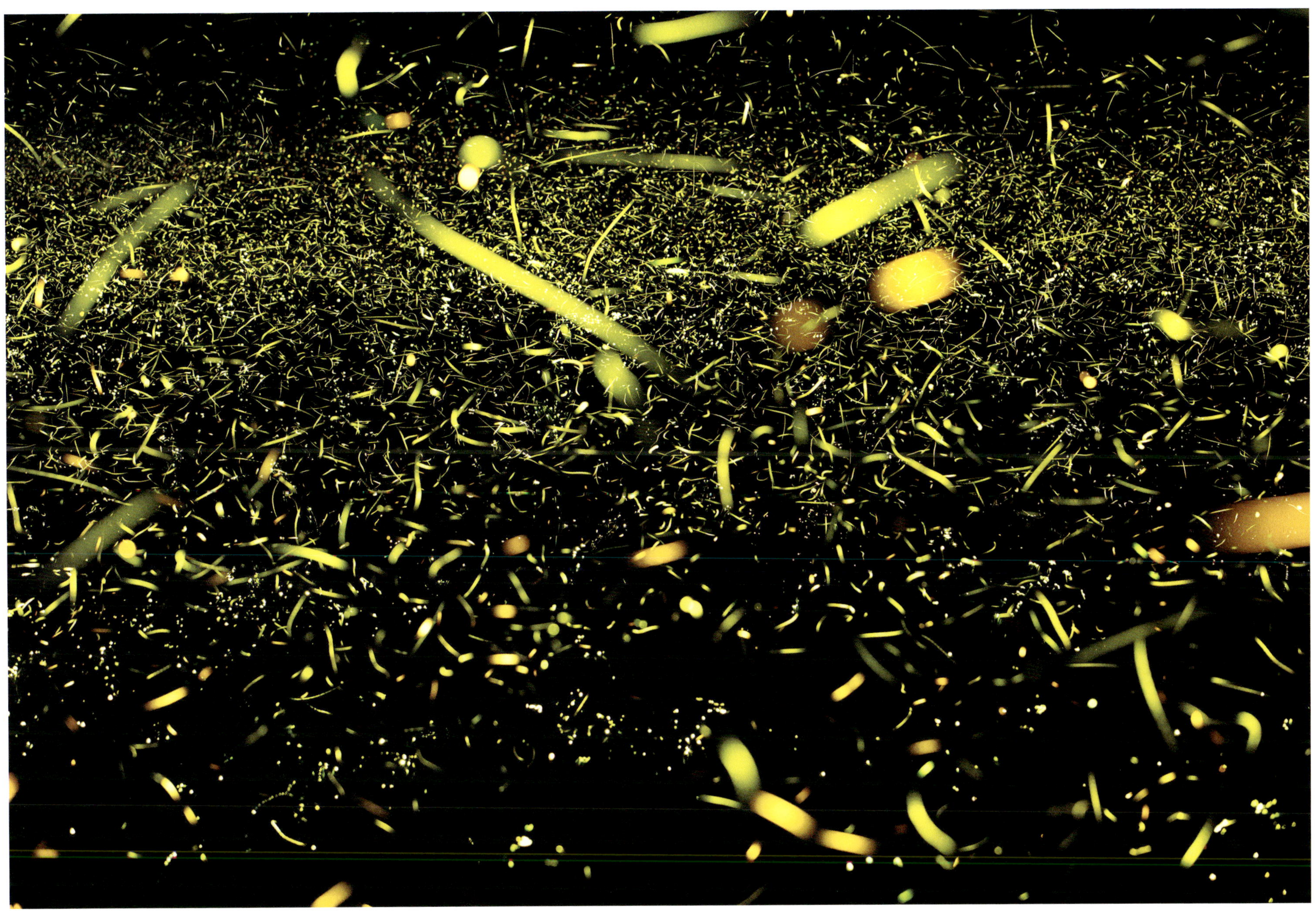

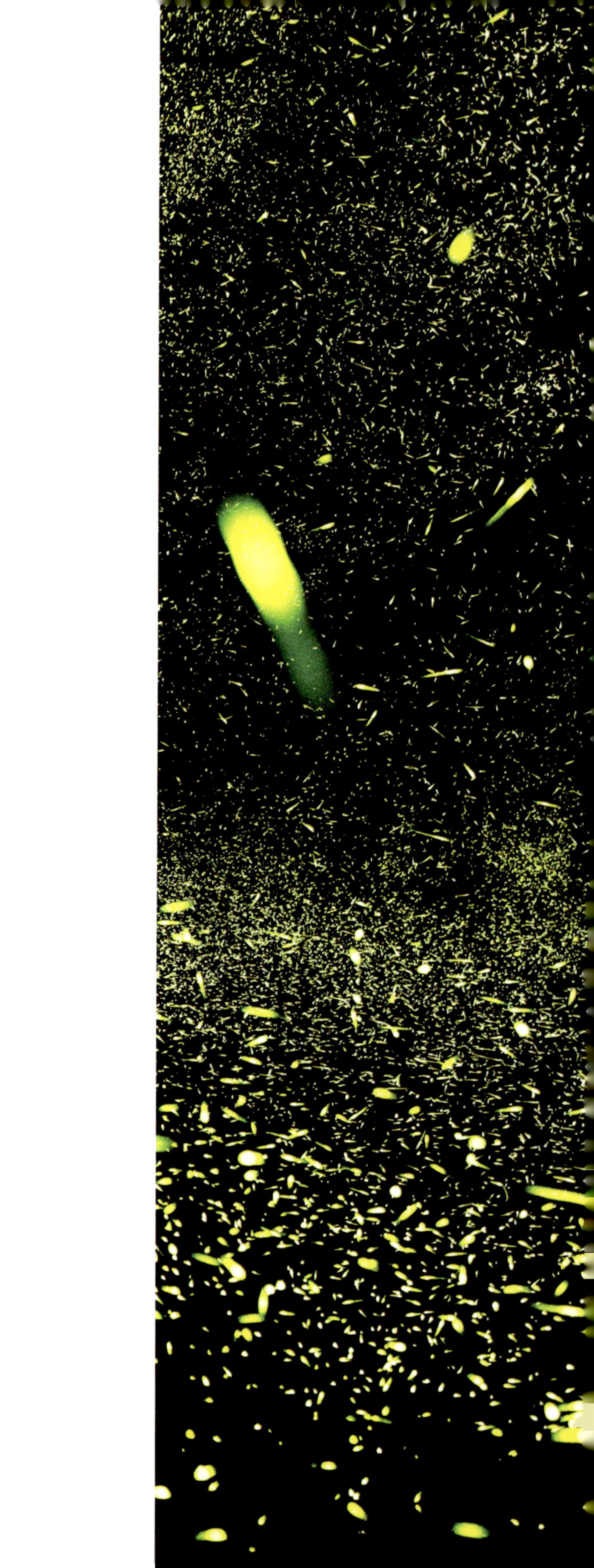

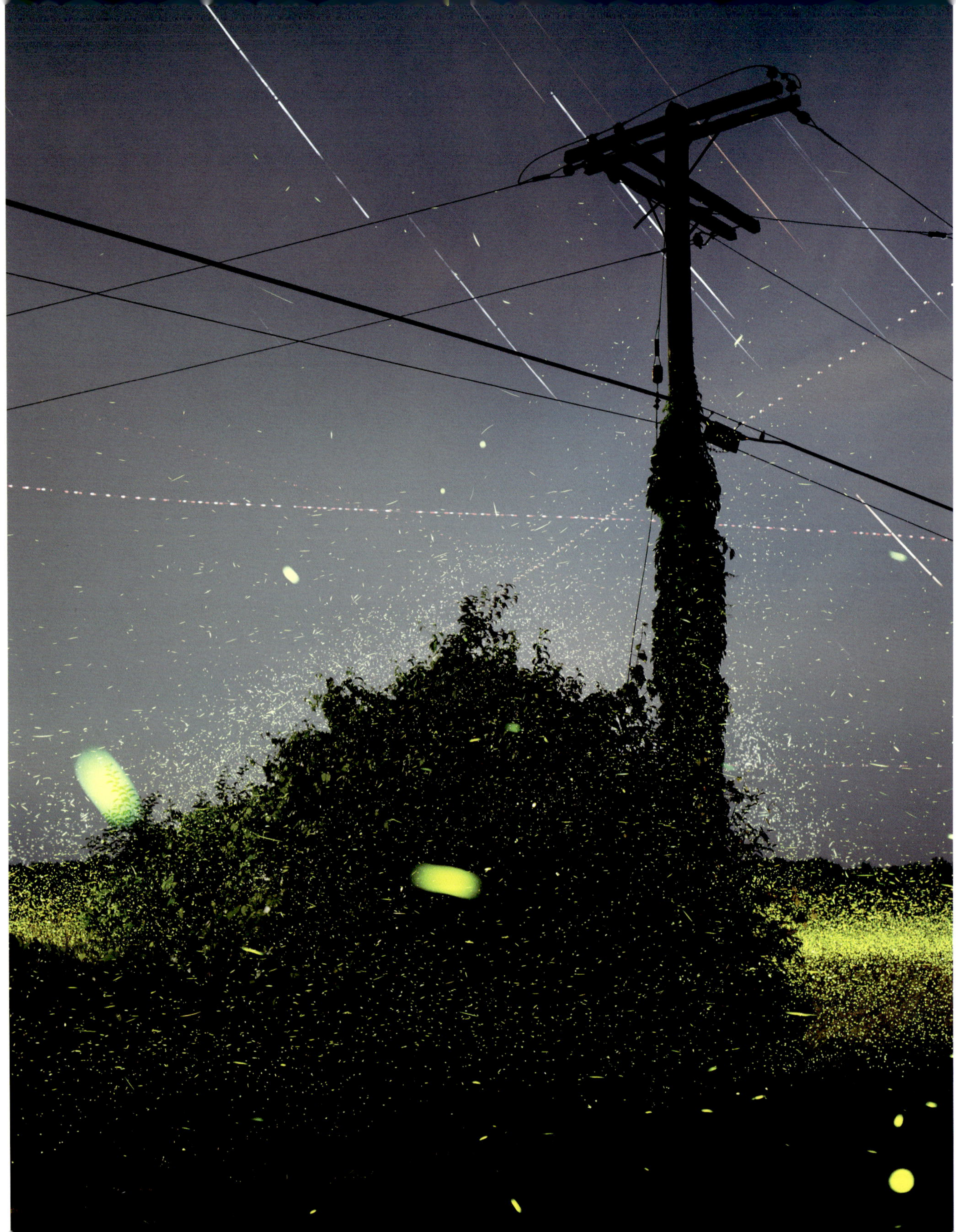

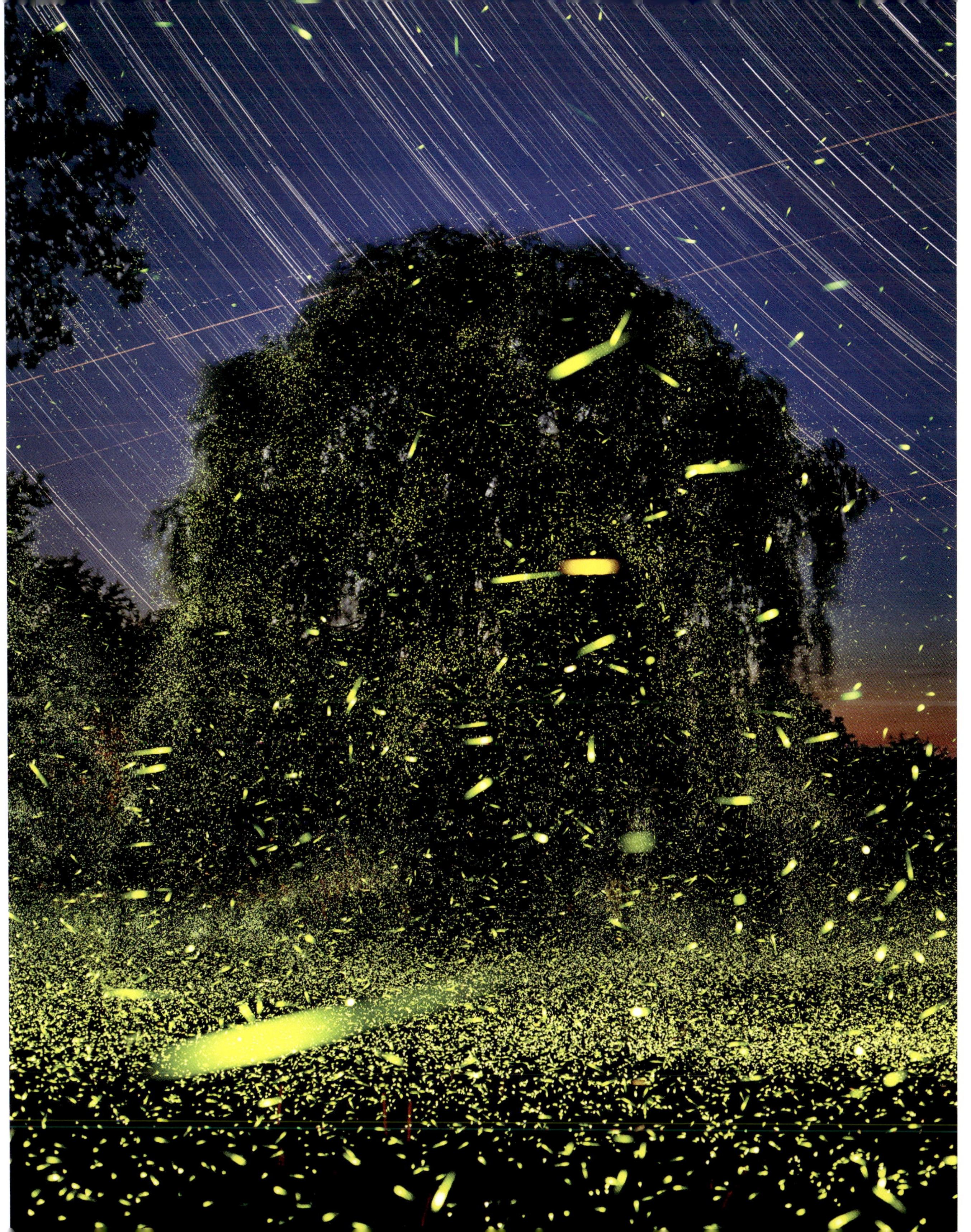

What keeps you going back out in the dark year after year?

Why do I continue going back? Because I haven't figured it out yet? I remember one day when I was excitedly showing my kids pictures on my phone that I had made the night before. I'm like, "Check out this one, check out this one." One of the kids, who shall remain unnamed for the record, looked at me and very wisely asked, "Daddy, when are you going to stop going out every night and making the same picture?" Turns out I'd asked myself that same question many, many times, and that always distressed me, because I never had an answer. In that moment, when I was directly asked that question by another human, I blurted out what was likely the only honest answer: "I don't know." And I still don't.

What keeps me going back? Something to do, something to quiet the noise, something to focus on, something that brings me significant joy and knowledge, something that brings me beauty instead of terror, something that shows me something invisible. I go back because it makes me feel better.

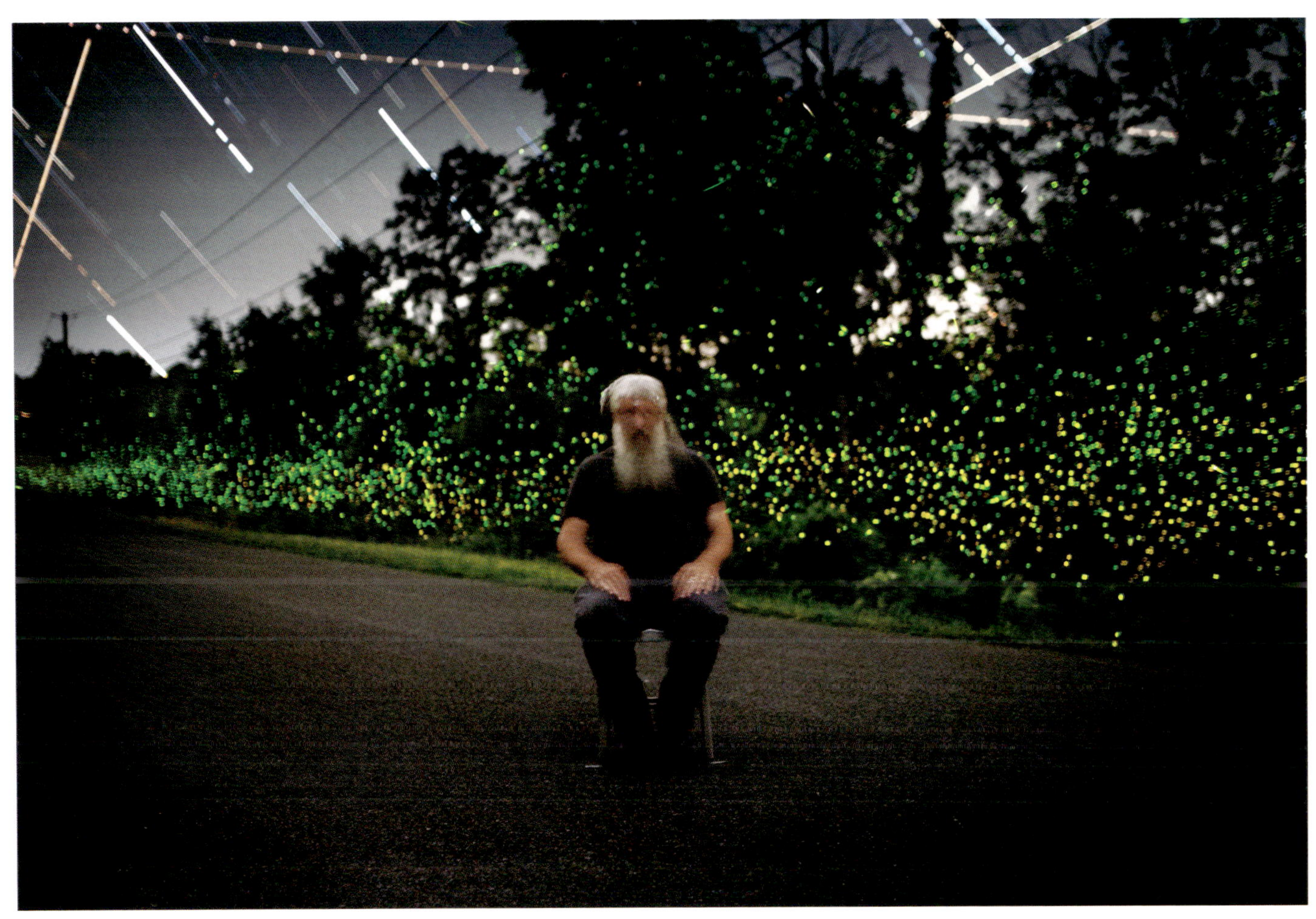

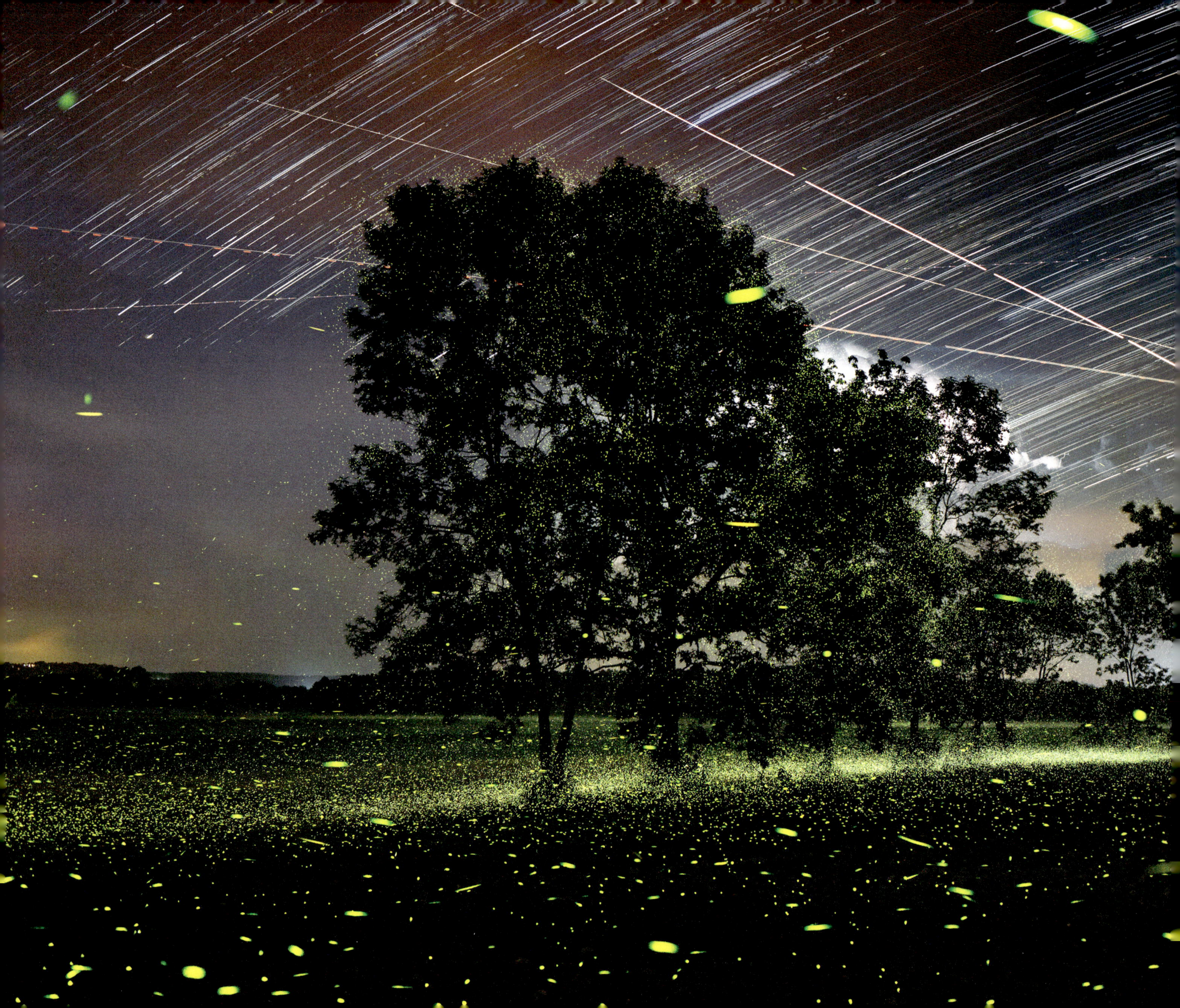

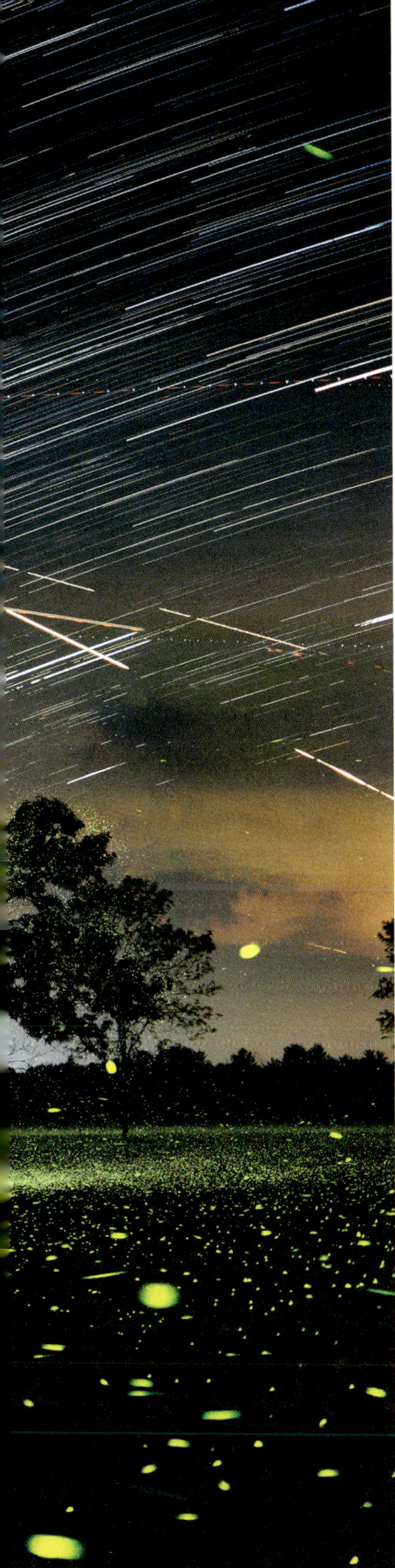

ACKNOWLEDGEMENTS

I don't even know where to begin, so…let's go:

This book is for my dad.

He was a huge book-lover and all-around amazing human. One of my great joys was being able to tell him soon before he died that I was finally doing a book and here it is.

Of course…none of this would have been possible without my family. My steadfast and extraordinarily strong mom and the supportive memory of my dad. I love you both so much. My super-smart and hard-working partner for her knowledge and honesty. And, while they don't really get why I do what I do and probably think it's stupid, my kids occupy more of my heart than anyone else on the planet and causes it to keep beating. It might not seem that way sometimes, but almost everything I do, I do with them in mind.

Thanks to Gordon and Jake for taking a chance on me!

David Kennerly for being an all-around awesome human. He is everywhere all at once, a distinct and unique force of nature. The definition of gracefully working hard. And I mean hard. His support has meant a lot and he got this particular ball rolling and gave me something really fun to spend a few months doing and he took serious time to write a wonderfully ebullient essay that made me reconsider some of my own work. Thank you. Thank you. Thank you.

I don't even know where to start with Jessica Chappe. On more levels than I care to count, this book wouldn't exist if not for her. From keeping me on track and on task, for always honest and insightful feedback, for her commitment and determination. For, at least once, bringing me up from the depths and out into the light. For listening to and recording my endless yapping and dragging coherency out of the chaotic noise factory that is my brain. Let alone that she was who introduced David Kennerly to my pictures. Small world. Can't wait to see your book someday sooner rather than later.

Tim Davis, neighbor and friend, not only wrote a great essay that makes me blush, but arrived in the middle of the picture edit process and casually threw a very productive wrench into my stiff gears that ended up liberating the book from my pedantry. I am not sure that I know anyone who is as smart and eloquent about photography as him, while also being an extraordinary image maker. That being said, the red barn is his fault.

Dr. Orit Peleg (the quantifier of the sublime, the counter of the uncountable, the systemic visionary, the decipherer of clouds, the data-tamer) for a wonderful essay. Deep gratitude for letting me help out a bit with the research, a dream come true for me. It was such an honor and I can't wait to see what she finds next, generally speaking, even if I won't be able to comprehend the enormity of it.

A huge thanks to Thomas for his excellent advice, hand-holding, and attention to detail. Let alone decades of friendship and visits to abandoned industrial sites. But mostly, I want to thank him for still talking to me after the 1980s happened and to confess, here and now, to the world, that my dish-washing skills are still horrific.

Speaking of decades, my longtime muses Aaron and Pete rank high on my list of favorite humans and may or may not have been present for the making of some of these images—if not these specific ones, then certainly many others.

Kelly Spencer for her transformative (without being disruptive) text editing, sensitivity, and guidance. Your help was essential and, well, very helpful.

Countless friends and family. Fiona, Janice, Joel, Carolyn, Raphael, Barry, Judy and Jake, Wendy, Stan and Lois, Jesse, Shamus, Tina, Jen, the weekend morning "church" crew and our many communions, Mikee and Rob for the carbs, Jim for convincing me to get in touch with Dr. Peleg...the list goes on and on.

Shout-out to Radim, Julian, Sriram and Garth.

Last but not least are all my social media followers. Even the bots. You all sustain me and encourage me. I have so much fun in that space and I have met some truly wonderful people there, even though I have never met the vast majority of them IRL. Someday.

Y'all are the best!

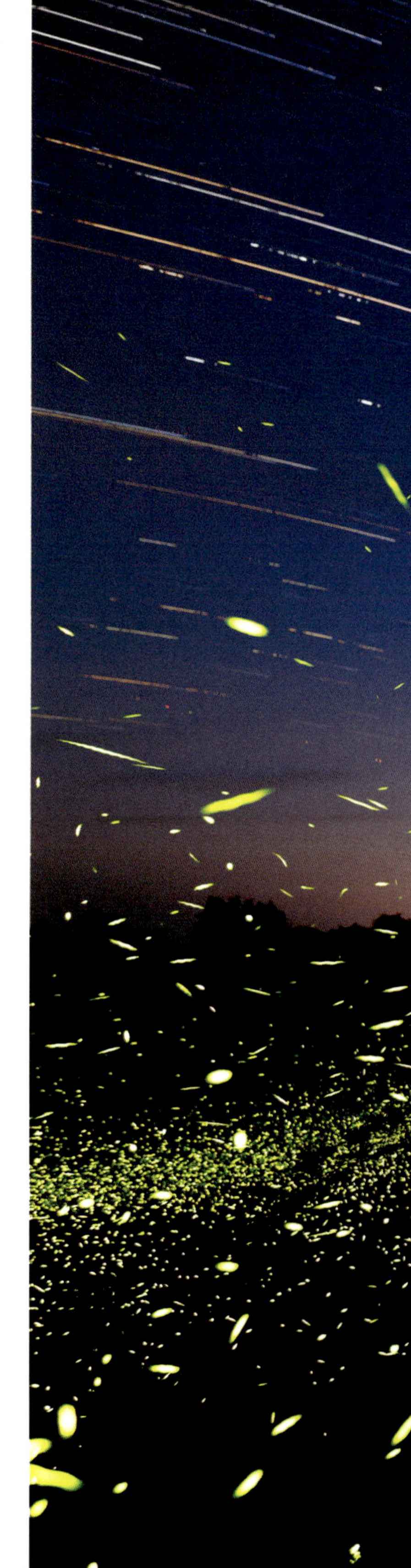

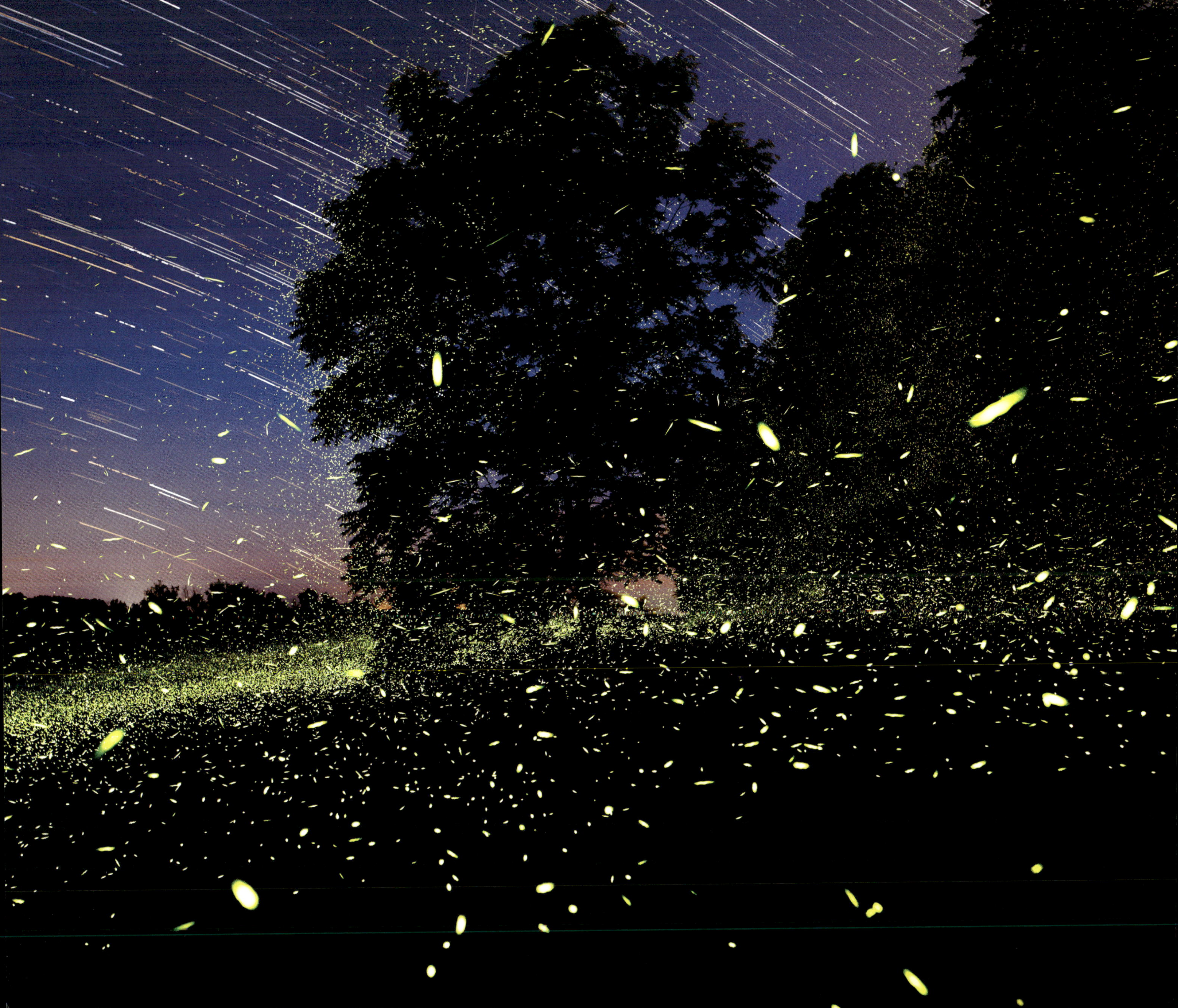

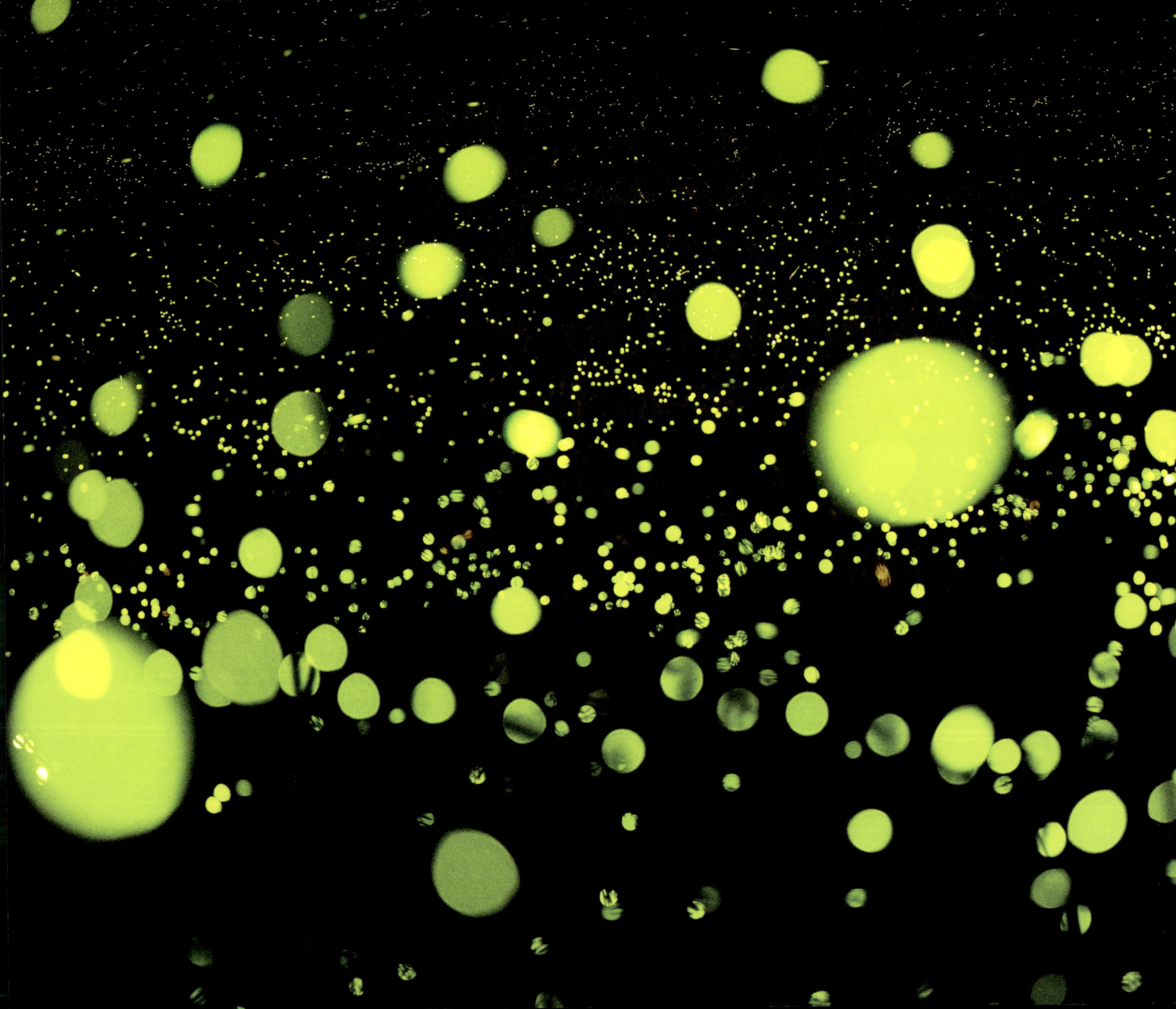

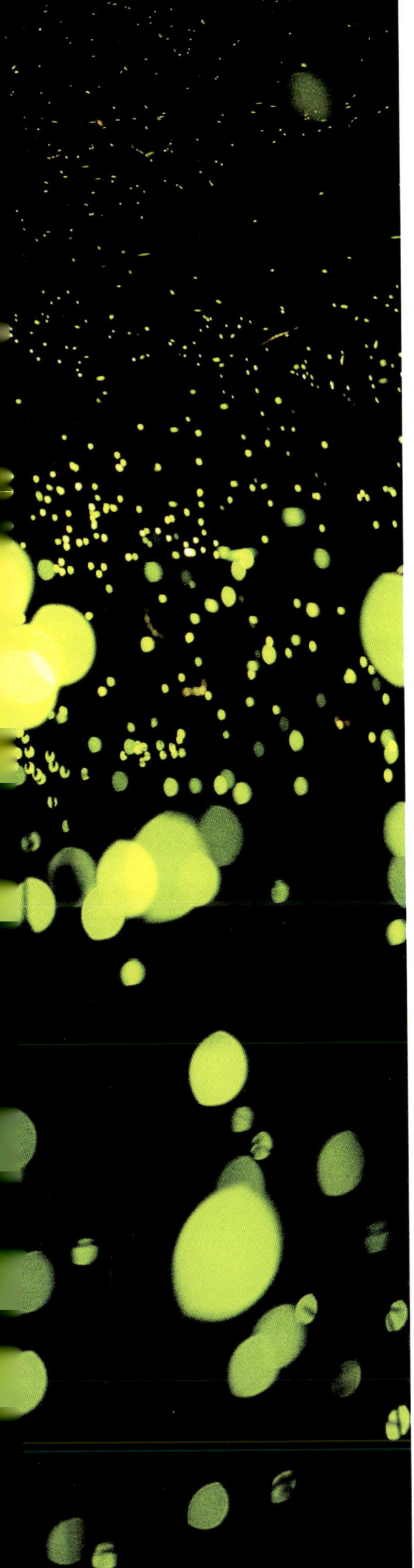

ABOUT THE AUTHOR

PETE MAUNEY (b. 1967) is a photographer and photographic technician. Mauney received his MFA and BA in photography at Bard College with a prior two-year stint at NYU in film. He has worked with a number of distinguished clients supporting them on a range of levels such as art reproduction photography, exhibition printing, and drum scanning. For the past decade, Mauney's personal work has focused on documenting fireflies and airplanes in the evening, applying his technical knowledge and skills to accurately depicting an accumulation of time in space. His work has been featured on NPR, Wired, Chronogram, and Colossal to name a few and is in multiple collections including the Morgan Library and The Black Gold Museum in Saudi Arabia.

CONTRIBUTING AUTHORS

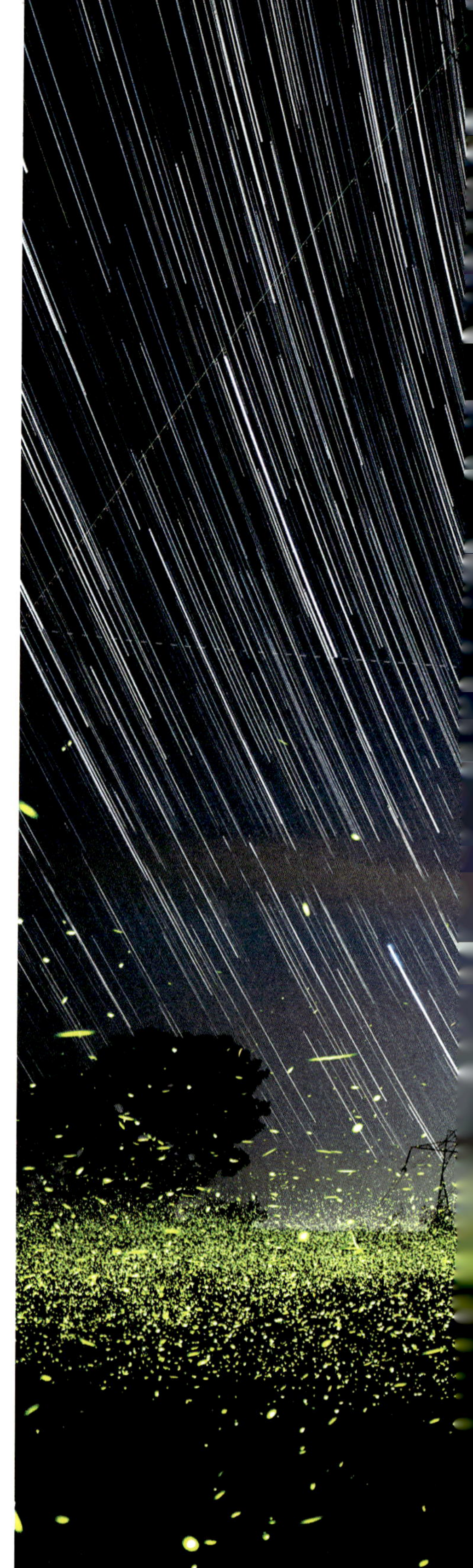

TIM DAVIS (b. 1969) is an artist, essayist, and songwriter living in Tivoli, NY, and teaching photography at Bard College. His latest books include I'm Looking Through You (Aperture, 2021) and the forthcoming Normaltown (Fall Line Press, 2024). His website is www.ohthattimdavis.com.

DAVID HUME KENNERLY (b. 1947) won the 1972 Pulitzer Prize for Feature Photography for images of the Vietnam War and other work he made in 1971. He has photographed every American president since Johnson. He is the first presidential scholar at the University of Arizona.

ORIT PELEG (b. 1983) is a computer scientist, biophysicist and associate professor in the Computer Science Department and the BioFrontiers Institute at the University of Colorado Boulder in Boulder, CO. She is known for her work on collective behavior of insects and the biophysics of soft living systems, including honeybees and fireflies.

JESSICA CHAPPE (b. 1994) is a mixed media storyteller and an oral historian based in Catskill, NY. Her projects focus on how people find belonging through community, place, and self. She received a BA in Photography at Bard College in 2016.

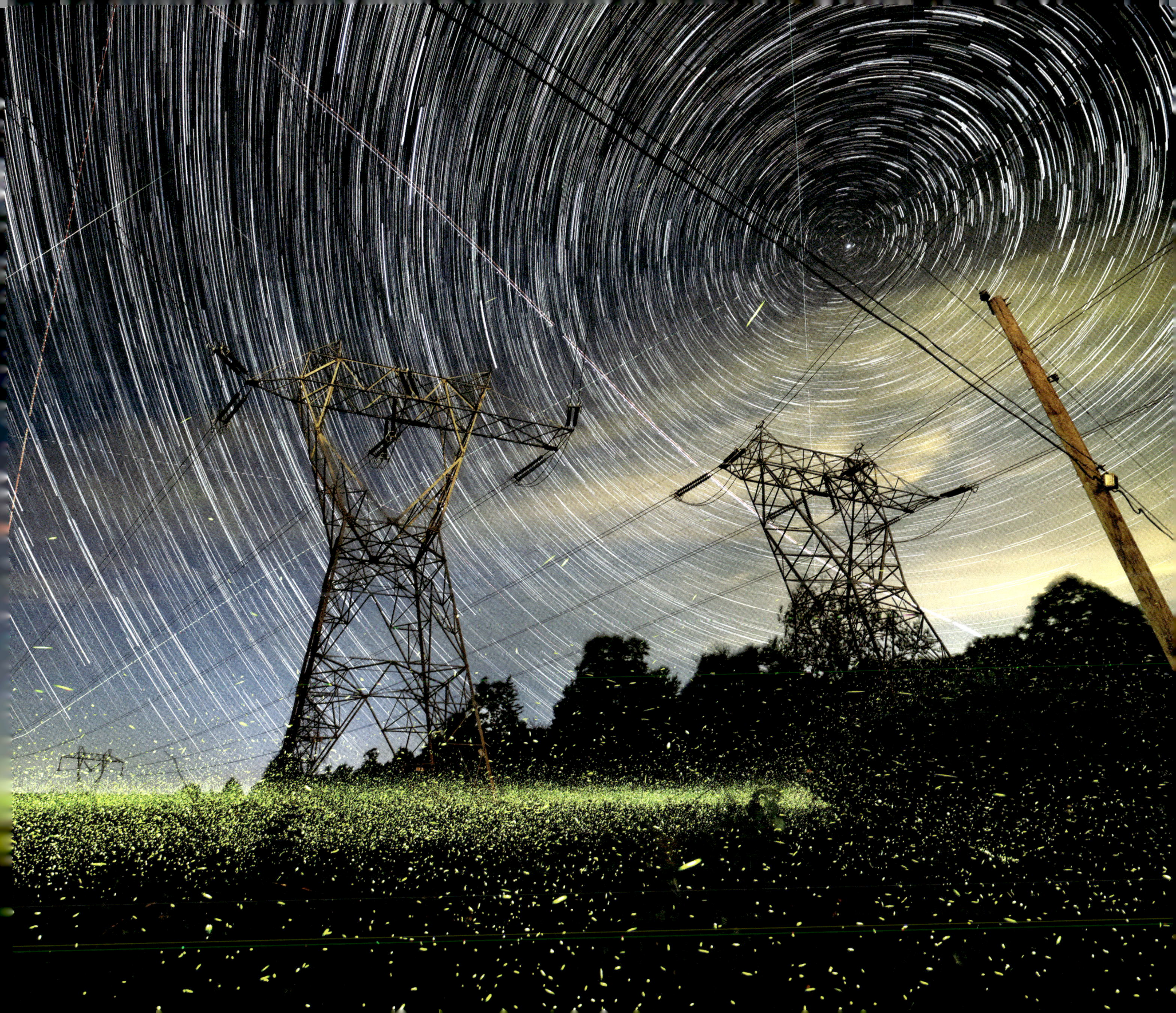

NOTES

BENEATH THE STARLIGHT, ORIT PELEG

[1] Bialek, W. Biophysics: Searching for Principles. (Princeton University Press, 2012).

[2] Lewis, S. Silent Sparks: The Wondrous World of Fireflies. (Princeton University Press, 2016).

[3] Faust, Lynn Frierson. Fireflies, Glow-Worms, and Lightning Bugs: Identification and Natural History of the Fireflies of the Eastern and Central United States and Canada. (University of Georgia Press, 2017.)

[4] Lewis, Silent Sparks: The Wondrous World of Fireflies.

[5] Ibid.

[6] Strogatz, S. Sync: The Emerging Science of Spontaneous Order (Hyperion, 2003).

[7] Sarfati, R. & Peleg, O. Chimera states among synchronous fireflies. Sci. Adv. 8, eadd6690(2022).

[8] Sarfati, R., Hayes, J. C. & Peleg, O. Self-organization in natural swarms of Photinus carolinus synchronous fireflies. Sci. Adv. 7, eabg9259 (2021).

[9] Sarfati, R. et al. Spatio-temporal reconstruction of emergent flash synchronization in firefly swarms via stereoscopic 360-degree cameras. J. R. Soc. Interface 17, 20200179 (2020).

[10] Lewis, Silent Sparks: The Wondrous World of Fireflies.

[11] Faust, Fireflies, Glow-Worms, and Lightning Bugs.

[12] Martin, O. et al. Embracing firefly flash pattern variability with data-driven species classification. Preprint at bioRxiv https://doi.org/10.1101/2023.03.08.531653 (2023).

[13] Sarfati, R. et al. (2023). Crowdsourced dataset of firefly trajectories obtained by automated stereo calibration of 360-degree cameras. Dryad. https://doi.org/10.5061/dryad.gb5mkkwvd

**PETE MAUNEY AND JESSICA CHAPPE
IN CONVERSATION**

[1] Wendy Ewald (b. 1951) has received great acclaim since her first project in 1969 for her collaborative photography projects with children, families, women, workers, and teachers all over the world. Mauney has worked closely with Ewald since 1993, assisting in the field with technical support and behind the scenes with exhibition prints and drum scans.

[2] Wendy Ewald. Portraits and Dreams. Danbury, CT: Writers & Readers, 1985.

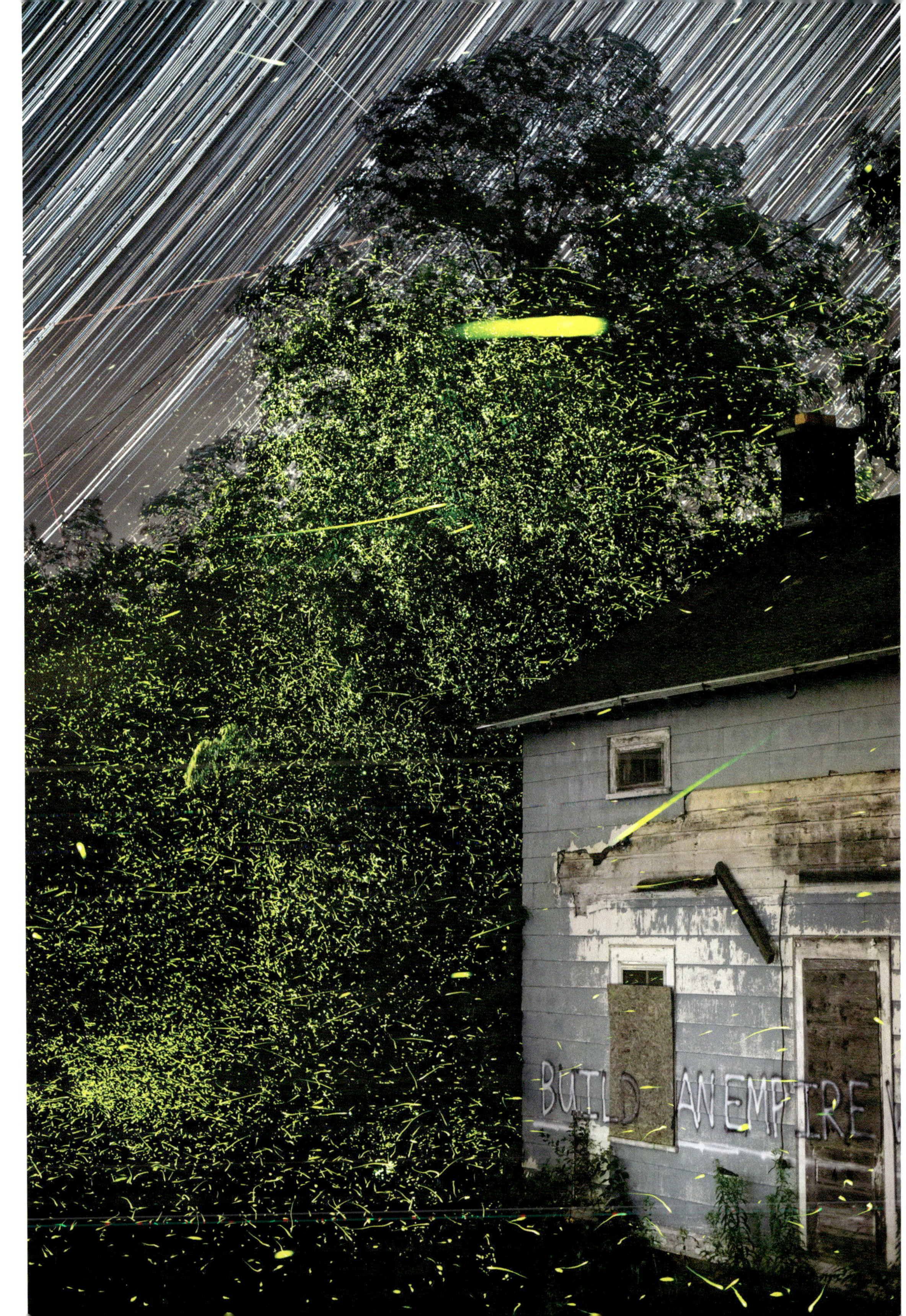
BUILD AN EMPIRE